100 Books
To Read Before
The Four Last Things

100 BOOKS

To Read Before
The Four Last Things

The Essential Guide to
Catholic Spiritual Classics

Compiled & Edited by
Marie I. George

✧ Angelico Press

First published by
Angelico Press, 2017
© Marie I. George, 2017

Grateful acknowledgment to the *Fellowship of Catholic
Scholars Quarterly* for permission to reprint the slightly
modified review by the editor/compiler on page 109.

For information, address:
Angelico Press
4709 Briar Knoll Dr.
Kettering, OH 45429
angelicopress.com
info@angelicopress.com

978-1-62138-268-3 paperback
978-1-62138-269-0 cloth
978-1-62138-270-6 ebook

Cover image: Lucy Iacoviello, Untitled, 2017
Cover design: Michael Schrauzer

CONTENTS

St. Louis-Marie Grignion de Montfort—*The World's First Love* by Archbishop Fulton J. Sheen

The Mystics 149

The Cloud of Unknowing by Anonymous—*Come be My Light* by St. Teresa of Calcutta—*The Complete Works* (Vol. 1) by St. Elizabeth of the Trinity, OCD—*Dark Night of the Soul* by St. John of the Cross—*The Dialogue* by St. Catherine of Siena—*Revelations of Divine Love* by Julian of Norwich—*Fire Within* by Fr. Thomas Dubay, SM—*Interior Castle* by St. Teresa Avila—*Spiritual Letters* by Dom John Chapman, OSB—*The Third Spiritual Alphabet* by Fr. Francisco de Osuna, OFM—*The Way of Divine Love* by Sr. Josefa Menéndez—*The Way of Perfection* by St. Teresa of Avila—*Words of Light* by St. Pio

Prayer 193

The Armenian Prayer Book of St. Gregory of Narek—*The Art of Praying* by Fr. Romano Guardini—*Essence of Prayer* by Sr. Ruth Burrows, OCD—*How to Pray Always* by Fr. Raoul Plus—*Opening to God* by Fr. Thomas Green, SJ—*Prayer and the Will of God* by Dom Hubert Van Zeller—*The Prayer of Love and Silence* by a Carthusian—*The Prayer of the Presence of God* by Dom Augustin Guillerand, O. Cart.—*The Practice of the Presence of God* by Br. Lawrence of the Resurrection—*Soul of My Soul* by Catherine de Hueck Doherty—*When the Well Runs Dry: Prayer Beyond the Beginnings* by Fr. Thomas Green, SJ

Retreats & Ignatian Spirituality 223

Consoling the Heart of Jesus by Fr. Michael E. Gaitley, MIC—*A Do-It-At-Home Retreat: The Spiritual Exercises of St. Ignatius of Loyola* by Fr. André Ravier, SJ—*The Examen Prayer: Ignatian Wisdom for Our Lives Today* by Fr. Timothy M. Gallagher, OMV—*Poustinia* by Catherine de Hueck Doherty—*A Retreat for Lay People* by Fr. Ronald Knox—*Retreat with the Lord* by Fr. John A. Hardon, SJ—*The Spiritual Exercises* by St. Ignatius of Loyola

The Spiritual Life 241

Virtues 271

Dedicated to the Sacred Hearts of Jesus and Mary

"You will not see anyone who is really striving after his advancement who is not given to spiritual reading. And as to him who neglects it, the fact will soon be observed by his progress."

—St. Athanasius

Introduction

Five or six years ago, in the space of a month, two different friends of mine recommended spiritual authors whom I had never heard of before. These authors' works proved extremely helpful to me. It then occurred to me that it would be useful to have a guide to spiritual reading, so that if providential suggestions from friends or spiritual mentors were not forthcoming, people would have another means of finding a book suited to them.[1]

I was convinced that if the guide were to be helpful, it would have to do more than summarize the contents of the various works. A priest once advised me to buy a certain book; while it looked promising from the point of view of the topics covered, it nevertheless left me cold. I was sure other people sometimes purchased books that did not meet their personal needs. Consequently, I envisaged a guide that would provide its readers with indications that would help them gauge whether the book was suited to them from the point of view of temperament, stage in the spiritual life, vocation, and other personal factors that account for why one person finds a given book stimulating, while another finds it boring. And this is what the contributors to this volume have attempted to do.

The above summarizes the purpose of this book. The rest of this introduction explains further the underlying principles guiding the volume's development. It also serves to refresh the reader's memory of the many benefits of spiritual reading.

The Purpose of Spiritual Reading

Certainly, God's word, especially the Gospels, is spiritual reading *par excellence*. Through the Bible we learn who God is, what His

---

1. A helpful guide I have come across is by Fr. Peter John Cameron, OP, *The Classics of Catholic Spirituality* (Staten Island, New York: Alba House, 1996). It covers fourteen spiritual works.

1

plan for our salvation is, and what we must do if we are to be with Him for all eternity. It is plain from the inclusion in Mass of three Scripture readings (plus the psalm response) that this form of spiritual reading is meant for all believers. As the *Catechism of the Catholic Church* (#133) states: The Church "forcefully and specifically exhorts all the Christian faithful . . . to learn 'the surpassing knowledge of Jesus Christ,' by frequent reading of the divine Scriptures. 'Ignorance of the Scriptures is ignorance of Christ.'"

The Scriptures, however, raise any number of questions that they do not directly answer. For example, St. Paul says that love is patient and kind. However, he does not spell out the many ways in which patience and kindness benefit our neighbor, nor does he tell us how to acquire the two. Yet, other spiritual writers do just this. Similarly, Christ often insists on the importance of trusting in Divine Providence and St. Paul teaches that all works for the good of the one who loves God (see Rm. 8:28). Here too their pithy message has been fruitfully expanded upon by a number of spiritual writers. Now, among those who desire intensely to follow Our Lord, there are simple souls who lack education and/or whose capacity for education is limited. This was the case of most of the Apostles, a number of whom were fishermen. For many such people the supernatural virtues, the gifts of the Holy Spirit, prayer, frequenting the sacraments, and meditating on Scripture suffice for them to achieve the perfection God intended them to achieve, and indeed, sometimes, a very high degree of perfection. However, for those who are capable of reading books written at an adult level and who desire more ardently than most to know, love, and serve God, spiritual reading is a means to holiness that has been counseled by many saints.[2] As St. Thomas Aquinas explains when commenting on John the Baptist's preaching:

---

2. See St. Alphonsus Ligouri, "Spiritual Reading": "To a spiritual life the reading of holy books is perhaps not less useful than mental prayer. St. Bernard says reading instructs us at once in prayer, and in the practice of virtue. Hence he concluded that spiritual reading and prayer are the arms by which hell is conquered and paradise won. We cannot always have access to a spiritual Father for counsel in our actions, and particularly in our doubts; but reading will abundantly supply his place by giving us lights and directions to escape the illusions of the devil and of

It is to be noted that instruction ought to be varied according to the state of the audience. For it suffices for simple people that those things that pertain to salvation be briefly spoken of; but to the knowledgeable, each particular ought to be explained. The Apostle indicates this in 2 Co. 3:1: "I could not speak to you as spiritual but as carnal beings." John did just that: he briefly admonished the crowds about repentance and announced the kingdom of heaven. Here he explains the particulars of these two things to the Pharisees.[3]

Spiritual reading, of course, is not to be done for the sake of erudition, but to acquire understanding that helps us better love and serve God.

In addition to providing us with knowledge helpful for our salvation, spiritual reading offers other benefits as well. In fact, like many good homilies, it may not always teach us anything new, but rather stirs up our affections, leading us to make acts of faith, hope, and love, or arouses contrition in us, or reanimates our desire to serve the Lord in gladness.

Spiritual reading, in virtue of the increased understanding of spiritual realities that it provides and the effects that it has on our hearts, naturally fuels prayer. Indeed, spiritual masters have called it "oil for the lamp of prayer,"[4] and it is a well-known fact that St. Ter-

---

our own self-love, and at the same time to submit to the divine will. Hence St. Athanasius used to say that we find no one devoted to the service of the Lord that did not practice spiritual reading. Hence all the founders of religious Orders have strongly recommended this holy exercise to their religious. St. Benedict, among the rest, commanded that each monk should every day make a spiritual reading. But before all, the Apostle prescribed spiritual reading to Timothy. *Attend unto reading* [1 Tim 4:13]. Mark the word *Attend*, which signifies that, although Timothy, as being bishop, was greatly occupied with the care of his flock, still the Apostle wished him to apply to the reading of holy books, not in a passing way and for a short time, but regularly and for a considerable time." The rest of St. Alphonsus' essay is well worth reading.

3. Thomas Aquinas, *Super Evangelium S. Matthaei,* ed. P. Raphaelis Cai, OP (Rome: Marietti, 1951), no. 263 (my translation).

4. See Fr. Frederick Faber, *Spiritual Conferences* (Rockford, Illinois: Tan Books, 1957), "On a Taste for Reading Considered as a Help in the Spiritual Life." This is a very fine essay on the importance of spiritual reading and reading in general in the spiritual life.

esa of Avila, a Doctor of the Church, was for many years unable to pray without the help of a book. The *Catechism of the Catholic Church* says in regard to meditative prayer:

> Meditation is above all a quest. The mind seeks to understand the why and how of the Christian life, in order to adhere and respond to what the Lord is asking. The required attentiveness is difficult to sustain. We are usually helped by books, and Christians do not want for them: the Sacred Scriptures, particularly the Gospels ... writings of the spiritual fathers, works of spirituality. ... (CCC, #2705)

Now oftentimes, those who are especially motivated to love God with their whole hearts find themselves a spiritual director, as is indeed advised by many spiritual writers. One's spiritual director is generally the person who is in the best position for suggesting spiritual reading. However, even good spiritual directors may not be familiar with certain books that might be of benefit to a specific individual. Moreover, many of us, for a variety of reasons, do not have access to a suitable director.[5] We need help in choosing our spiritual reading. There may be spiritual authors from whom we could be drawing great profit whose names we are not even familiar with. It is here that this guide can be of help.

The Importance of Sound Catechesis for Fruitful Spiritual Reading

It is desirable that individuals who do spiritual reading have a firm grounding in catechesis. The importance of catechesis, and that at an adult level, is twofold. First, spiritual authors, even saints, are not always right as to everything they say, or even if right, they may sometimes express themselves in a way that can be misconstrued.

---

5. See Roger J. Scheckel, "Hunting Big Game," *Lay Witness* (September/October 2010), 22: "Because you are entrusting your soul to your spiritual director, he must be a person whom you can trust without reservation and who can maintain the strictest confidence. It is important to choose carefully. Better that you not receive spiritual direction, relying on the basics that you receive through homilies and spiritual reading, than be misdirected. The old adage 'beggars can't be choosy' does not apply when seeking a spiritual director."

They sometimes give contradictory advice or at least seem to do so. Those who have received a solid and adult catechesis will not be led astray in these cases. Secondly, people need catechesis in order to know how they should act in order to please God. Some may have a sincere interest in becoming closer to our Lord, but engage in grave sins, such as skipping Sunday Mass or using contraceptives, which distance them from God, in some cases doing so because of ignorance resulting from the failure to seek out a mature understanding of the Church's moral teaching. What the latter need to do first and foremost to become holy is to acquire knowledge of Church teaching and strive to eliminate grave sin from their lives. As the *Catechism of the Catholic Church* notes: "The education of conscience is indispensable for human beings who are subjected to negative influences and tempted by sin to prefer their own judgment and to reject authoritative teachings" (#1793). What are the means the Church prescribes in order to perform this "indispensable" task?

> In the formation of conscience the Word of God is the light for our path; we must assimilate it in faith and prayer and put it into practice. We must also examine our conscience before the Lord's Cross. We are assisted by the gifts of the Holy Spirit, aided by the witness of advice of others and guided by the authoritative teaching of the Church. (CCC, #1785)

While we can, on occasion, find the advice we need for forming our consciences in spiritual writings, still most of us would do well to first read the *Catechism of the Catholic Church*,[6] which St. John Paul II "declare[s] to be a sure norm for teaching the faith,"[7] before embarking on spiritual reading. (Incidentally, reading the *Catechism* prayerfully is spiritual reading.)

The Contributors to this Volume

The first reaction of virtually every contributor to this guide was "I don't have any special competence, nor do I possess any special

---

6. The shorter *Compendium of the Catechism of the Catholic Church* may be better suited to some.

7. *Catechism of the Catholic Church*, no. 3.

holiness." As ordinary as they may claim to be, they are all well-cat-echized and have attained a certain level of education; they are all faithful to the Magisterium, and the very fact that they do spiritual reading indicates they are likely to be more devout than the average person. Whatever imperfections they have do not prevent them from identifying what readings have helped them and why, but rather make them helpful guides to those of us who are all too aware of our own imperfections.

The vast majority of works considered in this volume are reviewed by two different individuals. If there is anything that is obvious about spiritual reading, it is that what strikes one individual in a deep way may not resonate at all with another; indeed what strikes the same individual at one time may be quite different from what strikes him at another. (This parallels the fact that not all of us are equally inspired by the same saints.) To the extent possible I have included comments by individuals of both sexes and of different personality types.[8] This way, readers have a way of gauging not only whether the *topics* covered suit them, but also whether the *manner of presentation* is likely to suit them as well. A sanguine person might find the tight argumentation of a given spiritual author tiring, while a choleric person might find the more diffuse or poetic style of some other author boring. A woman might find enchanting the detailed account of the life of the Little Flower and be moved by it to a simpler, purer love of God, while a man might be find it tedious and struggle to draw spiritual profit from it. The length of each work is also noted, since individual preferences vary in that regard.

The reviewers not only provide help in selecting a suitable work, but may also aid us in gaining maximal profit from it. They do so by directing our attention to something the author is saying that we may have otherwise overlooked. I have been enlightened by their insightful remarks on a number of occasions. Appended at the end

---

8. Discerning your temperament or personality type is self-knowledge helpful for developing virtue; it can also guide one in part when it comes to selecting spiritual reading. Two books on temperament are Conrad Hock's *The Four Temperaments* (CreateSpace Independent Publishing Platform, 2010) and Art and Laraine Bennett's *The Temperament God Gave You* (Manchester, New Hampshire: Sophia Institute Press, 2005).

of the volume is a short biography of the contributors; there is also an index listing which books they reviewed.

A Few Final Observations

There are other sources of spiritual reading than the sorts of book found in this guide. For example, the monthly publication, the *Magnificat*, provides a short spiritual reading for every day of the year, and it can be very nourishing for someone who is constrained by time. In addition to being a good alternative for those suffering from time constraints, the *Magnificat* exposes one to a wide variety of spiritual authors, thus providing a great way of discovering authors best suited to oneself, whose works one can then acquire and read at greater length.

There are certain kinds of books that either are spiritual reading or are akin to it that are not going to be covered in this guide. In this category are included: commentaries on Scripture, lives of saints, encyclical letters, and books on confession, matrimony, and the Rosary. That they are not covered is in nowise a judgment on their utility, but is simply a consequence of a pragmatic decision regarding the length of this guide.

There are doubtlessly spiritual authors well worth reading who receive no mention in this guide. Sometimes this is due to the unavailability or high cost of their works.[9] In other cases, this is due to my ignorance or to my idiosyncrasies (*mea culpa*). Any suggestions will be seriously considered for a revised edition. Also, a choice had to be made as to which works of a given author are covered, given space constraints. However, a list of some of the other popular books in print by each author has been provided.

A final note: before one buys a book, it is worth checking to see if it is available online (a surprising number are). This way one can peruse its contents and gain first-hand knowledge of whether the book suits one.

---

9. At the time of the publication of this volume, every work reviewed could be found in print except one, and at a reasonable cost.

Autobiographical Works

Confessions by St. Augustine

St. Augustine's *Confessions* is not only a classic of Christian spirituality, but also a classic of world literature, as witnessed by its inclusion in the Oxford World's Classics. The work is divided into thirteen books, of which the first nine form an autobiography from Augustine's birth until his conversion and the death of his mother, St. Monica, while the remaining four are philosophical and theological. The reader may find these latter books much more difficult to read, and therefore not as useful.

The entire work is addressed directly to God, rather than to the reader. The author's formation as a teacher of rhetoric is manifest in the style and the numerous questions he asks. But it is also profoundly psychological: this is not a standard autobiography, but rather (to use the words of St. Thérèse of Lisieux) the story of a soul. In delving deep into his thoughts and motivations, Augustine does indeed "confess" his own sins and weaknesses; but his work is also a confession of the truth of the Catholic faith, found after so long a journey, and of the glory, mercy, and providence of God, who leads Augustine, despite himself, to the fullness of His revelation.

The autobiographical portion, books I through IX, reveals to the modern reader a boy and later a young man who, while growing up in a very different world from ours, had to confront the same basic human situations. We learn about his holy mother, Monica, his irascible pagan father, Patricius (who eventually converts), his faults as a child (of which the episode of the theft of the pears is a striking example of human psychology in a group of peers), but also his talents, which lead him from his home town of Thagaste in North Africa, to Carthage, Rome, and finally Milan, where he is converted through the influence of the holy bishop of that city, St. Ambrose.

We also see how he is ensnared both by his sensuality and by the appeal of Manichaeism, a dualistic Gnostic doctrine that saw in the world a struggle between a good god who created spirit and an evil one who created matter. His journey is therefore an intellectual as well as a spiritual one. Under the influence of various thinkers, he gradually drifts from the teachings of Mani to skepticism, and from there to a growing realization of the truth of the Catholic faith, a truth whose final acceptance is delayed only by his will, still reluctant to embrace the demands of the Faith. During this long journey, he lives with a concubine and begets a son, but is unwilling to marry her due to her low social status, and eventually sends her back to North Africa when she becomes an obstacle to his advancement. Finally, the voice of a child telling him to "pick up and read," completes the work that his mother and St. Ambrose began, and he is baptized. Shortly after, her work in this life accomplished, Monica dies.

The *Confessions*, although not an easy read due to the poetic language and the numerous references to a world of late Antiquity that is long gone, is well worth the effort. Its main value is the insight that it gives into the interior life of one of the great early saints of the Church. His progression from error to truth, from sin to holiness, and from worldly misuse of his talents to a Father of the Church, offers us a powerful example of how we can follow a similar journey. Here we have far more than just the "facts" of a saint's life—we have the inside story, told with a candor that allows us no excuses as we look through the lens of Augustine's soul into our own.

Finally, and on a more general level, we see in the *Confessions* the loving hand of God's Providence, assisted by the perseverant prayers of Augustine's mother Monica, leading him to his conversion. And so we also are inspired to turn to prayer and to trust in Providence to overcome human weakness.

(Review by Mark Murray)

Confessions by St. Augustine

This is arguably the greatest spiritual autobiography of all time. Though it was written more than one and a half millennia ago, and is obviously time-bound in some ways, the book nevertheless manages to read with a freshness and familiarity that few similar books have duplicated.

The man who ended up as a bishop (and later a Doctor of the Church) began as a proud, fornicating heretic, and this autobiography recounts not only the conversion but the decades before it, including the behind-the-scenes years of prayer that his mother

Monica devoted to it. Augustine is merciless to himself, as it were breaching the seal of the confessional to bare to the reader his darkest moments, his most revealing desires (the most famous of which is perhaps, "Give me chastity, Lord. But not yet"), for the sake of all the more gratefully praising God for His mercy in saving such a one.

Perhaps most resonant in his personal story is the gradualness of his conversion; it wasn't simply a matter of having a certain argument presented to him clearly, his counter-arguments being resolved, and him therefore asking for baptism. Rather, what we see with Augustine is the need to have both the intellect convinced by, and the heart give in to, the faith and its God. And neither does either part of his soul "convert" all at once; part of his heart is moved, then part of his mind, part of his mind, then part of his heart. The reader follows Augustine through his dabbling in the various schools of rhetoric, forsaking them for Greek philosophy, and then the quasi-Christianity of the Manicheans. Augustine's intellect, however, becomes Christian at a faster rate than does his will; he sees the absurdities of Manicheanism, what Manicheanism should be, before he can go all the way. Augustine does recount a watershed moment when, in a moment of spiritual crisis, he becomes committed to the faith, and this part of the book is as moving now as no doubt it was moving then.

Though autobiographical and largely chronological, the work is also meditative; throughout the author addresses God rather than the reader, wondering, with the benefit of hindsight, at the movements of Providence in bringing him back to his Beginning. For spiritual reading, this book is eminently accessible (with the possible exception of the last several chapters, which are an extended commentary on the first chapters of Genesis), and thus is recommended especially for the young or newly converted.

(Review by Chris Decaen)

Divine Mercy in My Soul by St. Faustina, OLM

Though I had been exposed to St. Faustina's message and had prayed the Divine Mercy chaplet on a few occasions, it wasn't until the death of St. John Paul II on the eve of Divine Mercy Sunday in 2005 that I encountered it in any real way. His passing, even if expected, shook me to the core; I found I needed to be with others who loved him as I did. So the next day, we attended the services at our local Cathedral, where I heard the Chaplet sung for the first time. The haunting melody sung in community touched me physically; it brought with it a force that reverberated throughout my whole body, sending shock waves into the deepest reaches of my soul. It was a profound experience of a communal plea to God our Father to have mercy on us. I had a palpable, perhaps mystical sensation of actually being heard—and of something important being given to us—to me, to my family, to those participating—and really, truly—to the whole world. The Chaplet became my devotion of choice and, eventually, I picked up the *Diary of Sister Faustina Kowalska.* Though at 700 pages it is not a quick read—it's occasionally repetitive prose can be daunting—the beautiful and sometimes alarming message it offers contains abundant material for personal meditation and an urgent reminder of our need for God's mercy and of the obligation we all have to extend that mercy to others.

St. Faustina was a Polish nun who lived in the 20th century; she was canonized by John Paul II on April 30, 2000, the first saint of the third millennium. Her diary is an account of the personal revelation she is said to have received from Christ himself as he instructs her on the nature of his divine mercy and his desire that all of humanity should come to understand its unfathomable mystery. Written in the form of a journal, the diary relates her many conversations with Jesus, a dialogue that began in February, 1931 and continued for many years. During that time he led her to a deeper insight into the mystery of God's mercy and gave her precise directions concerning the mission of proclaiming this message of God's mercy to the world. It was Jesus himself who gave us the Chaplet of Divine Mercy.

In her diary Sister Faustina conveys to us the message Jesus gave her. Its essence can be stated fairly simply, even starkly: Jesus desires to save us all. In the most urgent of terms, St. Faustina relays his fundamental message again and again, in every way possible. Jesus wants us to know that he came for everyone, even the greatest sinner—that the "greater the misery of a soul, the greater its right to

[His] mercy." There is but one condition: The sinner needs to ask for it. Jesus, she says, is mercy itself; he is a veritable ocean of mercy, just waiting for someone to whom he can give it. And the greatest sin is to not trust in him, in his mercy.

The Blessed Virgin makes several appearances in the course of the diary. And in one passage she reveals, perhaps most directly, what is at stake for those of us here below. Here Our Holy Mother tells the nun that, while she "gave the Savior to the world," it falls to Faustina "to speak to the world about His great mercy and prepare the world for the second coming of Him who will come, not as a merciful Savior but as a just judge. Oh, how terrible is that day! Determined is the day of justice, the day of divine wrath. . . . Speak to the souls about this great mercy while it is still the time for mercy. If you keep silent now, you will have to answer for a greater number of souls on that terrible day." It seems to me that in this passage we hear the anticipation of our own mission, in these days of difficulty and distress.

(Review by Deborah Savage)

Divine Mercy in My Soul by St. Faustina, OLM

I had heard of the *Diary* of St. Maria Faustina Kowalska many times before I finally read it, most notably from a friend who described it as one of the most "emo" saint books she had ever encountered. ("Emo" is a descriptive for someone filled with angst, highly emotional, and self-preoccupied; these people are usually associated with a specific genre of music, but not always.) This description intrigued rather than concerned me, since I have always found the works of St. Thérèse helpful, despite her sometimes childish and frilly style. And so I read the *Diary*, and have read it several times to date.

The first thing that struck me is that it truly is a diary. Some of St. Faustina's entries tell us about her life, struggles, and general events. Others are her letters to God: inmost, occasionally half-baked thoughts scribbled down in the moment. (His responses to her are distinguished by bold type.) Her style does tend to be melodramatic and, as she records even the smallest of her concerns and preoccupations with the utmost gravity, it can feel tedious. There is a great

lesson precisely here, however, in the story of a soul laid at least partially bare to our eyes—with all her awkwardness, boring stream of
consciousness, sincerity, and limitations—learning over a lifetime
to accept and love herself simply because God loves her. Not
because God reveals hidden beauties that belong to her alone; these
do not exist. Not because His Love affirms her personal worthiness
(though He often praises her efforts) or fills her with self-confi-
dence. No, simply because He loves His creature however fallen,
however weak, however lost, with an infinite passion. No matter
one's state in life or temperament, the theme of God as Lover and
soul as Beloved is timely.

A second thing in the *Diary* is Faustina's feistiness, which stands
tirelessly to attention despite her passive, nervous temperament and
her vow of obedience: a balance that many of us struggle to believe
could even exist. Yet we see it in her despite depression, anxiety,
weakness, sickness, limitations, discouragement, and a myriad of
other obstacles. How often her soul laments these things! Yet her
desire to remain "on the battlefield" with weapons in hand, even if
the "mortal sweat" should break out upon her brow, is undimin-
ished; and she eagerly follows her Lord's suggestions on how to manage. Gradually, God brings her from one battle to the next, until she
is about the great work of heralding a new emphasis on His Divine
Mercy. She sees darkly the mysterious intertwining of suffering, the
demands of justice, the work of redemption, and the infinite tenderness of Divine Mercy in the lives of those around her and most especially her own; and she records all these things for us to take to heart.

A final thing, and perhaps the one that I most enjoyed about the
Diary, is its portrayal of prayer: the dialogue between God and the
soul of Faustina. Often, God addresses her: "But, my child, we
should talk in more detail about the things that lie in your heart. Let
us talk confidentially and frankly, as two hearts that love one
another do." And she speaks just so, without artifice, without the
desire to appear one way rather than another, unconcerned with
maintaining distance or dignity. Temperaments inclined to stillness
and silence will be inspired by her unflinching activity and intense
focus on the needs of the world around her, and those predisposed
to flourish while being in the thick of things will find in her life a

reminder of the absolute necessity of stillness, silence, and interior detachment.

(Review by Angela Fuhrman)

The Life of Teresa of Jesus: The Autobiography of St. Teresa of Avila

I had a variety of reactions to this book. Being attracted to saints whose lives initially were less than exemplary, I found a friend in Teresa who by her own accounts was a rather worldly nun. She spent a good deal of time socializing, and not always with people apt to lead her closer to God; at one point she even abandoned mental prayer for about a year. However, when Teresa went on to describe four types of prayer, her detailed descriptions of the higher forms were largely lost on me. The comparison she gives of a person praying to a gardener, in its broad lines, is not hard to understand. In the first degree of prayer, a lot of work is involved on the part of the gardener to carry buckets of water with which to water the plants, whereas in the fourth and last degree, the gardener does nothing at all, but all the work is done by God who provides rain. However, the details she gives about higher forms of prayer mean little to those who have not experienced them, although it good to have some clue as to how to recognize them, in case we should ever be recipients of such. It is also good to know that they are free gifts of God that we cannot merit, and also that it is not wrong to hope for them and to do what we can to make ourselves more worthy to receive them by detaching ourselves from the world.

If I was unable to entirely follow what Teresa said about prayer, I was even more lost when she went on to speak of her locutions, various types of visions, ecstasies, levitation, and the like; I confess skimming some of those sections. Even Teresa's more mundane account of the difficulties and persecution she faced in founding a house for Carmelites who would follow the original rule included supernatural events, such as apparitions both of Our Lord and of the deceased St. Peter of Alcántara. The end of her biography is chock-full of supernatural favors, such as a vision of her parents in heaven, a vision of angels, and many cures, both physical and spiritual, wrought by God in answer to her prayers. While how to tell whether or not a locution is from the devil is not the sort of problem I have, those who have had religious experiences that they are trying to understand may well derive guidance and reassurance from Teresa. I did find sobering her description of the vision she had of the place in hell that would have been hers, save for God's mercy.

Given that this fairly long book is filled with accounts of supernatural phenomena that the majority of us are unlikely to experience, some may find that the time it takes to read Teresa's biography is better used reading something that relates more closely to their own life. That said, interspersed between the narratives of supernatural occurrences is some very down earth advice concerning excessive attachment to others and to one's health, spiritual friendship, spiritual directors, and humility. Somehow it is easier to take this advice from someone who from the beginning of her spiritual life to the end is so honest about her faults and failings; in the beginning, for instance, she speaks about her attachment to worldly pleasures, and toward the end she confesses that she briefly went back on her intention to hold the reformed community to living on alms, despite Christ having told her to do so. Teresa has a lively and engaging personality. I could hear her speaking to me from above: "For some years now I have felt like this—I never see a person whom I like very much without immediately wishing that I could see him wholly given to God, and sometimes this yearning of mine is so strong that I am powerless against it." There is a reason she is a Doctor of the Church.

(Review by Marie George)

Other works by St. Teresa of Avila are *Interior Castle* and *The Way of Perfection* (both reviewed in this volume).

The Secret Diary of Elisabeth Leseur: The Woman Whose Goodness Changed her Husband from Atheist to Priest by Elisabeth Leseur

Elisabeth suffered most of her adult life from bad health, including breast cancer. She suffered even more from not being able to share her spiritual life with her husband and with others in their social ambit. Indeed, at one point Elisabeth abandoned the practice of the faith for a couple of years, worn down by her husband and his friends' arguments against religion. Prefaced by a touching tribute by her husband Felix, this collection of her journals, letters, and essays is recommended reading for those who suffer physically as well as for those who are surrounded by non-practicing friends and/or relatives. I suspect the book will appeal more to women than to men, and especially to those of an affectionate nature, though Leseur is by no means anti-intellectual. In "Christian Womanhood" and elsewhere Leseur insists that women should study both secular and spiritual authors, both for the sake of acquiring knowledge and in order to discuss the truths of the faith in an intelligent manner. Leseur loved all the good things in life and loved people, but saw the need to subordinate these loves to the love of God through which they find their true meaning.

The book can get repetitive at times, which is understandable since a good part of it is Elisabeth's personal diaries. This detracts but little from the book's impact. After her death, her non-believing husband was so moved by these writings that he went from being a non-believer to becoming a Dominican priest. Some of the recurring themes include advice as to how to draw people to the faith and how to deal with suffering. On the former point she speaks of the importance of speaking gently and tactfully with those who reject Christ, and notes that often one is more successful attracting such people to the faith by one's serenity, joy, and charity. She insists upon the necessity of a robust interior life if one is to be an apostle, a person non-believers are going to be attracted to listening to. As for suffering, she advocates keeping silent concerning one's trials— obvious but needed advice for those of us prone to complain. Leseur reiterates many traditional teachings concerning suffering such as offering it as reparation for one's sins and for others' salvation, and viewing it as an opportunity to exhibit a purer love toward God. Her example of living out these truths is there to inspire us, and herein lies the special strength of the book.

A time-line of the major events in Elisabeth Leseur's life is provided in the beginning of the book and a short biography at the end.

(Review by Marie George)

The Secret Diary of Elisabeth Leseur: The Woman Whose Goodness Changed Her Husband from Atheist to Priest by Elisabeth Leseur

I have led many book clubs for Catholic women though the years in different states. One of the books I have discussed recently with my current book club was *The Secret Diary of Elisabeth Leseur*. Few books in all of my years of leading book clubs provoked such diverging opinions and reactions from the members. Some women had been expecting a fun, calendar-type journal of activities, or a tale of life in Paris at the time. Some women were nearly angry at Elisabeth's seeming passiveness, and some women said they just could not finish it because it was so repetitive.

Yet a few of the Book Club members, like myself, were amazed by the book. I have read many books in my lifetime, and many of them were spiritual. This one stands in a unique place among others, perhaps because it enters into the depths of a heart longing for a life of intimacy with the Lord.

The diary of Elizabeth Leseur is not an ordinary diary. Perhaps this is why the book disappointed so many women. Elizabeth is a married woman with a busy social life in Paris, but in her diary we do not read about her outings and meetings and recipes served at the many social functions; instead, we read the intimate journaling of her interior quest for holiness. Elizabeth loves her husband, a husband who is charming and wonderful but does not share her spiritual life. So she writes in her journal as to have in it a companion on her journey: she writes of her sacrifices, offerings, and interior struggles.

The book consists of four main parts: first, the reader is given a chronology of her life, which proves to be a very useful go-to resource since the body of her writing is broken into separate parts and the dates may overlap at times.

The second part is perhaps the most interesting to many readers, and it is the account of her life written by her husband Felix. An atheist, he found her journal after her intense suffering and subsequent death, and eventually underwent a complete conversion. The reader can just imagine with what amount of love the religious Felix writes about his late wife, the one who was an instrument of his conversion, having veiled both her intense spiritual and physical suffering from him during her lifetime.

The third part is the body of her writing: the journal, resolutions, prayers, and the spiritual-content letters she composed for beloved relatives. These writings form the main bulk of the book, and they can be read in order, but also in spurts, in parts, at random.

The fourth and final part of the book is a biographical note containing a quick overview of the lives, tying everything together and bringing the book to a rewarding closure.

In my own life as a wife and mother at home for over thirty years, I too have been on this spiritual quest. It was comforting and encouraging to me to read about Elizabeth's struggles—and conquests—in advancing toward our Loving Lord. As I finished the book I felt that I had made a new friend in my own journey, one that is much more courageous and spiritually developed, but a friend on the journey nevertheless.

(Review by Ana Braga-Henebry)

The Story of a Soul: The Autobiography of Saint Thérèse of Lisieux, edited by Mother Agnes of Jesus

Pope St. Pius X called St. Thérèse "the greatest saint of modern times," and Pope St. John Paul II declared her a Doctor of the Church. These titles are given to a woman who lived a short and hidden life, and whose simplicity is disarming. But she offers a newly profound understanding of living the gospel by having complete confidence in God. Her spiritual poverty—going to God with empty hands—is combined with her heroism in the context of an ordinary life, filled with mundane routines. This makes her a great heavenly friend and guide for someone like me, a wife and mother whose spiritual battlefield is at home.

St. Thérèse was the youngest of five daughters in a devout 19th century French family. Her mother died when she was four years old, and her two older sisters, Marie and Pauline, entered Carmel when she was still a child. Thérèse also entered at fifteen. Later, Pauline, as her Mother Superior, asked Thérèse to write her child-

21

hood memories, and this constitutes the first and largest part of her autobiography. The second part recounts her life as a Carmelite nun, and was written for another Superior. The third is an explanation of her little way, written at Marie's request.

The fond memories of childhood, shared by one sister with another, plunge the reader into a family living life on a different plane. This opens up a world for those of us trying to create a home culture in which children grow up with the reality of the spiritual world. The preparation for Sacraments is lovingly and thoroughly done by those closest to her, who know her completely. There is a fierce determination not to let sin sully the soul, and immediate contrition when it does. Small but effective ways to develop virtue are diligently pursued.

One could read any number of books that distill St. Thérèse's spirituality, but reading her own words allows one to see it in action. Many touched me, charged as I am with the welfare of a husband's and children's souls. For example, her thought on how to guide the novices placed in her care: "Just as a mighty river carries with it all it meets into the ocean's depths, so, my Jesus, a soul which plunges into the boundless ocean of Your love bears all her treasures with her. You know what my treasures are; they are the souls You made one with mine, treasures which you Yourself have given me." And when all else fails: "all my strength lies in prayer and sacrifice. They are my invincible arms, and I know from experience that I can conquer hearts with these more surely than I can with words." St. Thérèse's daring confidence when confronted with her failings is so encouraging! For example: "I must admit that I am far from doing what I know I ought to do, but the very desire to do so brings me peace."

I think that women of all ages would enjoy *The Story of a Soul*, and men would as well. Thérèse's doctrine of spiritual childhood (complete confidence in God's tender, personal love) is universal, and represents real deepening of Christ's words to us all: "Amen I say to you, unless you be converted, and become as little children, you shall not enter into the kingdom of heaven" (Mt. 18:3). Beneath what may at first glance seem childish language, one readily encounters a soul of strength and profound insight.

(Review by Lise O'Reilly)

Story of a Soul: The Autobiography of Saint Thérèse of Lisieux

Thérèse of Lisieux's spiritual memoir has captivated readers since its posthumous publication in 1898. *The Story of a Soul* is at root a story of Thérèse's experience of being loved by God and loving God and others in return. The first epistle of John states that "God is love," but this characterization of God is not an end but a beginning of human knowledge of God. What Thérèse does is to remind readers that love is inherently dynamic and relational. Love always impels persons toward one another. In the last chapter of this autobiography, Thérèse uses the metaphor of iron and a fire to illustrate this point: "If fire and iron had the use of reason, and if the latter said to the other: 'Draw me,' would it not prove that it desires to be identified with the fire in such a way that the fire penetrate and drink it up with its burning substance and seem to become one with it?". In Thérèse's world, love changes everything, for it is not possible for either the lover or the beloved to remain in place. Love is not a possession that a person has and can subsequently employ for all types of endeavors, but it is a relation that depends upon a particular context to be revealed.

Love's relationality serves as its basic framework, but what is the nature of this relation? Thérèse claims over and over again that the relation of love is one of service, and the theme of loving suffering is vividly portrayed in *The Story of a Soul*. Thérèse writes that "the divine call was so strong that had I been forced to *pass through flames*, I would have done it out of love for Jesus." She claims, "Love for mortification was given me, and this love was all the greater because I was allowed nothing by way of satisfying it."

What is the goal of such mortification? Since love is dynamic, it helps to look at the eschatological goal Thérèse has in mind for a loving relationship. Love is a dynamic mystical communion where the lover serves the beloved without any self-conscious reflexivity, and thereby becomes an image of the beloved. Thérèse speaks of this mystical experience in terms of a conflagration that consumes the lover. This fire is the goal toward which suffering accepted in love tends: "It seems to me that if You were to find souls offering

23

themselves as victims of holocaust to Your Love, You would consume them rapidly." At the end of her life Thérèse could write, "I no
longer have any great desires except that of loving to the point of
dying of love."

It would be a mistake to see Thérèse's willingness to be consumed
in the fire of love as stoic obedience due to a divine command. She is
willing to be consumed in fire, but not because she resigns herself to
an inexorable and impersonal fate. Thérèse breaks off *The Story of a
Soul* in mid-sentence: "It is not because God, in His anticipating
Mercy, has preserved my soul from mortal sin that I go to Him with
confidence and love." Thérèse only wants to do her beloved's bid-
ding.

The saint known as the "Little Flower" died at the age of twenty-
four, and by the standards of the world she was not well versed in
the exigencies of what many twenty-first century readers would
consider a normal, happy life. She did not travel widely; she did not
go to a selective college; as a Carmelite nun she neither married nor
had children; her final years were racked by the agony of tuberculo-
sis. But her spiritual story has moved countless people before and
after her canonization in 1925, almost all of them outside the walls
of a Carmel. Thérèse's unassuming simplicity makes her writing
accessible to anyone who has ever pondered the question of what it
means to love, and yet her experience was so profound that it provoked Pope St. John Paul II to declare her a Doctor of the Church in
1997. In a fast-paced world seemingly too busy for prayer, Thérèse
distills a Christian's relationship to God down to its essence: "He
has no need of our works but only of our *love*."

(Review by Christopher Denny)

Those who are fond of the Little Flower's autobiography may also
enjoy *The Letters of St. Thérèse of Lisieux* and *St. Thérèse of Lisieux:
Her Last Conversations*.

Christ

Christ, the Life of the Soul by Dom Columba Marmion

The book is composed of notes taken and edited by people who attended various conferences given by Dom Marmion, published with his approval. Two things are striking about this book: the first, not surprisingly, is its insistence on the centrality of Christ in our spiritual life; the second is how Marmion's manner of teaching inspires us to seek the things that are above. There is no philosopher's paradise; we are made for heaven, and without Christ we cannot attain our ultimate end: "God is not content and never will be content, since He has resolved on making us His children, with a natural morality or religion; He wills us to act as children of a divine race. But it is through His Son, it is in His Son and by the grace His Son, Christ Jesus, has merited for us, that He gives us power to attain this holiness." The book contains a lot of doctrine (similar to *That Tremendous Lover*) and scriptural exegesis—things which may be wearying to some. The book is long. However, if one puts out of one's head the idea that one has to "get through" the book, and meditates on a few pages at a time, there is immense spiritual profit to be derived from it. As Cardinal Mercier puts it: "The perfume of Holy Scripture, to be breathed in at each page of this volume, gives the impression that it was conceived and prepared during prayer, at the foot of the altar before being given to the public."

The main theme of this work is God's divine plan as enunciated in Ep. 1:4-6: "God, the Father, chose us in his Son to be his adopted children for the praise of the glory of his grace." The first part outlines our sublime calling and devotes a chapter each to the central roles that Christ plays in its realization. Christ is our model, the exemplary cause of our perfection; he is our redeemer and infinite source of grace. The Church is his mystical body. And the Holy Spirit is the Spirit of Jesus. The second part presents the foundation of the Christian life, namely, faith in Jesus Christ, and then proceeds to articulate the twofold aspect of the Christian life, starting with baptism. The Christian life consists of death to sin and life for God. The section on death to sin outlines sin's effects and emphasizes the importance of the sacrament of Penance. The section on life for God includes chapters on the truth in charity, the Eucharist, the Church's public worship, private prayer, love of neighbor, the Mother of the Word Incarnate, and coheirs in Christ.

To gain some idea of the richness of Marmion's teaching, consider what he says in his treatment of the Divine Office in the chapter entitled "Vox Sponsae" ("Voice of the Spouse"). Marmion begins by noting that we do not know how to pray as we ought, but the Spirit himself helps us in our weakness (see Rm. 8:26). He continues: "God alone knows the way in which we should call upon Him. . . . To praise God worthily, it is necessary that God Himself should compose the expression of these praises. And that is why the Church places the psalms upon our lips. . . . At the same time as they celebrate the Divine perfections, the psalms *wonderfully express the sentiments and needs of our souls.*"

(Review by Marie George)

Christ, the Life of the Soul by Bl. Columba Marmion

Christ, the Life of the Soul by Blessed Columba Marmion is a long-form trope on the centrality of Christ to the spiritual life, especially under the aspect of Divine adoption. Marmion's intense Christo-centrism and his exuberant style make it easy to see a certain kinship between the beloved turn-of-the-century Benedictine abbot and Pope St. John Paul II, who beatified him in 2000. Though *Christ, the Life of the Soul* has all the theological rigor of a Christology textbook, it nonetheless maintains the accessibility of a preached retreat, all of its contents having first been delivered orally by the author.

"Divine adoption," by which Christ draws all humanity into His own inner life, forms the great tent under which Marmion gathers us for a tour de force of the principal dogmas of the Catholic faith. Through this approach, Bl. Columba is able to weave each doctrine into the inner life of the reader in a way that is quite compelling. There is an unhurried, full-blooded savor to his approach to doctrine that lifts the reader from the realm of dry exposition into his solicitous spiritual guidance. He cautions that "We cannot really glimpse the grandeur of these dogmas and their fruitfulness for our souls unless we prolong the contemplation somewhat." As a gifted spiritual director, Bl. Columba never misses an opportunity to interject a probing question directly to the reader, or to pause to "relish" (*sapere*) a particular passage of Scripture. In describing the Holy Spirit's gift of wisdom, Marmion seems to reveal something of his own approach throughout: "What does 'wisdom' signify here? It is a 'flavorsome knowledge of spiritual things,' a super-natural gift for knowing or esteeming Divine things through the spiritual *taste* with which the Holy Spirit inspires us in this matter."

Marmion contrasts this savory approach against the "joyless labor" of those who find themselves scandalized by the utter simplicity of the Divine plan. Citing St. Francis de Sales, he teaches such sour Christians that even a "small amount of virtue" in "the little simplicities of life" can be more pleasing to God than martyrdom for a soul whose love is "languid, weak and slow."

Throughout *Christ, the Life of the Soul* we hear from Marmion's favorite guides, especially Paul, Augustine, Thomas Aquinas (whom he names "prince of theologians"), Teresa of Avila, and Gregory the Great. A handful of Scriptural figures also play central roles in Marmion's winsome Christology. Mary Magdalen and the Good Thief are each uniquely illustrative of the beautiful excesses of Christ's Divine plan of adoption. Marmion reserves a place of honor for the Blessed Mother by dedicating the book's entire penultimate chapter to her essential part in Redemption.

The sheer delight in the person of Christ to be found in the pages of this great spiritual work is clearly the fruit of Marmion's own joyful spiritual inebriation. There is a kind of immediacy to Bl. Columba's approach that never gives into the temptation to achieve relevance by shifting focus away from Christ. Best savored slowly, Bl. Marmion's classic is a worthy aid for the journey toward our inheritance. The inheritance here is none other than Christ Himself who is "more than a model, more than a High Priest." Acting within the intimacy of the soul, He is, above all, its very *life*!

(Review by Christopher Candela)

Bl. Marmion is also author of *Our Way and Our Life: Christ in His Mysteries.*

Conversation with Christ by Fr. Peter T. Rohrbach

A certain number of us are intimidated by the thought of reading works by mystics. Fr. Rohrbach does us a great service in presenting St. Teresa of Avila's teachings on personal prayer in a manner that is accessible to a beginner. He draws out of St. Teresa's works what is most readily understood, supplementing it with relevant passages from spiritual masters such as St. Francis de Sales.

Part I states the purpose of meditation, quoting St. Teresa: "Mental prayer is nothing else than an intimate friendship, a heart-to-heart conversation with Him [i.e., Christ]." An outline is given of the five steps in the method St. Teresa recommends for mental prayer: preparation, selection of the material, consideration, conversation, and conclusion.

Part II explains the different steps. The first step, preparation, consists in a "humble admission of one's weakness and a keen realization of Christ's presence." Next comes the selection of material. Sometimes the events of daily life provide sufficient matter for conversation. Often needed, however, is the help of a book that speaks of Christ (the prime example being the New Testament). However, one does not read the book in the manner one would if one were seeking instruction about the spiritual life. One reads slowly and with an eye to finding material for conversation with Christ. The third step, the consideration, consists of applying one's memory, imagination, and intellect on the subject matter chosen. Rohrbach discusses a variety of views expressed by spiritual authors on representing the subject of meditation by means of imagination. Once the scene is represented, one uses one's intellect to consider the different circumstances surrounding it (who, what, when, etc.) as is conducive to conversation with the Lord (and not in the manner that a theologian would consider them). Then comes the conversation. Whereas the consideration took the form of "He said, He did," etc., the conversation takes the form of "You said, You did." The last step of the meditation is a conclusion suitable for ending a conversation with one's Savior. Later in Part V Rohrbach gives a sample demonstration of the method.

Part III takes up some alternative methods of meditation, the first consisting in a meditative recitation of prayers, and the second, meditative reading of passages from a book apt to help one directly communicate with our Lord.

Part IV provides useful advice as to how to handle distractions which affect the imagination and/or intellect, and aridity which afflicts the will.

Part VI takes up "indispensable aids to meditation." Recollection of God throughout the day (sometimes called the practice of the presence of God) and detachment from creatures and from self (i.e., humility) are needed if one is to be friends of Christ. Spiritual reading is necessary if one is to have an intelligent companionship with Christ, as this supposes knowledge of him and of his teachings. Rohrbach notes that spiritual reading is especially important in our age to counterbalance the pervasive influences of the secularized world we live in.

Part VII addresses progress in prayer and describes a more advanced form of mental prayer that God sometimes calls people to. Part VIII emphasizes the importance of mental prayer, and hence of persisting at it despite difficulties one might experience, especially at the beginning.

This book is very accessible; it is clear and has an engaging tone. Even certain high school students could read it with profit. The importance of its theme can hardly be overstated.

(Review by Marie George)

Conversation with Christ by Fr. Peter T. Rohrbach

Living an active, service-oriented life is fine, but without care, one's prayer life can gradually grow weak and filled with distractions. To exchange this for a meaningful conversation with Christ needs serious application and a reliable guide.

This is a simple "How-To" Manual for using meditative prayer to reach intimacy with Christ, based on the teachings of St. Teresa and St. John of the Cross. Fr. Rohrbach speaks to both beginner contemplatives (God bless them!) and also active Christians, including those of us who try to pray, but whose minds just aren't able to slow down. If we are going to pursue a deeper prayer life, one filled more with serenity than distractions, we need to be told, "Sit still a moment and listen to me!" and even before that, we need to be taught *how* to sit still; how to find a moment away from the lists that run through our heads from daybreak until we fall asleep at night. Those of us so caught up in the whirl of life won't bother with anything less than a very straightforward and accessible guide. This one will do.

If the language and style of the saints seem daunting, here is an appealing alternative. The language is conversational and easy to read, but lacking the overly simple style of a best seller, in which you can usually infer all the contents of a chapter by a quick perusal of the first and last paragraphs. Each topic is presented, analyzed, and developed thoroughly, and yet, after finishing a chapter, one can still come away with an uncomplicated, clear idea that can be remembered in a simple sentence or two.

The whole book travels gently from a general preparation for contemplation to a hint at the life changing experience of achieving it. On the way, it presents demonstrations of different approaches and assorted aids, as well as difficulties and an arsenal of advice and techniques for attacking them. There are enough variations upon the method to address the needs of a large range of ordinary folks with all their different tastes, strengths, and weaknesses. Not a big reader? No problem! Easily distracted? Apply mortification and humility. And St. Teresa and St. John of the Cross will tell you how.

As in any really accessible manual, the chapter titles are just one word or brief phrases. So if we want to work on a particularly difficult step, or fix a certain problem, we can look up, say, "Detachment" as easily as we could search for "Brake Fluid" in our car owner's manual. This is quick and easy enough.

And finally, after endeavoring to visit with Christ through one of the many ways suggested, there still will be failure. Fr. Rohrbach is very encouraging and supportive of those of us who feel discouraged by early or persistent failure. We are fully assured that just to attempt a conversation with Christ, no matter how sorry an attempt it happens to be, is a good and successful start at the application of the techniques presented. He then provides a list of causes for the failed attempt, arming us with the skills to avoid them the next time. He invites us to come, prepare, and give it a go, and if we fail, to take up these tools and try again. We are promised that eventually the goal will be achieved, and one will be welcomed "into a new life of friendship with Christ."

(Review by Maureen Coughlin)

The Friendship of Christ by Fr. Robert Hugh Benson

Fr. Benson opens the book with a chapter containing considerations on friendship in general, followed by quotations from Scripture that make it clear that Christ desires to be our friend. Here I have a couple of quibbles with him, e.g., he says friendship is an emotion. Benson then goes on to treat in three sections the different aspects of an individual's friendship with Christ: Christ in the interior soul, Christ in the exterior, and Christ displaying friendship in his historical life.

As for the first part, Christ in the interior soul, it makes me wonder whether descriptions of "stages" in the spiritual life finally do all that much good, for it seems that before people have experienced the stages for themselves, they are unable to appreciate to any significant extent a book account of them. I suppose it is good to know that there are these stages, and to know that even if we are on the purgative way, we are on the path human beings normally follow. It is also useful to understand why we get stuck in this stage. Benson, for example, notes how we find our consolation in much that is not God, and how when one area of our life crumbles we tend to look to satisfaction in some other area.

The section on Christ in the exterior addresses Christ's presences other than that which he has in our hearts. Benson starts first with the Eucharist, and then goes on to treat Christ in his Church. Here he speaks about how Christ speaks authoritatively and exteriorly through his Mystical Body, the Church, quoting appropriate scriptural verses regarding the Magisterium. Benson then speaks about Christ's presence in his priests. I do not understand this topic, and did not find Benson that helpful. Christ's presence in saints, on the other hand, is easier to understand: "It is not I who live, but Christ who lives in me" (Gal. 2:20). As for Christ's presence in sinners, Benson maintains that Christ is present as one who is mocked and crucified in those who are not in the state of grace. It is our responsibility to seek to restore the image of Christ in such persons. Christ's presence in the average person evokes our care: "As long as you did it to one of these my least brethren, you did it to me" (Mt. 25:40). Christ's presence in those who willingly suffer lies in their being parts of his Mystical Body who "fill up those things that are wanting of the sufferings of Christ" (Col. 1:24).

The final part on Christ in his historical life opens with reflections on the seven words of Christ.

There is a lot of good material in this book. Here and there are some minor philosophical and theological slips (e.g., Benson's unnuanced affirmation that it is a greater act to restore than to create; see *Summa Theologiae*, I-II, q. 113, a. 9), but overall it is a solid work. I do not know what sort of reader would draw most profit from this book; it is written in a style that is not contemporary, but not stuffy either. I do think that everyone would get something out of this short work whose goal is to help us cultivate our friendship with the One who does not call us servants, but friends.

(Review by Marie George)

The Friendship of Christ by Fr. Robert Hugh Benson

If John Henry Newman was the prize of Anglican converts to Catholicism in mid-nineteenth century England, then Robert Hugh Benson (1871–1914) has a virtually equal claim for the beginning of the century that followed. His pedigree was arguably even higher than Newman's given that Benson was the son of the Archbishop of Canterbury. Ordained into the Catholic priesthood in 1904, Benson also ranks as one of the unsung heroes of the Catholic literary revival, a movement that included Newman, Gerard Manley Hopkins, G. K. Chesterton, and Evelyn Waugh. Benson's prolific writings included novels, short stories, plays, poetry, apologetic and devotional works, essays, and sermons. Benson's *Confessions of a Convert* still stands among the classics in the literature of conversion, along with such masterpieces of the genre as Saint Augustine's *Confessions*, Cardinal Newman's *Apologia Pro Vita Sua*, and Ronald W. Knox's *A Spiritual Aeneid*.

The Friendship of Christ (1912) is a devotional work consisting of a series of somewhat shortened sermons from those delivered by Benson in Rome, England, and New York between 1910 and 1912. Published during the year in which the Titanic sank, the book vigorously attempts to raise the reader with rhetorical relish into a personal bond and friendship with our Lord, Jesus Christ. While Christians are constantly told that Christ is priest, prophet, and king, it is spiritually salutary to be reminded that the Savior who took our human nature craves to include us into his circle of friends.

Studded with biblical references that anchor its reflections, *The Friendship of Christ* is divided into three parts, each of which represents a different perspective on friendship with the second person of the Trinity. In Part I Benson pushes Aristotle's famous line that "a friend is a second self" to its limit by instructing us how to enter into a personal relationship with Christ. This is accomplished by illustrating how Christ inhabits the human soul wherein he summons us through purgative and illuminative measures into a reciprocal dyad of familiarity and companionship. Part II switches from an interior to an exterior tactic and calls us to witness the many disguises of friendship that Christ wears in the world: the Eucharist, the Church, the Priest, the Saint, the Sinner, the Average Man, and the Sufferer. These external modes of friendship allow us to love Christ in all his aspects and to meet him in all of his "trysting places." Part III showcases the depth of Christ's friendship with us both by elaborating on his sacrifice upon the cross via an analysis of the Seven Last Words and by articulating the ways in which he raised his friends into everlasting life.

The Friendship of Christ adopts an innovative strategy for a work of spirituality in that the bond of friendship functions as a surrogate for the unitive summit that usually stands atop the mountain of the mystical ascent. It succeeds in being accessible to the reader of modest learning, especially as the rhetorical flourishes of the sermon format aim at the heartstrings of our emotions more than at our theological knowledge and intelligence. In Part I, Chap. 2, Benson reminds us of the unique character of any friendship between a human soul and Christ: "For this indeed is the one Friendship in which final disappointment is impossible." Benson's contemporary,

Helen Keller, mirroring a famous line from Milton's *Paradise Lost* tells us that: "I would rather walk with a friend in the dark, than alone in the light." Christ is that friend who remains with us in the brightest of days as well as the darkest of nights.

(Review by Glenn Statile)

Other works by Benson include *Lord of the World* and *Paradoxes of Catholicism*.

He and I by Gabrielle Bossis

Gabrielle Bossis (1874–1950) was a single French lay woman. In the later years of her life, Christ began to speak with her on a regular basis, and he had her write down and publish their conversations. There is no book that as quickly draws me into conversation with Jesus as this one does. I immediately recognize that the words Jesus spoke to Gabrielle he also addresses to me. The book helps break down barriers to having a loving relationship with our Lord, and indeed this is the book's very purpose:

> Write! I don't want people to be afraid of Me anymore, but to see My heart full of love and to speak with Me as they would with a dearly beloved brother. For some I am unknown. For others, a stranger, a severe master or an accuser. Few people come to me as to one of a loved family. And yet My love is there, waiting for them. So tell them to come, to enter in, to give themselves up to love just as they are. Just as they are. I'll restore. I'll transform them. And they will know a joy they have never known before. I alone can give that joy… (Voice full of yearning).

He and I began to have the desired effect on me upon reading the very first words Jesus spoke to Gabrielle: "My little girl." The book is to be savored a page or two at a time.

He and I covers all the essential elements of the spiritual life: suffering, relying on Christ alone, humility, love of neighbor, Mary; nothing is left out. And the beauty of it is how concrete it is. In place of a treatise on contemplative prayer (as valuable as it may be), we see Christ gradually leading Gabrielle to contemplative prayer, especially in the later parts of the book. In place of general talk about union with God, we see how Christ accomplishes this with Gabrielle's cooperation. Always in the forefront is the love which Christ has for her (and for us) and the love he seeks from her (and us) in return. And this mutual love is also not only expressed in general statements, but is spelled out in the concrete events of Gabrielle's life: in minor misfortunes like losing her reduced fare pass or traveling on a freezing train, to her sufferings during the war, and finally in the illness that leads to her death. Christ continually encourages her, despite her weakness: "Take a steady look at your failures and stains, and offer them to Me so that I may wash them away. Tell Me how weak you are and how often you fail. Say: 'My great Friend, help me. You know only too well how helpless I am, but with You I can do anything.'" Even when Christ chides her, it is never harshly, though sometimes it is firmly, for example: "Who is your God, you or I? Then why don't you think of Me more than yourself?". On another occasion, when she was distracted after receiving Communion, he says to her: "When a beloved person is in your living room, you don't stand at the window watching the people pass by, do you?".

I did not doubt before reading this book that "no greater love has a man than this" and that "God so loved the world." However, like many of us, I tended to conceive of Christ as only dying for humankind in general rather than as also dying specifically for me. *He and I* has broken down this conception and allowed me to experience Christ's personal interest in me. I strongly recommend this book to all (except perhaps those very advanced in the spiritual life), be they young or old. I'm not sure, however, whether most men would relate to this book; those who, like St. Alphonsus Liguori, are of tender heart definitely could.

(Review by Marie George)

He and I by Gabrielle Bossis

This extraordinary gem of a book has been on my nightstand for years. If I were exiled to an island and could only take with me three books, they would be the Bible, the *Catechism of the Catholic Church*, and *He and I*.

He and I is the recorded sayings of a "Voice" heard by Gabrielle Bossis, an older, upper middle-class French laywoman, between 1936 and her death in 1950. Unlike so many alleged locutions, this Voice, recognizable as the voice of Christ (or even, on one occasion, God the Father), speaks to Gabrielle—and through her to us—as the greatest Lover, the most faithful, caring, and attentive of friends, in the normal living of day-to-day life.

Gabrielle was a single woman by choice, at a time when living single was unusual. She turned down several proposals for marriage, and also resisted pressure from her spiritual director to enter a convent. During the period in which the Voice's words were recorded, Gabrielle traveled the world, performing the plays that she wrote. But this backdrop to her life is evident only from the notation of where she is at the beginning of some entries, and sometimes by a brief note that gives a context to that entry.

Otherwise, the Voice's supplications, advice, and gentle admonitions can easily be applied to the situations and challenges faced by every follower of Christ. Perhaps this is one of the most convincing facets attesting to the authenticity of the Voice—the sayings can apply to anyone, in any state of life, and can have varying applications and profundity that apply at different times in different ways.

Although there are entries in which the Voice addresses Himself to Gabrielle, other entries refer to the reader in the plural (e.g., "you, my children"), making it clear that the Voice intends the messages to be for everyone. As the Voice says at one point, "Each soul is My favorite. I choose some only to reach others." The earlier messages were published anonymously prior to Gabrielle's death. When she was marveling (January 12, 1950) at how quickly the first edition of the book sold out, Jesus responded: "That's because I wanted it to be so, and the sorrowful and immaculate heart of My mother shared My desire . . . what a joy for Me and for you if at last all people became My faithful friends, trustfully calling for Me and offering Me the most secret chamber of their hearts for My permanent home."

One so often hears about the difficulty in our time of finding a good spiritual director. This book can help to address the need for spiritual guidance when an expert human guide is not available.

The reader will find ways both big and small to advance in the spiritual life, if one takes the messages seriously and strives to put the advice they contain into practice. Perhaps most importantly, the Voice constantly reminds the reader how much He loves each one of us and desires constant and profound union with every person He has created. All the practical advice that is given is in furtherance of this ultimate calling to union.

There is a natural tendency, once a person starts reading this book, to continue turning the pages in an ongoing fascination with the depth and attraction of the messages. But my recommendation would be to read it slowly, and to take time to meditate on the words. The Voice at one point (July 10, 1948) asks that the messages be read once in the morning and then again a couple times later in the afternoon, to help foster the habit of "oneness" that the Voice—Jesus—so clearly desires with each one of us.

Another recommendation is to read the book, at least for the first time, from front to back, and to make notations in the margins when one comes across a subject that is particularly important or meaningful to the reader. My dog-eared copy has many underlined sentences, together with such margin notations: suffering, surrender/trust, the Eucharist, Divine Providence, Mary, death, charity, humility, etc. I find this makes it easier to find a certain passage when I remember it and want to re-read it later on.

However, it can also be helpful to randomly open the book at the end of the day. On occasions too numerous to count, I have happened on precisely the words of encouragement, comfort, or even correction that I needed at that particular time.

This book is unique, and it has the potential to transform anyone's life. I strongly encourage you to obtain a copy, and see what it can do for your relationship with God.

(Review by A. M. Desprit)

Imitation of Christ by Fr. Thomas à Kempis, CRSA

I had hoped in rereading the *Imitation of Christ* after the space of thirty some years that I would come to see why this work is beloved by so many saints. Overall this hope was disappointed. As the titles of the first two of four sections indicates, the work consists largely of admonitions or advice as to how to think and act. The various things counseled are left undeveloped—rarely are there more than two sentences in a paragraph and most topics receive less than two pages. Consequently, one is often left saying to oneself, yes, this is important, but how does one go about achieving it? E.g., "Ah! If man had but one spark of perfect charity he would doubtless perceive that all earthly things are vanity." Moreover, for the most part, the *Imitation* does not have the kind of power to move that one finds in the pithy and well-turned phrases of a work such as the book of Proverbs. A lot of what is said is pretty obvious to any serious disciple of Christ and tritely put, e.g., "Whensoever a man desires anything inordinately he is presently disquieted within himself." Some of what is said is puzzling since Thomas offers little by way of any explanation for anything he says, e.g., "Keep not much company with young people." Doubtless important themes are treated, such as desolation and trust in providence, but to my mind these topics are treated at greater length and in a more compelling manner by other authors. Thomas comes across as somewhat anti-intellectual. Certainly, he rightly criticizes a pursuit of knowledge that detracts from the love of God, and calls to our attention the temptation to "master" the ins and outs of the Bible as one would the works of secular sciences, instead of humbly receiving spiritual nourishment from it. Still, there is not a necessary opposition between philosophical or theological investigations and faith animated by charity. Yet Thomas never has anything positive to say about intellectual pursuits. Part III contains a number of dialogues with Christ. Some of them are partly scriptural, either quoting or referencing Christ's own words. I have my doubts, however, about the other lines that Thomas puts in the mouth of Christ, given that he did not receive them from Christ himself, as did St. Catherine of Siena (as recounted in the *Dialogue*). I did find some of the chapters in Part IV on the Eucharist helpful, especially those concerning the reverence with which Christ is to be received, our self-offering, the devotion we ought to have, and what to do when lacking devotion. Again, apparently a number of saints have found this work helpful; that I haven't may be due to some limitation on my part.

Perhaps, though, the *Imitation* was simply the best of the spiritual writings available to the saints in question.

(Review by Marie George)

The Imitation of Christ by Thomas à Kempis

The Imitation of Christ is an early 15th-century Latin handbook for the spiritual life attributed to Thomas à Kempis. Born in a Rhineland town in either 1379 or 1380, he died in 1471. Thomas of Kempen spent his mature years in the Netherlands as a member of the Brothers of the Common Life, whose founder was Gerard Groot. While the *Imitation* is among the most popular spiritual and devotional works in the Christian canon, counting such saints as Thomas More, Ignatius of Loyola, and Thérèse of Lisieux among those who took its spiritual counsels to heart, it did not emerge from a vacuum. It formed an important link in the practice known as the *Devotio Moderna* (Modern Devotion), a renewal movement calling for a return to pious practices such as humility, obedience, and simplicity of life. A reinvigoration of the weakened monastic tradition and a call to clergy to live in accordance with gospel precepts and Church doctrine were also among its chief aims. It is fair to characterize the *Devotio Moderna* as a Christian humanist counterpoint to the rise of secular humanism in the early renaissance. The popularity of the *Devotio Moderna* was undermined by the advent of the Protestant Reformation.

The sometime ascription of anonymity to the author of the *Imitation* is a testimony to the actual humility of Thomas à Kempis, as various biographical sources attest. As the title of the book indicates, spiritual advancement and enlightenment should be grounded in the imitation of Christ. St. Augustine taught that the imitation of Christ is the fundamental purpose of a human life, a view later echoed by St. Francis of Assisi, who distinguished between spiritual and physical *mimesis* in advocating the practice of preaching and poverty respectively. The Stoic emperor Marcus Aurelius recognized the efficacy of imitation as a virtue even earlier. "You should consider that Imitation is the most acceptable part of Worship, and that the Gods had much rather Mankind should Resemble, than Flatter them."

The *Imitation* is divided into four parts. The book begins with advice about the spiritual life in general, then moves onto a focus upon the interior life of the soul engaged in an actual dialogue or encounter with Christ, and concludes with an exhortation to recognize the sacrificial splendor of the Holy Eucharist. The one hundred and fourteen chapters are brief and the content is quite accessible. One caveat is that the book's tone retains an early Church emphasis upon the utter sinfulness of human nature and the need to withdraw from the world, ideas that might seem at odds with a post-*aggiornamento* mindset. Aristotle espoused the belief that one becomes good by doing good. *The Imitation of Christ* facilitates such a worthy goal. In Book IV, Chap. 11, Thomas à Kempis writes: "For in this life I find there are two things especially necessary for me, without which this miserable life would be insupportable. Whilst detained in the prison of this body, I acknowledge that I need two things, namely, food and light." By the latter is meant the spiritual edification that sustains us on our journey toward salvation. This emphasis of the spiritual over the scholastic is complemented by another text: "a good and pure conscience bring more joy than learned philosophy." Since such a joy is guaranteed to all who follow what the title of the final chapter in Book Two calls "the royal road of the holy cross," it is a godsend to have such a guide as the *Imitation of Christ*.

(Review by Glenn Statile)

Other works by Thomas à Kempis include *On the Passion of Christ: According to the Four Evangelists: Prayers and Meditations* and *The Valley of Lilies & The Little Garden of Rose.*

Little Book of Eternal Wisdom by Bl. Henry Suso, OP
My Daily Bread by Fr. Anthony J. Paone, SJ

There are a couple of other books similar to the *Imitation* in that they take the form of a dialogue of sorts between God and the individual: *My Daily Bread* by Fr. Anthony J. Paone, SJ and the *Little Book of Eternal Wisdom* by Bl. Henry Suso, OP. In form they also resemble *He and I* except that the latter is composed of actual conversations between God and a real person (Gabrielle Bossis), rather than fictive ones. If I compare these three works, some people, such as myself, are able to readily relate to Gabrielle, and so are likely to find *He and I* more helpful than the other two works. Others, however, may find that the latter's more universal mode of discourse makes it easier to relate what is being said to their own lives; the fictive character in both works represents "any believer" wishing to grow close to God. Some other differences are: *My Daily Bread* and the *Little Book of Eternal Wisdom* are more didactic, somewhat sterner in tone, and try to motivate us in part by talking about the pains of hell (which certainly our Lord himself often mentions).

The chapters in Suso's *Little Book of Eternal Wisdom* vary in length from a couple of pages to a dozen pages; they lend themselves to being read a few paragraphs at a time. The first part has many chapters on our Lord's Passion and Death on the Cross, including several chapters in which Mary takes Christ's place as interlocutor. The topic of suffering is frequently addressed, e.g.: "*The Servant*: Lord, if Thou wouldst send me ordinary sufferings, I could bear them, but I do not see how I can ever endure such extraordinary sufferings as these.... *Eternal Wisdom*: Every sick man imagines that his own sickness is the worst, and every man in distress, his own distress the greatest. Had I sent thee other sufferings it would have been the same. Conform thyself freely to My will under every pain which I ordain thee to suffer, without excepting this or the other sufferings. Dost thou not know that I only desire what is best for thee, even with as kindly a feeling as thou thyself? Hence it is that I am the Eternal Wisdom, and that I know better than thou what is for thy good. .... Why then dost thou so complain to Me? Address Me rather as follows: O my most faithful Father, do to me at all times what Thou wilt!" Throughout the work the Servant respectfully addresses pointed questions to God, for example, as to why God allows us to fall into desolation when this seems to increase the likelihood that we fall into sin. One thing I find somewhat off-putting by Suso's work are the Servant's effusive exclamations issuing from his love or admiration of our Lord. Though of course such expressions of fervor are appropriate, the written text has the effect of blocking my own spontaneous expressions of this sort. Some may also find Suso's medieval style an obstacle to appreciating the content of his work.

In the second part, Suso treats the unprovided for death, prayer, practice of the presence of God, the Eucharist, and praise of God. In the third part, he proposes: "One Hundred Meditation and Prayers, Comprised in Few Words"—nine pages worth of meditation topics a sentence or two long.

Here are a few additional comments about *My Daily Bread*: the brevity of its chapters (2–3 pages), along with its comprehensive treatment of the various aspects of the spiritual life, makes it suitable for use all year long and even by those who have limited time. Each chapter begins with a message from Christ, after which there is a reflection on it, and lastly there is a prayer. Here is a representative example of a reflection: "So often when I thought I was doing something for God, I became angry, spiteful, or uncharitable toward those who interfered with my plans! The fact that I lost my self-control was proof that I was not working for God at all. My worst enemy is within me—this blind, puny, selfish self! Only when I act for God alone, will my action be at its best. I must pray daily with humility and with hope that I may overcome this contemptible self within me."

(Review by Marie George)

The Practice of the Love of Jesus Christ by St. Alphonsus Liguori

St. Alphonsus, a Doctor of the Church, wrote over a hundred works on spirituality and theology; his works have been widely disseminated in many languages. The *Practice of the Love of Jesus Christ* alone has appeared in over five hundred editions. St. Alphonsus himself regarded it as his "most pious and practical" work. The piety at times might prove a bit much for some; there is a vehemence of his expression of affection for God that some may find is not their style. St. Alphonsus recounts anecdotes such as: St. Francis broke into tears upon seeing a lamb or any object reminding him of Jesus; St. Wenceslas warmed snow-covered paths so much after making a visit to the Blessed Sacrament that his companion did not feel the cold. There is no doubt St. Alphonsus has a heart, but he also has a head, and can be hard-nosed and very practical, and this is why he is a favorite for some (including me). Also characteristic of St. Alphonsus's work are frequent references to Scripture and to the writings of other saints.

The first four chapters of the work's seventeen chapters (most of which can be read in one sitting) are ordered to showing us how much we ought to love Jesus. The first chapter contains a teaching I'd heard from the good nuns: Christ would have suffered all the pains of the cross for each of us alone. In Chapter 4, we are told: "Nothing in the world should trouble us, for the hands that dispose the circumstances of our lives are those that for love for us were nailed to the cross." Chapters 5 and 6 are on patience and meekness; the latter chapter contains healthy advice about being gentle with ourselves when we fall into sin. Chapter 7 contains a to-the-point treatment of purity of heart. Chapter 8 makes an important distinction between inadvertent venial sin and deliberate venial sin; the former we should not obsess over, but the latter is sort of lukewarmness we need to flee; five remedies for lukewarmness are suggested. The next four chapters are on humility, vain glory ("you are who you are before God"), detachment (just as a bird attached by a string ever so fine cannot fly, so too souls that do not break their attachment to some worldly thing do not attain union with God), and mildness. Chapters 13 and 14, which cover the conformity to the will of God especially in the face of things particularly hard to bear (sickness, poverty, and scorn), are to be ranked with *Trustful Surrender to Divine Providence*; indeed, I suspect that work drew upon St. Alphonsus. The one thing I take exception with is his view that spiritual directors are to be shown unreasoning obedience. The discussion of four reasons for why God lets us suffer is concise and helpful. And his treatment of what one should do if one is so sick one seems unable to pray is short, but very helpful. Another outstanding chapter is the final chapter directed to those afflicted by temptations or experiencing desolation. In Chapter 15 on faith, St. Alphonsus points out that those of us who believe in the mysteries of our faith and in the utility of the sacraments, but don't really accept that it is a blessing to be poor, afflicted, and maltreated, have little faith in

Christ. In the following chapter, on hope, he reiterates Aquinas's teaching that even if it were revealed to one that one was damned, one should take this as a warning, not as an expression of certain condemnation. The work concludes with a summary of the main points.

(Review by Marie George)

The Practice of the Love of Jesus Christ by St. Alphonsus Liguori

In *The Practice of the Love of Jesus Christ* St. Alphonsus Liguori provides an extended meditation on the famous passage in 1 Cor., Chap. 13 ("Love is patient, love is kind..."). Not overly long, this book is very accessible and quite ideal for spiritual reading, perhaps as a bedside book or as a companion to visits to a chapel for prayer. In small chapters, which are easily read in one sitting, St. Alphonsus elaborates on how, by following the precepts presented in 1 Cor., we will learn to think and act like one who loves Jesus Christ. He concludes each chapter with a prayer to help interiorize what was learned.

This book will most benefit those who are seriously committed to the faith and would like to deepen their spiritual life, but are not sure how to proceed. St. Alphonsus's admonitions are very demanding, but can provide the reader with a new resolution to grow in holiness. His counsels are indeed hard: we read of the need to love suffering, to disavow worldly ambition and worldly esteem, and of the danger of damnation. His words can be shocking at times to our modern sensibilities, but are very valuable as a corrective to prevailing laxity. His best chapter reflects on "Charity Dealeth not Perversely." In it he provides practical advice on avoiding lukewarmness, including cultivating a desire for perfection and the importance of mental prayer or meditation. This chapter alone is worth reading if nothing else. St. Alphonsus presents a very inspiring vision: he assumes in a straightforward manner that everyone should strive to be, and can become, a saint. It is perhaps common to hear people snicker at efforts at improvement even in secular matters, let alone with respect to religion. Given this,

St. Alphonsus's words are encouraging, "Those who really desire perfection never stop advancing toward it? and if they don't give up, they finally get there."

Especially helpful and practical is a recap of St. Alphonsus's major points near the end of his meditations on Corinthians. He provides a quick overview of the main themes which can serve as points for prayer and meditation. St. Alphonsus also includes a list of short and poignant maxims dealing with the spiritual life, such as "Whoever wishes for God alone is rich in every good," "He that loves God, finds pleasure in everything; he that loves not God, finds no true pleasure in anything," and "He that desires nothing in this world is master of the whole world." Since these points are short and may be consulted daily, this book is greatly valuable, not just as a work to be read once, but as one that may be referenced with profit over many years.

The Practice of the Love of Jesus Christ is a first rate work by a Doctor of the Church. A prayerful and engaged reading will be extremely beneficial for anyone who desires to deepen his or her faith. It is recommended without reservation.

(Review by Michael McCaffery)

St. Alphonsus Liguori's many works include *The Twelve Steps to Holiness and Salvation, Uniformity with God's Will, How to Pray at All Times,* and *Visits to the Most Blessed Sacrament and the Blessed Virgin Mary* (reviewed in this volume).

This Tremendous Lover by Dom M. Eugene Boylan, OCR

This book comes highly recommended by people such as Joseph Cardinal Bernadine and Fr. Benedict Groeschel, CFR. I think that this is partly because Boylan relies heavily on Church documents and on the writings of the saints, especially Thomas Aquinas. I also think it is because of the commonsensical and balanced character of his advice. For example, in speaking of the need to reflect on spiritual reading he counsels: "To us it seems quite sufficient that a man should, say, sit down at his own fire . . . or that he should go out for a walk. . . . As far as thinking goes, there are many men and women who will achieve much more in such a way than by trying to think on their knees in the cold of the morning before breakfast. . . . However, men and their minds vary, and each should do what suits him best in the matter." One exception to Boylan's usual attentiveness to individual differences is his seemingly categorical rejection of married women having careers.

Boylan's work follows his own advice that we need to first educate ourselves as to revealed doctrine, especially as to the Lord's life and teaching, along with the general principles of the spiritual life, and then we should do spiritual reading that fosters union with our Lord more directly. Accordingly, there is a lot of doctrinal instruction in this book, especially in the earlier chapters (Chapters 1–4 are on the fall, the plan of restoration, the redemption, and the mystical body). Those who are well-catechized may find the early chapters a bit dry.

Chapters 5 and 6, on partnership with Christ and membership of Christ, build directly on the previous chapters. Chapter 7 contains an excellent discussion of humility, elaborating on how God resists the proud and gives grace to the humble, and tying humility in with obedience to God's will. In Chapter 17 Boylan returns to this important theme, discussing at length the human tendency to "want to be conscious of our own strength" and to place our hopes for happiness in ourselves. Chapters 8 and 10, on prayer, contain a lot of sound advice for beginners, e.g., to be careful not to decide to say so many prayers that they become a burden to us, potentially resulting in us giving up praying altogether. (Later on, Chapter 19 presents clearly and succinctly the saints' teachings on more advanced forms of prayer.) Chapter 9, on spiritual reading, begins by highlighting its importance and then gives flexible suggestions as to its frequency and content. Chapters 11–14 treat the Sacraments in general, the Eucharist, the Mass, and Divine Providence. Chapters 15, 18, and 20 on abandonment, Christ's Cross, and confidence in Christ are hard hitting, and Chapter 16 on union with Christ in our neighbor contains a lot of balanced advice. In the latter chapter Boylan mentions a point that he returns to in Chapter 21 on marriage, namely, that a person's idea of God has a great influence on his spiritual life, and "that idea is formed chiefly by the example and model of one's parents' love and kindness, and in later years by the love and kindness of one's spouse." Chapter 22 is on Mary, and includes a discussion of consecration to Mary. Chapters 23 and 24 wrap up the book by reiterating its main themes, God's great love for us and our need to trust in His plan for our lives and to "cast ourselves on His mercy in our complete poverty and powerlessness, joyfully accepted and gladly acknowledged, so that all may come to us from Him."

(Review by Marie George)

This Tremendous Lover by Dom M. Eugene Boylan, OCR

This Tremendous Lover, written in 1947 by the Trappist monk M. Eugene Boylan, is a spiritual guide written primarily to help and encourage the layperson to develop a spiritual life that fosters daily growth in closeness with Christ. Boylan describes Christ as our "tremendous lover" who seeks to make us happy forever by joining in spousal union with us. Our part is to have faith in Him, hope in Him, love Him, have true humility, and abandon ourselves to God's will. Once we are in union with Christ we can rely on Him in us to love God perfectly.

Boylan gives practical advice on how to accomplish our part of faith, hope, charity, true humility, and abandonment to God's will. Of utmost importance are daily spiritual reading, reflection, and prayer. Reading spiritual works, especially the Gospels, will lend to reflection that will help us in prayer, and prayer will fuel our love for Christ. Boylan encourages those of us who spend our prayer time battling distractions to persevere, saying that "our very inability to pray is a perfect prayer" and our relentless efforts are extremely pleasing to God. In time, what started off as prayer predominantly with words will evolve to affections and eventually to prayer of love with no words, a total movement of the heart. In addition to praying and meditating daily, we must also frequent the sacraments. These are the special channels through which we are supplied with graces, merited by Christ, necessary to maintain a vital union with Him. Participating in the Eucharist results in our greatest union with Christ because He is our food, and this food has the power to transform us into it. In this way we gain Christ's power to love God.

To receive the graces from prayer and the sacraments, the dispositions required of us are true humility and submission to God's will. True humility consists in lovingly accepting our own weaknesses or aridity in our daily attempts at prayer, and it opens us to God's mercy. God helps the humble, the poor in spirit, thereby rendering Himself glorious and sanctifying us. Humility in our interactions with others, such as accepting criticism, not insisting on our own opinion, and yielding to the will of others, helps us ultimately to abandon ourselves to God's will, which is the greatest way to be united to Christ. God's greatest desire for us is to be united with Him in perfect happiness, and there is nothing that happens in our lives, no matter what mistakes we've committed in our past, that is not permitted or supervised by God for the ultimate end of uniting us with Him. Cheerfully accepting our present situation is the highest way of accepting His will and is all that is necessary for complete sanctification and perfect union with Christ.

I highly recommend this book to the laity, particularly married laity. Not having the gift that the religious have in being required to follow a daily regimen of prayer, the layperson can benefit from this book's insistence on the necessity of daily prayer for the vitality of the spiritual life. Further, an entire chapter is dedicated to the vocation of marriage. Boylan goes so far as to say that "in some mysterious way husband and wife share in the reality their union symbolizes," the union of Christ and the Church. Married people are called to and can arrive at the perfection in love that is between Christ and his Church, because in the sacramental union of marriage, there is not only natural but supernatural love. Boylan gives specific advice to both the husband and the wife to achieve that end, but also gives encouragement to those whose love is given but not returned. The chapter dedicated to humility is full of wisdom that could be applied directly to the married man and woman, for what is at the root of many failed marriages but pride? In the ideal Christian marriage, as in the ideal union between Christ and his "lover," each must, in faith, hope, love, humility, and abandonment, see and love and serve the other, as, in the words of St. Augustine, "One Christ loving Himself."

(Review by Lucy Iacoviello)

Boylan is also author of *Difficulties in Mental Prayer*.

Divine Providence

Abandonment to Divine Providence by Fr. Jean-Pierre de Caussade

As John Beevers points out in his introduction to the Image Books edition of *Abandonment to Divine Providence*, many of de Caussade's teachings are found in the works of earlier and later spiritual authors. At times I find de Caussade's formulations extreme. Also, overall, I find *Abandonment* less motivating than *Trustful Surrender to Divine Providence* because it speaks comparatively little of God's love and care for us and makes fewer references to Jesus.

De Caussade's advice boils down to: carry out the basic duties of Christianity and of one's state of life, accept God's will in all one does and suffers, and God will take possession of one's heart. However, those of us who are not simple souls need guidance if we are to do those things. De Caussade does offer some pointers. He insists repeatedly that spiritual reading and practices are useless unless they are done in accord with the will of God. This is doubtlessly true, but most of us need a daily spiritual to-do list if we are to keep ourselves from being preoccupied with worldly affairs and pleasures. De Caussade's legitimate concern here is that we compartmentalize our spiritual life.

De Caussade's central theme again is that God speaks to us at every moment through the events of our lives and that by surrendering ourselves to Him we will achieve holiness. De Caussade thus warns us that planning may lead us to becoming attached to attaining our own goals, when our sole goal is to love God and serve as tools for his projects: "We must give ourselves to whatever God wishes and for as long as he wishes and yet never get personally involved in them." Type A that I am, he seems to me at times to go too far in speaking against planning, which after all is often a manifestation of the virtue of prudence. De Caussade speaks of souls abandoned to God's will as having special sensitivity to God's promptings to speak to a given person, read a given book, etc. He says we should obey such promptings without reflection. But can we always be sure that they really are from God without rationally examining the matter? Still, he is right that we often ignore the promptings of grace to follow our own lights: "Jesus is our master to whom we do not pay enough attention." De Caussade notes that we often do not understand God's ways. According to him, all we need to know is that God knows what He is doing with us and that His work is the best possible. De Caussade gives the famous comparison of our lives being a tapestry that we see from the messy side and God sees from the beautiful side. We need to stay focused on loving God and doing what He requires of us in the present moment, and not fret over the reasons why God allows us to undergo certain sufferings. While *Abandonment* is not a book I am drawn to rereading, there is doubtlessly profit to be drawn from it, especially its central message that God, at every moment, provides us the guidance we need to become holy, and we need to be attentive to Him.

(Review by Marie George)

Abandonment to Divine Providence by Fr. Jean-Pierre de Caussade, SJ

Abandonment to Divine Providence is a collection of retreat conferences, which the great Jesuit spiritual writer gave to the Nuns of the Visitation in Nancy (France) in the early 18th century. The book is divided into two books, "On the Virtue of Abandonment" and "On the State of Abandonment."

Abandonment is a remarkable book, and is quite different from most any other book of spiritual direction that I have ever read. You will search its pages in vain for any reference to Holy Mother Church, to the Holy Sacrifice of the Mass or the Eucharist, to the Divine Office, or to ascetical practices. The book contains only scant references to the Fathers and Doctors of the Church, the lives of the Saints, or the great spiritual writers.

What you will find is one of the most simple and sublime methods of achieving sanctity that you may ever read. This book came as a shock to me, given that I had spent the last decade reading about Roman Catholic spirituality, Church history, the lives of saints, theology, etc., before I read it. "No one becomes learned in the science of God either by the reading of books, or by the inquisitive investigation of history." According to de Caussade I have been missing the entire point of how to achieve a life of holiness. Why? For the simple reason that "When one is thirsty one quenches one's thirst by drinking, not by reading books which treat of this condition."

Instead, de Caussade argues that "Perfection consists in submitting unreservedly to the designs of God, and in fulfilling the duties of one's state in the most perfect manner possible." This fidelity is achieved in two ways: active and passive abandonment to the Will of God. The former consists in fidelity to the duties incumbent on us from the laws of God or the Church, while the latter is the loving acceptance of all that God sends us at each moment. The term "duties of the present moment" is a common thread woven throughout this great work. Though the book is primarily intended for religious, it is easily adaptable to the life of a layperson. For abandonment, as described by de Caussade, is a spiritual first principle, a foundation upon which to build a life that is ordered toward Christian perfection. Once the foundation is laid, it will support the spiritual life of a layperson or a religious. The point he is making is that once a soul abandons himself to Providence, God will make a saint of him, much as an artist of sculptor creates a masterpiece.

The beauty of de Caussade's method is that it can be practiced everywhere and at all times. For, he assures us, "there isn't a moment in which God does not present himself under the cover of some pain to be endured, of some consolation to be enjoyed, or of some duty to be performed. All that takes place within us, around us, or through us, contains and conceals his divine action." And the result of such abandonment, of submission to the will of God, is that He "changes into divine gold all [of our] occupations, troubles and sufferings."

I think that a person needs two qualifications to read this work with profit, the first of which is a good understanding of basic Catholic doctrine, particularly as it regards the duties and obligations of one's state in life. Without this, a person could slip into laxism, or quietism, and actually fall away from the path of perfection. De Caussade warns against such dangers, in seeking to discern God's will, and counsels that "souls should only attend to those inspirations which it believes it has received from God, *by the fact that these inspirations do not withdraw it from the duties of its state*" (emphasis added). Secondly, the person should have at least a moderate understanding of Divine Providence; otherwise it may be difficult for him to truly understand why we should trust in it.

(Review by John Stehn)

Other works by de Caussade include *Spiritual Counsels* and *Letters on the Practice of Abandonment to Divine Providence.*

He Leadeth Me by Fr. Walter J. Ciszek, SJ

He Leadeth Me is the second book written by Fr. Ciszek, a Jesuit priest who suffered for nearly twenty-three years in the Soviet Union, first in solitary confinement, then at a Siberian labor camp. His earlier autobiography, *With God in Russia*, recounts the events of those years living under the atheistic communist regime. He wrote this later book to better respond to the question he often was asked as to how he survived all those years under such horrific conditions. In this book, he shares his "conversion" that allowed him not only to survive, but to grow into an extraordinary vessel of God's grace.

Fr. Ciszek's spirituality is reminiscent of that of earlier Jesuit writers, Fr. J.-P. de Caussade, SJ (1675–1751) (*Self-Abandonment to Divine Providence*), Fr. Jean Baptiste Saint-Jure, SJ (1588–1657), and St. Claude de la Colombière, SJ (1641–1682) (*Trustful Surrender to Divine Providence*). But Ciszek demonstrates through his personal experience how absolute confidence in God's presence, providence and power can be lived in even the most abject of circumstances. And in living out this radical dependence on and trust in God, he provides an avenue of hope to anyone in any circumstance, since it would be difficult to imagine a situation in which it would be more impossible to do so than his.

Ciszek reveals why trust in God is fundamental to the Christian faith. He gives practical advice and valuable insights as to how radical trust in God can be incorporated into the ordinary and not-so-ordinary events of anyone's life. Throughout the book, he masterfully relates his personal experience to trials and temptations faced by every committed Christian.

It is important not to skim over the few but critical passages that he devotes to what allowed him to accept and then persevere in a radical dependence on God—humility and prayer. It is apparent that Ciszek developed his deep prayer life before undertaking his mission into the Soviet Union, and it was through prayer that he allowed God to speak to him and to change his heart throughout his experience. He sheds new light on why prayer and scripture meditation are essential, and how we can overcome common difficulties in prayer. The book includes a beautiful exposition on the significance of the *Our Father*.

Other passages address common challenges in the spiritual life: temptation when a project we have undertaken out of love for God does not play out as we anticipated; physical suffering in the mystery of salvation; the importance of witnessing by the way one lives; and, the fear of death. Other aspects of the book provide profound thoughts for meditation on such subjects as the Eucharist and the Mass, the priesthood, and the sanctifying nature of work.

There are parts of the book that are repetitious and that obviously were not written by a professional author, but I found this reinforces the authenticity of the author's convictions and the sense that he is earnestly trying to convey the lessons he learned for the benefit of others. As he points out on several occasions, they are not easy lessons to learn, but having Fr. Ciszek's example, advice, and encouragement lends hope that we might follow to where Christ led him.

(Review by Sheri Richert)

He Leadeth Me by Fr. Walter J. Ciszek, SJ

The previous review so thoroughly treats the contents of *He Leadeth Me* that I will only add a few comments by way of emphasis. The book is not a treatise on themes pertaining to the spiritual life, but rather is autobiographical. It portrays failings that most sinners can easily identify with, only then to show how God meets us in our misery by forgiving, healing, and strengthening us. Ciszek, as many of us do, overlooked God's will in the ordinary events of his life because of his idea of what God ought to will. He became discouraged about dismal situations that he could do little, if anything, to change, instead of focusing on changing himself, something that would have had a positive effect on those around him (sound familiar?). And he relied on his own strength. Through the grace and mercy of God, Ciszek's failings ultimately turn into the means of his conversion to a whole-hearted trust in His Providence. *He Leadeth Me* is without doubt the most inspiring story concerning Divine Providence that I have ever read.

(Review by Marie George)

Let Go by Archbishop François Fénelon

I was a bit leery about reading Fénelon, as his *Maxims of the Saints* had been condemned by the Inquisition. However, I found nothing unorthodox in *Let Go*, a collection of letters written by Fénelon for the purpose of spiritual direction. His main message is that we need to abandon ourselves to God in our sufferings, trusting that He sends them in order to excise the self-love that prevents us from dying to ourselves and living for Him. Virtually everything Fénelon says develops one aspect or another of this theme. For example, he notes that our resistance to suffering is worse than the suffering itself. We need to trust that God knows how to proportion our sufferings so that we can accomplish His purposes. We tend to praise ourselves, more or less overtly, for the good we do, failing to acknowledge that we can do nothing without God. We nourish our selfishness in a myriad of other ways as well. God sends us sufferings that hit us at our most tender spot, at the part of us that most clings to a life that is not rooted in God: "The great Physician who sees in us what we cannot see, knows exactly where to place the knife. He cuts away that which we are most reluctant to give up. And how it hurts!" Sometimes it is fairly obvious why we need to suffer a certain way; as one heading affirms: "Sensitivity to Reproof is the Surest Sign We Need it." Sometimes suffering helps us by exposing our self-sufficiency. Other times, however, we do not understand the purpose of the specific suffering that has been sent us. Fénelon insists that we need to abandon ourselves to God and not second-guess Him. Sometimes we fail to see the purpose of our suffering because our self-love blinds us, but other times God intentionally acts in a hidden way, because if we knew the sanctifying work that God was doing in us, we might become proud. Fénelon notes that suffering is not only a necessity if we are to be striped of our self-love, it is also something we should welcome and bear out of love for Christ. Christians know that they are called to carry their cross each day.

Let Go sheds light on how "crosses are God's means of drawing souls closer to Himself." While this short book treats a fundamental matter of our faith, it seems to me better suited to someone who is not a beginner in the spiritual life. The book presupposes some depth of conviction about certain truths, e.g., concerning God's immense love for us, as well as a certain degree of self-knowledge obtained through regular examination of conscience; it also presupposes a certain lived experience of suffering.

(Review by Marie George)

Let Go by Archbishop François Fénelon

I describe this compilation of forty letters as a motivational book with a spiritual perspective that will speak differently to each reader's circumstance. Although the crux of the message is the same throughout, each letter delivers the message in a way that appears to address different sets of circumstances in which we may find ourselves, and each serves as a reminder to help us realize that we cannot do it alone. In my opinion, the book should be read more than once to fully grasp the message. In fact, it would be a good idea to make note of a letter(s) that particularly speaks to you and refer to it as needed. For me, that was Letter 38 (and others). My review of *Let Go* could best be summed up by my own experience. Namely, it will minister to you if you let it.

Whether because of my own shortcomings or my conscious resistance, as I began reading it I thought, "To whom is he writing?" It seemed to me as if the letters were addressed to an audience straight out of the seventeenth century; one which would better appreciate and understand a theme based in something akin to self-flagellation. Letter 4, for example, read as something macabre, not spiritually uplifting. The "dying of one's self" came across to me as if some form of punishment, not the more spiritually peaceful message of "let go and let God." My initial reaction was to put it down. I've got nothing against a "smack in the face" type of enlightenment; it's just that it did not speak to me at all.

My thoughts then turned to "this is intended for those desirous of living a deeper, Christian life." Even then it seemed to me that while these letters might reach an audience in a seventeenth century setting, they were not meant for people living in the modern world, and especially not parents such as myself who are raising children in the face of the pressures typical of our era. With the burden and responsibilities of raising four active children in this day and age, how could I "let go" as expressed in these letters?

I am not sure if the editor intended the letters to be placed in any particular order, but the farther along I read, the clearer the message was coming to me. It wasn't until I read Letter 30 that I began to realize he was speaking to me, not some reader in the seventeenth century. Letter 30 spoke to me, particularly the first two sentences, because they described me. But, it wasn't until Letter 38 that I truly understood and appreciated the message. At that point, I wanted to re-read the letters to see what I must have missed because it was finally beginning to sink in. It took this reader nearly until the end of the book to realize that to better appreciate *Let Go*, one should first, well, let go.

Like most spiritual writings, the message is timeless and is intended for all readers whose goal is to attain an inner peace. I'd like to (respectfully) elaborate on this with my own interpretation of the message: resistance to the circumstances that we face makes the difficulty we are meant to bear even more burdensome than God intended it to be. As my wife has been saying for many years, "learn to let go and let God" and things will work out as they should.

To put it another way, "Trust in the Lord with all thine heart and lean not unto thy own understanding. In all thy ways acknowledge him and he shall direct thy path" (Pr. 3:5–6).

(Review by Sabino Biondi)

Another work by Fénelon is *The Seeking Heart.*

Trustful Surrender to Divine Providence: The Secret of Peace and Happiness by Fr. Jean Baptiste Saint-Jure, SJ and St. Claude de la Colombière, SJ

Although Fr. Saint-Jure and St. Claude de la Colombière did not write this book together, one can readily see why an editor put their writings together. St. Claude often repeats the same points Fr. Saint-Jure covered, but without sounding redundant; he heightens the importance of what Saint-Jure said and he adds some profound insights. Both authors engage the mind by their logic, clarity, use of Scripture, excerpts from the writings of the saints, examples, and simple comparisons; and they engage the heart by their warmth. Their accessible treatment of the important reality of divine providence makes this a must-read for anyone who does spiritual reading.

Saint-Jure first quotes the Scripture that says even if a woman could forget her child, God will never forget us. He then explains that nothing happens unless God wills it, and so if you are the victim of someone's evil-doing, although God does not will the evil of sin, He does will that you suffer. God who is supremely wise and loving knows what is best for you. God is like the surgeon who sometimes causes pain in order to cure, and like the father who punishes his child for the child's good. The trials and sufferings God sends us are perfectly suited to our advantage, if only we cooperate with Him. God is trying to sculpt us into a living image of Himself, and will never send us a trial that is not conducive to this end. Our sanctification lies in loving God with all our heart, and since mutual love involves the union of hearts, our will should be in accord with God's will. Conforming our will to God's will not only will bring us eternal salvation, but brings us peace in this life, for since everything happens according to God's will, if our will is conformed to His, everything will happen in accord with ours. Saint-Jure elaborates on all the different circumstances in our lives in which we are called to practice conformity to God's will and of the benefit we thereby gain.

St. Claude begins by affirming: "It is one of the most firmly established and most consoling of the truths that have been revealed to us that (apart from sin) *nothing happens to us in life unless God wills it so.*" It is consoling because God wants the best for us, and knows better than we do what we need in order to save our souls. St. Claude goes through all the things that God has done for us that ought to inspire our trust (dying on the Cross, providing us with a guardian angel, etc.), and he answers the complaint that God sometimes strikes us with cruel blows, observing: "What have you to fear from a hand that was pierced and nailed to the cross for you?". St. Claude points out that if we are to trust Divine Providence in great trials, we need to practice trusting it in the small trials that occur in daily life. He also points out that few of us are able surrender our whole lives to God, and that God helps us detach ourselves from what is holding us back from perfect love by sending us a trial that affords a propitious opportunity for doing so. We too often have an eye to our material well-being when this in fact is what keeps us from loving God and neighbor as we ought. St. Claude thus urges us to pray: "Either give me so much money that my heart will be satisfied, or inspire me with such contempt for it that I no longer want it." He ends on the note of God's great love for us, to which he appends an exercise of conformity to Divine Providence.

(Review by Marie George)

Trustful Surrender to Divine Providence by Fr. Jean Baptiste Saint-Jure, SJ and St. Claude de la Colombière, SJ

I am not exaggerating when I state that this book saved my life . . . at least my spiritual life and perhaps my sanity. It was providentially given to me by a friend on the eve of some dreadful upheavals in my life. It was shortly after reading it that my father became ill and died. The very next year, my wife filed for divorce. Either one of these events would have sent me into a spiritual tailspin, had I not previously read *Trustful Surrender*. And while they were accompanied by much sadness and suffering, nevertheless, the lessons that I learned from this remarkable little book help me not only to survive, but to grow spiritually, as a result of these events.

Trustful Surrender is very small book, and it consists of a chapter taken from separate spiritual works that were written by each of the authors. The first part, by Fr. Saint-Jure, demonstrates the premise of God's absolute governance over the created world with ample quotations from Scripture. From there, he develops the principle of trustfully abandoning and conforming ourselves to the will of our Heavenly Father. He follows this with practical examples of doing so, for various circumstances and situations that occur in our everyday lives:

- Public calamities
- Adversity and disgrace
- Defects in our nature
- Poverty and hardships
- Sickness and infirmity
- Interior trials

What is so nice about these situations is that they do not just apply to religious. Most, if not all of them, apply equally to those in the lay state as well.

The second part is by St. Claude, who does a remarkable job of developing a sure understanding of why we should have absolute faith, confidence, and above all trust in God's providential care over us. He does this with just a few quotations from Scripture. For the rest, he relies on elegantly developed conclusions drawn from the Scriptural passages. In the process, he answers critical questions such as "Why does God allow suffering?" and "Why aren't my prayers being answered?"

To me, the wisdom imparted by this book is more than a foundation for a fruitful spiritual life, it is a metaphysical first principle of reality. As St. Claude notes:

> It is one of the most firmly established and most consoling of the truths that have been revealed to us that (apart from sin) nothing happens to us in life unless God wills it so. Wealth and poverty alike come from Him. If we fall ill, God is the cause of our illness; if we get well, our recovery is due to God. We owe our lives entirely to Him, and when death comes to put an end to life, His will be the hand that deals the blow.

This principle, illuminated by the sure knowledge that God is a Father who loves us and wants us to be intimately united with Him for eternity, is the point of departure for this book. Our authors skillfully unfold from these truths that learning how to trust in

God's providence and abandon ourselves to His will is the key to happiness in this life and in the next. Trusting Divine Providence is easier said than done; it takes great patience, particularly during painful trials and tribulations. It is impossible without the grace of God, which, however, our loving Father desires to bestow on us, if only we ask Him.

The two authors are careful to point out that this doctrine is not an invitation to throw up our hands and say "who cares"—just the opposite. We are to do what we can, and always act in accordance with virtuous moral principles, but we can be sure that the outcome of our actions are guided by a loving Father who wills to be united with us for eternity.

I think this book is indispensable to anyone who seeks to make progress in the spiritual life, and it is particularly so for those of the melancholic or choleric temperaments, as they tend to have great difficulty in trusting Divine Providence.

(Review by John Stehn)

Some of St. Claude's letters and retreat notes can be found in *The Spiritual Direction of Saint Claude de la Colombière* (reviewed in this volume).

Mary

The Glories of Mary by St. Alphonsus Liguori

This work is long, a good 700 pages; however, it is a work that one can draw profit from, even if one skips around and only reads parts of it. It contains some fairly protracted discussions of theological questions such as whether Mary is the Mediatrix of grace, but also offers a great deal of material for meditation, including meditations on the Hail Holy Queen, on the principal Marian Feasts, on the Litany of the Blessed Virgin Mary, and on the Seven Sorrows of Mary. St. Alphonsus is a bit saccharine and flowery at times, although one can be sure that his words spring for a sincere love for our Lady. Some may have a hard time following the theological battles he engages in. The book is full of pious stories, which some readers may find engaging and others pietistic. There is no doubt that you will understand Mary better after you read only parts of this book, and most likely, you will realize (as I did) that you ought to increase your devotion to her.

I came to the book with a couple of questions. As for whether Mary is Mediatrix of grace, St. Alphonsus answers this in a resounding affirmative, both in a section devoted to this topic and in the section on the Visitation. This somewhat surprised me given the comparatively circumscribed understanding that the *Catechism of the Catholic Church* (see nos. 969–70) presents us with. In response to the obvious objection that there is only one mediator between God and man, St. Alphonsus says that "Mary was made the mediatress of our salvation; not indeed a mediatress of justice, but of grace and intercession." He addresses other objections that had occurred to me, and quotes many authorities, such as St. Bernard, on this matter.

Another question I had was whether St. Alphonsus had a view on St. Louis de Montfort's Marian consecration. He does mention Marian consecration a number of times, but never exactly in the form de Montfort presents it. Also, unlike de Montfort, when St. Alphonsus speaks of Marian devotions, he recommends that we pick the ones we like best and stick to them and makes no claims about the superiority of one over another.

(Review by Marie George)

The Glories of Mary by St. Alphonsus Liguori

Perhaps St. Alphonsus Liguori's greatest work, this monumental tome about the Blessed Mother is not for those squeamish about the dignity of Mary in creation, salvation history, and the estimation of the Church. The work is divided into, first, a line-by-line commentary on the *Salve Regina*, second, discourses on Mary's feasts, third, her sorrows, fourth, her virtues, and last, devotions to her, especially the Rosary. Nevertheless, St. Alphonsus's goal here is not hyperbole: he cannot be accused of waxing so poetical that he goes overboard, to the point of superstitiously divinizing a virgin from Nazareth, mistaking creature for Creator, as Protestants sometimes complain. Rather, Alphonsus argues from reason, from revelation, and from the Doctors of the Church to defend each praise he heaps upon Mary. *The Glories of Mary* is not only a panegyric for the Mother of God, but a theologically erudite defense of the honors the Church has never been hesitant to bestow on her. Likewise, then, it is an exhortation to nurture our own devotion to her, and a meditative practice of that devotion.

This is no short work (my copy is about 700 pages) and it is not methodologically systematic. Although it often repeats itself, it generally manages not to be repetitive as each return to an old theme usually adds fresh insights. Since it is for the most part focused on prayers and poems in praise of Mary, it never becomes so abstract or theologically abstruse that it appeals only to academics. Like Don Quixote with his devotion to Dulcinea, Alphonsus never loses sight of the goal of sharing our Lady with whomever is listening; his goal is to move the mind *and* the heart, so even the theological rigor is coupled with rich poetic imagery, drawn from the Gospels, Doctors of the Church, or the liturgy's use of the wisdom literature of the Old Testament. Given its size, however, this book would probably be best only for someone exceedingly comfortable with Marian devotions, so it would not be ideal for a new Catholic. There are more suitable—that is, briefer—introductory works on the Blessed Mother.

(Review by Chris Decaen)

St. Alphonsus Liguori is the author of many works, including *The*

Practice of the Love of Jesus Christ and *Visits to the Most Blessed Sacrament* (both are reviewed in this volume).

33 *Days to Morning Glory* by Fr. Michael E. Gaitley, MIC

Fr. Gaitley's 33 *Days to Morning Glory* is a less demanding alternative to St. Louis de Montfort's method for preparing for Marian consecration. De Montfort advises prayers, readings from both Scripture and spiritual authors, along with specific spiritual exercises for each of the four weeks leading up to making the consecration. Fr. Gaitley's approach is to offer for each of the four weeks a short daily reflection on Marian teachings drawn from four saints.

Week one draws on St. Louis de Montfort. One of the main themes is that this consecration involves turning everything we have over to Mary, and thus giving her the right to dispose of the graces we gain by our good works (a theme I examine in my review of *True Devotion to the Blessed Virgin Mary*). Week two draws on St. Maximilian Kolbe who offers some ideas not presented by de Montfort, e.g., the notion of having a militia that seeks to conquer all the souls in the world for the Immaculata. According to Fr. Gaitley, Kolbe maintains that the Holy Spirit is the uncreated Immaculate Conception. Does this square, though, with the Church's Trinitarian theology? The Son is begotten, whereas the Holy Spirit proceeds; conception has to do with begetting. Week three draws upon St. Teresa of Calcutta. Here we are offered reflections on Christ's thirst and also on suffering: "Suffering, pain, sorrow, humiliation, feelings of loneliness, are nothing but the kiss of Jesus, a sign that you have come so close that he can kiss you." Week four draws on Pope St. John Paul II. Fr. Gaitley is not entirely clear as to how authoritative he thinks John Paul II's Marian teachings are when they do not simply echo Vatican II and other traditional Church teachings. Be that as it may, a teaching of John Paul II that Fr. Gaitley highlights is that we "take Mary into our home" by entrusting ourselves to her in a filial manner.

Fr. Gaitley offers a review and synthesis section for the final five days before consecration. I was glad to see a quotation from John Paul II affirming that true devotion to Mary can take many forms and no particular mode of devotion to her can claim "a monopoly over the others." It seems to me exaggerated to claim, as Fr. Gaitley does, that "Marian consecration is not just the quickest, easiest, and surest way to holiness for you and for me but for everyone."

Fr. Gaitley has a final chapter on the day of the consecration. There he addresses a tacit objection to the notion that we should do everything with Mary, namely, we are already having a hard time keeping God in mind. He suggests a middle position between saying once you are consecrated you need never explicitly think about Mary when performing actions in your daily life, and saying that you need to be continually thinking of Mary.

Fr. Gaitley's informal tone may be grating to some. However, the book is not short on content and has proven helpful to many who were preparing for Marian consecration. It comes recommended by Mother Assumpta Long, OP, among others.

(Review by Marie George)

33 *Days to Morning Glory* by Fr. Michael E. Gaitley, MIC

Fr. Michael Gaitley wrote this "Do-It-Yourself Retreat in Preparation for Marian Consecration" in 2011 to provide an "updated" way to make the consecration to Jesus through Mary that traditionally has been the hallmark of St. Louis Marie de Montfort. In the introduction, Fr. Gaitley notes that he personally finds it spiritually more fruitful to meditate on teachings about Marian consecration than to recite the long prayers contained in de Montfort's preparation. This short book, which has become widely popular in just a few short years, is intended for others with the same inclination.

The title of the book refers to the thirty-three days prescribed for the preparation and "morning glory" to, in Fr. Gaitley's words, "a new way of life in Christ. The act of consecrating oneself to Christ through Mary marks the beginning of a gloriously new day, a new dawn, a brand new morning in one's spiritual journey. It's a fresh start, and it changes everything."

The book is divided into five segments. Each of the first four are dedicated to meditations on the Marian spirituality of, respectively, St. Louis de Montfort, St. Maximillian Kolbe, St. Mother Teresa of

Calcutta, and St. John Paul II. The fifth segment of five days consists of a one-day summary of each of the four weeks and a final day to meditate on the prayer of consecration proposed by Fr. Gaitley (or the opportunity to write one's own prayer).

The meditations throughout the book are gems of Marian spirituality. The long quotes from the Saints provide fertile ground for deepening one's understanding of the theological basis for consecration to Mary and the benefits to be derived from it. Fr. Gaitley includes the writings of: St. Kolbe, on the profound union between the Holy Spirit and Mary (written only hours before his arrest by the Gestapo); St. Mother Teresa, on how Mary teaches us about the thirst of Jesus on the Cross; and St. John Paul II, on the scriptural basis for understanding Mary's motherhood and mediation.

The brevity of the meditations may be disappointing to some, but they can easily be supplemented by referencing the original source materials that are readily available. Some readers may also be distracted by Fr. Gaitley's overly casual writing style, but one can still benefit from the quoted materials. And finally, those who believe that prayer is an integral part of the preparation for consecration, particularly those who have previously followed and appreciated the formula of de Montfort, may find Fr. Gaitley's reliance solely on meditation materials to be insufficient. The solution to this last objection, time permitting, is to combine the two methods on a daily basis.

In any case, it is worth reading 33 *Days* for the purpose of understanding and better appreciating the recent developments in Marian theology that are the basis of the spirituality of some of the greatest saints of our time.

(Review by A. M. Desprit)

Others works by Fr. Gaitley include *The One Thing is Three: How the Most Holy Trinity Explains Everything* and *Consoling the Heart of Jesus* (reviewed in this volume).

True Devotion to Mary by St. Louis-Marie Grignion de Montfort

Far be it from me to disparage a devotion that has been put into practice by many saints. At the same time, not every devotion is for everyone. This one does not appeal to me. I agree that we should choose to offer everything we have to God, our liberty, memory, understanding, and will (as St. Ignatius puts it), and it makes sense to call this "voluntary slavery" (as de Montfort does; see also Rom. 6:22). However, I do not think that it follows that God wants us to offer everything we have to Mary on the grounds that she is the Mother of God and Queen of Heaven. After all, He does not want us to worship Mary on those grounds, nor has He made the beatific vision consist in knowledge of her. God has a right to demand of us nothing less than ourselves; we were made for Him. This does not seem to me to be the prerogative of any creature, no matter how sublime. De Montfort acknowledges that Mary is not the final end of our services. However, he makes it seem at times that the only way we can be entirely dedicated to God's service is by becoming a slave of Jesus in Mary. De Montfort does recognize that the greater number of saints have not embraced this practice; however, he maintains that for this reason they "had to pass through ruder and more dangerous trials."

A particular aspect of the slavery to Mary that de Montfort exhorts us to that I find especially unappealing is that we are supposed turn over all the value of our good works to Mary and let her dispose of them as she will. De Montfort insists that this does not mean we can't pray for specific people. However, it appears that we are not to offer up our suffering for a specific person or a plenary indulgence for a departed loved one, but are to turn their value over to Mary to distribute. It seems counterintuitive that while we can choose to benefit a specific person by our concrete benevolent actions, we are not to make such a choice when it comes to our sacrifices and sufferings. De Montfort holds that this sort of detachment is what renders this devotion so excellent, and he points out that Mary will do even more for our loved ones than we could do through our sacrifices. I don't doubt that. Still, that I personally direct the value of my sufferings to a specific person does not prevent me from also praying to Mary for that person. St. Thérèse prayed for a specific convict for weeks and had Masses said for him without going through Mary. Would she have become a greater saint if she had? Was she deficient in proper devotion to Our Lady?

Whatever we may finally decide as to the Marian consecration, the book is worth reading in order to better appreciate Mary's role in the divine economy and why we need to have recourse to her. Those interested in the notion that Mary is the Mediatrix of all graces will find quotations supporting this view taken from a number of saints. I found the book a little tedious, as it presented many things that I already knew about Mary and did so in a manner that did little to fan the flames of my love for her. But again, saints like John Paul II would beg to differ with me here.

(Review by Marie George)

True Devotion to Mary by St. Louis-Marie Grignion de Montfort

St. Louis Marie de Montfort, whose larger-than-life statue looks down on visitors at St. Peter's Basilica in Rome, wrote this book in the early 1700s about a devotion that is a "smooth, short, perfect and sure way of attaining union with our Lord, in which Christian perfection consists." The devotion is essentially a consecration of oneself and all one possesses to the Blessed Virgin Mary. De Montfort argues that because Mary is the most conformed to Jesus of all of God's creatures, it follows that devotion to her leads to "the most effective consecration and conformity" to Jesus.

In *True Devotion* itself, de Montfort states that he clearly foresaw "raging beasts" that would cause the book "to lie hidden in the darkness and silence of a chest and so prevent it from seeing the light of day." The manuscript, in fact, was hidden away in a chest to preserve it during the French Revolution, and was not discovered until 1842. Since it was first published in 1843, it has been issued in hundreds of editions and translated into about twenty languages.

The consecration that de Montfort proposes requires one to give oneself entirely to Mary—in order to belong entirely to Jesus through her—by giving her: our body with its senses and members; our soul with its faculties; our present material possessions and all we will acquire in the future; and, our interior and spiritual possessions and all we will acquire in the future. In return, de Montfort assures us that Mary will not be outdone in generosity, but will give herself entirely to the one so devoted to her, together with all the graces necessary to achieve union with her Son.

De Montfort strongly defends the efficacy of this devotion. He asserts that after extensive research into Marian devotions:

> I can now state with conviction that I have never known or heard of any devotion to our Lady which is comparable to the one I am going to speak of. No other devotion calls for more sacrifices for God, none empties us more completely of self and self-love, none keeps us more firmly in the grace of God and the grace of God in us. No other devotion unites us more perfectly and more easily to Jesus. Finally no devotion gives more glory to God, is more sanctifying for ourselves or more helpful to our neighbor.

The theological basis and practical application of the devotion are explained in several chapters. These include: the necessity of devotion to Our Lady; in what the devotion consists; reasons for pursuing the devotion; a presentation of the Old Testament figures Rebecca and Jacob as an allegory of True Devotion; the wonderful effects one should anticipate from faithfully practicing it; and, particular practices of the devotion.

Some will no doubt find certain of de Montfort's examples, arguments, and assertions outdated or even dubious. Extensive footnotes in the Montfort Publications edition of the book provide source references and occasional historical explanations of the text that are helpful. As with any spiritual classic that is centuries old, the discerning reader will detect the treasure contained in de Montfort's wisdom while appreciating the different cultural and temporal milieu in which it was written.

Perhaps the strongest endorsement of *True Devotion* in recent times came from St. John Paul II, who claimed that reading this book when he was a young man was "a decisive turning-point in my life." Like many when they first are exposed to the ideas presented by de Montfort, Karol Wojtyla was concerned that an excessive devotion to Mary may overshadow the supreme worship due to Jesus Christ. However, the future saint eventually understood that, "if one lives the mystery of Mary in Christ, such a risk does not exist."

Not only did St. John Paul II conclude that true devotion to Mary is not harmful to the spiritual life, but "this 'perfect devotion' is indispensable to anyone who means to give himself without reserve to Christ and to the work of Redemption." A key phrase in the book, "*Totus Tuus*" (*Totus tuus ego sum et omnia mea tua sunt*, meaning "I am all yours, and all that is mine is yours"), became his papal motto. The fact that this motto and the devotion behind it helped St. John Paul II to reach heaven should be encouragement enough for us to adopt them for our own.

(Review by A. M. Desprit)

Other works by St. Louis de Montfort include *The Secret of the Rosary* and *The Secret of Mary*.

The World's First Love by Archbishop Fulton J. Sheen

This book on Mary is my favorite among the books by Sheen that I've read. This is not to say that it lacks the shortcomings typically found in Sheen (described in other reviews). Also, the book does make a statement or two about Mary that seem questionable. However, this is not unusual even in good Marian theology which, while guided by authentic church teaching, ventures beyond it.

The strengths of the book are twofold. First, Sheen avoids excess pietism; secondly, he is not shy about speaking of the complementarity of the sexes. Some are going to find Sheen "sexist." However, I find that if one reads the nuances he adds, what he says corresponds closely to the teachings of the encyclical *Casti Connubii* on man and woman, teachings that sadly have largely been forgotten in recent times. For example, Sheen says: "Here is the essence of womanhood—acceptance, resignation, submission: 'Be it done unto me.'" Sheen points out, though, that Christ himself was subject to his parents, and that being subject does not mean pure passivity, but active cooperation. The chapter "Equity and Equality" is particularly insightful. Sheen notes that as a backlash from the subjection of women that took place in the seventeenth century not only did woman claim back the rights that were hers, "she fell into the error of believing that she ought to proclaim herself equal with man, forgetful that a certain superiority was already hers because of her functional difference from man." Sheen does not condemn women for pursuing careers, but notes that this pursuit must not squelch the basic instincts of womanhood, which he sees as being for devotion, sacrifice, and love for persons. When it comes to the home, Sheen sees man as governing it through justice, while woman reigns in it through love.

In the book's twenty-two short chapters, Sheen covers traditional themes associated with Mary, e.g., the Marian dogmas and the Seven Sorrows, while adding reflections that either are original with him or less commonly come across. For example, in the chapter "The Madonna of the World," Sheen tries to show that in many non-Christian religions there is a feminine principle, which he sees as expressing a universal desire for the Woman, Mary. And in the chapter "Mary and the Moslems," he tries to make a case (perhaps unsuccessfully) that the missionary should try to reach the Muslims by expanding on their devotion for Mary. Sheen also defends the notion that St. Joseph was a young man, and not aged as most art depicts him as being. As noted above, a significant amount of space is devoted to discussing the nature of woman. Other more general themes are treated as well, such as what genuine freedom consists in. Many of the book's chapters lend themselves readily to meditation. Sheen's love for Mary comes out on every page, inspiring like love in ourselves. Thus, the reader can profit from this work in multiple ways. Sheen's down-to-earth style makes this book accessible to people who might find more "lofty" treatments of Mary off-putting, while at the same time complementing them.

(Review by Marie George)

The World's First Love by Archbishop Fulton J. Sheen

The unsuspecting reader who picks up *The World's First Love* intending only to reinvigorate his devotion to our Lady is in for a big surprise. This book not only manages to supply the mind, heart, and imagination with fuel for a lively devotion to our Lady, but it contains at least a semester's worth of Catholic Apologetics as well.

Delightful for his eloquent prose and knack for turning a phrase (reminiscent of G. K. Chesterton), Sheen provides us with his own rich exegesis of many significant passages in Scripture relating to Our Lady. He also provides, by his frequent allusions, an introduction to the thought of many significant philosophers, good and bad: Plato, Thomas Aquinas, Marx, and Freud, to name a few.

The first part, "The Woman the World Loves" develops the idea that Mary is, indeed, the world's first love. She is the one person "in all humanity of whom God has one picture, and in whom there is a perfect conformity between what He wanted her to be and what she is." Throughout the book, Sheen continually refers to Mary as the "blue print," the paradigm to which we must turn to restore ourselves and the world to God. She is the blue print of freedom that comes from a "total abandonment to God," which Mary teaches us by her "Fiat" at the Annunciation. She is the blue print of love of neighbor in her Visitation, in her motherhood, and in her marriage to Joseph.

In the second part, "The World the Woman Loves," Sheen teaches us the centrality of Mary's role in the conversion of the modern world. Beginning with "Man and Woman" (Chapter 12), Sheen explains compellingly that the modern world needs "above all things else, the restoration of the image of man." Having explained how the image of man had been demolished through the erroneous philosophies of modernity especially "Monopolistic Capitalism," Socialism, and Communism, Sheen explains that "Mankind will find its way back again to God through the Woman who will gather up and restore the broken fragments of the image."

In Chapter 15, "Equity and Equality," Sheen masterfully traces the complementarity of the sexes and debunks the myth that women began to be emancipated in modern times. Sheen asserts that women abandoned their unique superiority to men largely because of the error "in the bourgeois-capitalistic theory of women, namely, the failure to make a distinction between mathematical equality and proportional equity."

Encyclopedic in his familiarity with the religious beliefs of China and Japan, Northwestern Uganda, Rwanda, India, and other various Hindu nations, Sheen demonstrates that all these religions have a devotion to a feminine principle that finds its consummate expression in Mary, the blue print. Mary is the "Madonna of the World," and she is already among the peoples of these places "preparing hearts for grace." "She is the Advent where there is not Christmas." Likewise Sheen demonstrates in "Mary and the Moslems" that Mary is the key to converting the Moslems. Interestingly, Sheen dwells on Our Lady's apparitions at Fatima (which, not incidentally, is the name of Mohammed's daughter) and demonstrates how the devotion to Mary is already rooted in the Koran.

Sheen closes the book with a beautiful explanation of the Rosary, its origins, and its extraordinary usefulness in the lives of ordinary Christians. He provides a short meditation on all fifteen decades and on the "Seven Dolors" of Mary. The last chapter reminds us that in the age of weapons of mass destruction, increased devotion to Mary is all the more pressing, and that we should heed Mary's call for "repentance, prayer, and sacrifice" at Fatima.

This book has given me a renewed appreciation for Archbishop Fulton J. Sheen's wisdom, his ability to speak to ordinary lay Catholics, his charm and his wit, his pervasive good-natured sense of humor . . . but most of all his contagious love for Our Lady!

(Review by Mark Langley)

Other works by Sheen include *The Cross and the Beatitudes, The Way to Inner Peace* (reviewed in this volume), and *Way to Happiness* (reviewed in this volume).

The Mass and
the Blessed Sacrament

How to Get More out of Holy Communion by St. Peter Julian Eymard

Years ago, one could find in the back of Saint Sacrament church in Quebec City a series of pamphlets on the Eucharist drawn in part from the writings of the 19th century French saint, Peter Eymard. I used to enjoy reading them, and so was glad to discover that eighteen of Eymard's reflections have been made available to an English speaking audience in *How to Get More out of Holy Communion*. However, after reading the first three reflections, to my chagrin, I found myself unmoved. As I continued reading, it eventually dawned on me that this was because St. Eymard devoted the first few chapters principally to convincing the reader of the desirability of daily Communion, and I didn't need convincing. Happily, in the next fifteen chapters, Eymard not only put things about the Eucharist that I already knew in a fresh light, but also pointed out some things that I had never thought about or at least not in quite that way. For example, Eymard explains:

> If at times Communion does not give us that rest and refreshment, it is because we make of it a difficult act of virtue. We exert ourselves to the utmost in it, making countless exhausting acts—in short laboring when we should be taking repose and nourishment. Receive the Lord, and be at peace. Why all this agitation? You do not go to a banquet to transact business. Enjoy this celestial Food, then, and since you are receiving the Bread of angels, give yourself, like the angels, to contemplation for a while. You do not take the time to taste our Lord, and then you withdraw full of anxiety over having felt nothing! Follow in spirit the example of the Carthusians, who lie prostrate at the foot of the altar throughout the time of their thanksgiving.

And in regard to what to many of us is the frustrating hiddenness of the Lord in the Eucharist, Eymard observes: "The glory of Jesus in the Eucharist, if revealed to us, would make us like Moses. But would there be friendship and intimacy? Moses, dazed with glory, was scarcely desirous of speaking or opening his heart! Yet Jesus insists on our friendship. He wishes us to treat Him as our Friend, and to that end, He takes the appearance of bread. No one is frightened; all think they see what has been familiar to them from their childhood: bread."

The chapters in *How to Get More out of Holy Communion* are short—four to five pages on the average. Each is preceded by a salient verse from Scripture. Eymard's style is simple and direct. He exhorts us in an understanding and kindly manner. The very love with which he speaks of Christ in his Eucharistic presence is an example for us. The book is suitable reading for every Catholic. If one is blessed with the leisure to prepare oneself before weekday Masses, this book would be very helpful for doing so.

(Review by Marie George)

How to Get More Out of Holy Communion by St. Peter Julian Eymard

How to Get More Out of Holy Communion by St. Peter Julian Eymard (1811–1868) is like a window into the relationship between God and one of his dear saints. As such, it is a guide to the sanctity of the communion with Our Lord: "Oh yes, happy fault! When man was in the state of innocence, God was our Lord and Master; now He is our Friend, our Guest, and Our Food."

The 142-page book consists of eighteen chapters of three to four pages each. The title pages of each chapter have pertinent scriptural quotations from the Douay Rheims translation, cross-referenced with the RSV. This book is not a "page turner," but rather provokes meditation: the thoughtful consideration of so great a Mystery, so great a Gift.

It is not a book to read and put on a shelf. Well, all right, I did do that, but then I couldn't leave it there. Now it travels with me to adoration, and when I am distracted I pick it up and read and ponder and pray and even write down my favorite passages. The chapter titles are informative enough that if on a particular day you have a specific need, you can find the chapter to address it. Some samples follow: "Your spirit will find joy in Communion," "Communion sustains and refreshes you," "Through Communion you regain your dignity," "Communion drives sadness from your soul."

The text is written in easily understood, simple sentences. Yet each sentence is profound. The author often is overcome by his own words to the point that his discourse becomes a meditation, which becomes an ecstatic devotional outburst. The frequent use of the exclamation point gives the less than fervent reader a glimpse into the energy, the pure zeal, that is the level on which a man truly cognizant of his goal of complete communion with Our Lord leads his life.

While I love this book (don't let the somewhat clunky title turn you off), I do think that it is a book that might appeal differently at different times. I recommend it wholeheartedly, feeling that everyone would benefit from it, but with the *caveat* that it is a book that will meet needs perhaps off and on. Like so much spiritual reading, the fact that you were not a fan ten years or even ten months or ten days ago does not mean you would not like it now. I believe this book reveals both the tools to achieve our goal of union with Christ and a glimpse through the writings of St. Eymard into the saint's very soul in its sanctity. That is a nourishing place to rest one's eyes. Not least of all, the book leads the reader to a deeper understanding of how much Christ desires union with us.

(Review by Ann Turner)

Other works by St. Eymard include *The Real Presence* and *My Eucharistic Day.*

Jesus Our Eucharistic Love: Eucharistic Life Exemplified by the Saints by Fr. Stefano M. Manelli, FI

This short book on the Eucharist is replete with stories of various saints' reverence towards the Eucharist. Some readers will be inspired by their examples of emphatic piety, e.g., St. Lawrence of Brindisi walking forty miles in order to get to a Catholic chapel where he could celebrate Mass, St. Francis Cabrini spending twelve hours in adoration, Bl. Agatha of the Cross visiting the Blessed Sacrament one hundred times a day, and St. Pio hearing many Masses every day. Others, however, seeing the bar set so high may feel discouraged, and may wish the book contained fewer pious stories and more by way of counsel as to how to attain such levels of devotion, as well as more advice as to what people are to do when their state in life does not allow for such displays of reverence. Fr. Manelli does offer some helpful advice for people who are constrained by time and/or distance from a church, by proposing that they make spiritual Communions. Given that many Catholics are unfamiliar with this practice, Manelli's explanation of how one makes a spiritual Communion and of its value is one of the most useful sections of the book. Manelli also points out that while daily Mass attendance may seem unrealistic for some people, more often than not, this is due to poor time management. He rightly insists that: "If we but appreciated the infinite value of the Holy Mass, we would be very desirous of assisting and would try in every way to find the necessary time."

Some of the other topics covered in this devotional work include the respect we ought to show priests, visits to the Blessed Sacrament, the various ties between the Eucharist and our Blessed Mother, and the purity of soul necessary for the reception of Holy Communion. A chapter and an appendix are devoted to prayers before the Blessed Sacrament. Another appendix treats of the Eucharistic miracle of Lanciano.

(Review by Marie George)

Preparing Yourself for Mass by Fr. Romano Guardini (Formerly entitled: *Meditations Before Mass*)

Pope Benedict XVI greatly admired Guardini's works. As for myself, Guardini gets on my philosophical nerves at times both because his manner of expression sometimes makes it unclear what he is getting at and because he disagrees with Aquinas on a number of points. For this reason, I chose to review *Preparing Yourself for Mass* rather than his lengthy and more popular work, *The Lord*. I find that Guardini belabors certain points in *Preparing Yourself for Mass* and, even after doing so, does not leave us with as much of the practical advice we were hoping for. Guardini's theological reflections are abstruse at times. Nevertheless, if one *patiently* applies oneself to this work, it is apt to affect one's participation in Mass for the better.

The book is divided into thirty-two meditations, each about eight pages in length, which originated as talks Guardini gave before Mass. The first six meditations concern stillness (understood as attentive presence) and composure/recollection (understood as reining in our thoughts so that we are really present at Mass). Guardini observes that people are often absent in church in the sense that they act in church the same as if they were anywhere else when instead: "Everything we do—our entering, being present, our kneeling and sitting and standing, our reception of the sacred nourishment—should be divine service." Our composure enables our participation. Too often some of us tend to zone out during part of the Eucharistic Prayer, when we should be mentally following all the words and actions of the priest. Our lack of composure not only affects us individually, but prevents us from actively forming part of a holy people, of the communion of saints, united in praise of God.

Advice that Guardini gives at several points is that before each Mass we should study one of the Mass prayers in advance, be it a proper prayer, such as the Collect, or a prayer that forms the Ordinary of the Mass.

Guardini sagely advises that in cases when Mass is not properly celebrated due to some failure on the part of the priest or congregation that "the individual should do everything in his power to perfect a practice or remove an abuse. Beyond that, he must accept the Mass he attends as it happens to be. He must not be unduly upset by its limitations.... He should remind himself that the essential remains untouched, should enter into it and help to accomplish the sacred act."

Guardini points out how Christ's institution of the Eucharist has become stylized in the liturgy; e.g., "the bread assumes a new, special aspect; it becomes host . . . the table, altar." He then astutely observes that this leaves the believer with the task "of discerning the essential in what meets his eye." So for example, at the Offertory, "we should say to ourselves . . . 'What the Lord instructed His disciples to do when he told them to prepare for the Feast of the Passover, and what the first congregations did when each believer stepped forward with his offering of bread, wine, oil, is being done—now.'"

In Chapters 25, 28, and 30 Guardini makes a clear and vigorous case that the Eucharist is not a symbol: it is Christ.

I will only mention one of the couple of points where Guardini disagrees with Aquinas: "Revealed truth is neither a continuation

nor a new dimension of earthly truth; it's something that completely overthrows earthly truth. And not only does it overthrow it;
it brands it as untruth." Aquinas maintains that truth cannot con-
tradict truth. Accordingly, while Aquinas puts forth rational arguments to defend the possibility of the Eucharist, Guardini affirms:
"We can neither say that it is possible nor that it is impossible."

(Review by Marie George)

Preparing Yourself for Mass by Fr. Romano Guardini

[How] genuinely disastrous is the disorder and artificiality of
present-day existence. We are constantly stormed by violent and
chaotic impressions. At once powerful and superficial, they are
soon exhausted, only to be replaced by others. They are immoder-
ate and disconnected, the one contradicting, disturbing, and
obstructing the other. At every step we find ourselves in the claws
of purposes and cross-purposes that inveigle and trick us. Everywhere we are confronted by advertising that attempts to force
upon us things we neither want nor really need. We are constantly
lured from the important and profound to the distracting, "interesting," piquant.

These words were surprisingly not written to describe modern life
with its many distractions (think—internet), but rather the pre-tele-
vision world of 1939. Fr. Romano Guardini provides this image early
in his book to highlight our need to grow silent and composed
before participating in the Mass. The book is a collection of lectures
he gave to educate his parishioners about how best to prepare themselves for, and participate in, the Mass. In thirty-two chapters,
Guardini methodically walks us to and through the Mass, from
preparation to thanksgiving, and concludes by taking up several
overarching topics.

The volume is a mixture of both wonderfully expressed common
sense advice, and some occasional turgid stuff. (Guardini was a university professor, and sometimes it shows.) The structure of his presentation is based on the Extraordinary Form, the Old Mass. This
reviewer happens to regularly attend the old rite, so it posed no difficulty, but certain liturgical references may be lost on a reader who
does not.

Fr. Guardini does not hesitate to express his peeves. He freely shares a wish list for changes in the Mass, eerily prescient of eventual Vatican II alterations. He bemoans the use of Latin and the use of missals. And when explaining the language of liturgy as necessarily clear, concise, and chaste, he uses the opportunity to take a swipe at the widespread but debased devotions to the Sacred Heart "characterized by an intolerable effeminacy and unnaturalness."

In the second half of the book, Fr. Guardini discusses discrete liturgical topics. Picking a chapter at random, which we'll call "Congregating is Hard to Do," Guardini describes both our need for and resistance to, forming a congregation for worship. He begins with a humbling description of the various inappropriate states of mind most of us bring to church as would-be congregates. He points out how the word "I" appears rarely in the Mass, limited mostly to when we each individually confess our sins. Thereafter, "we" predominates, and for a reason. And the "we" is not limited to those within the physical church structure, but includes all who believe, even across time, and "beyond the borders of death." This chapter pricks those of us who are tempted to think of Mass as private prayer.

The chapter on the New Covenant is a brief but compelling description of the ancient Passover liturgy, and how Christ fulfilled it, and sealed a new Covenant with his blood. Another on "Time and Eternity" focuses on our ephemeral earthly existence, on the mystery of Christ's ability to "step from eternity into place and hour" when he appeared to the Apostles, and repeatedly at each act of Consecration. And another discusses the liturgical tension between the practice of Adoration and the Mass, one "giv[ing] an impression of permanence quite opposed the act of Jesus's commemoration, into which the believer is meant to enter."

This volume will reward most diligent (and even repeat) readers with a new and more profound understanding of the dynamic encounter that is the Mass, and the consequent importance that we push away earthly distractions and compose ourselves for it every time, as though we truly understood that we are special guests at a heavenly banquet.

(Review by William Short)

Guardini is also author of *Learning the Virtues: That Lead You to God*, *Meditations on the Christ*, and *The Art of Praying* (reviewed in this volume).

Visits to the Most Blessed Sacrament and the Blessed Virgin Mary by St. Alphonsus Liguori

This short book contains prayers and meditation topics for thirty-one visits to the Blessed Sacrament. The format of each visit is as follows: firstly, there is a preparatory prayer (the same for all visits). Next there is a meditation of a page or so. After the meditation, one is to make a spiritual communion. After that there is a "visit with Mary." Lastly, there is a concluding prayer addressed to Mary (the same for all visits). Each visit takes ten minutes or so.

St. Alphonsus has an hyperbolic style that some will find suitable given it is Our Lord and His Mother who are being addressed and spoken of, whereas others will find it pietistic. And then some may find his manner of speech appropriate when speaking of or to Christ in the Eucharist, while finding it excessive, at times, when speaking of or to Mary. Indeed, a person without a proper understanding of the role of Mary in our salvation might misunderstand certain statements of St. Alphonsus, such as: "I place in you all of my hopes." He, of course, is not meaning to deny that we should place our hope primarily in Christ.

The content of each meditation is geared toward inflaming our hearts with love for Christ present in the Eucharist, and most of the meditations involve imploring Christ for greater love of Himself. The "visit with Mary" complements the meditations by asking for her aid in coming to a greater love of her Son. I have found this book helpful while making a Holy Hour, and think it may motivate certain people to make short visits to the Blessed Sacrament on a more regular basis, as well as providing those already accustomed to doing so with a means of increasing their devotion.

(Review by Marie George)

St. Alphonsus Liguori is author of *The Practice of the Love of Jesus Christ* and *The Glories of Mary* (both are reviewed in this volume).

Meditation Topics

Classic Catholic Meditations: to enrich your faith & help you to pray by Fr. Bede Jarrett, OP

The subtitle added to Sophia Institute Press's edition of *Classic Catholic Meditations,* namely, "to enrich your faith & help you to pray," accurately describes the book's contents. Many of the meditations are largely didactic, focusing on a truth of the faith or a point of morality, and not primarily on the life and person of Christ. For this reason, a person whose catechesis has been somewhat wanting is more likely to derive profit from Fr. Jarrett than someone who is well-catechized; Fr. Jarrett's manner of approaching topics bears some resemblance to Fulton J. Sheen's. For those unfamiliar with meditation, a very traditional "Scheme of Meditation" is handily located inside the back cover.

All of the 120 or so meditations are only a few pages long. They are grouped under fifteen headings, which makes it easy to find one suited to one's need. Some of the topics covered are: the Trinity, Mary, the Church, the Sacraments, prayer, dealing with others, and forming oneself. The work's generally instructive character is marred by some philosophical mistakes. For example, Fr. Jarrett speaks of a concept as being a "kind of mental picture," tells us that a habit does not incline to anything (contrary to what Aquinas says), and suggests that one can learn philosophy without books. Also, Fr. Jarrett's assertion that "God does not desire our perfection" is theologically questionable, given that Christ says: "Be ye perfect as your heavenly Father is perfect" (Mt. 5:48). Occasionally Fr. Jarrett's practical advice is one-sided, e.g., he speaks of responsible almsgiving, but fails to address the contrary problem, that of the neglect of the corporal works of mercy in the name of saving for future expenses that may never materialize, or if they do, may well be covered by an increase in income. However, on the whole Fr. Jarrett is helpful. He calls to our attention points we otherwise may not have thought about, e.g., on the effect our acquaintances have on us, and he gives sound practical advice, e.g., "friendship must be based on sincere confidence and trust, but this does not justify constant correction, which is an overly hasty attempt to reach the results of friendship." Fr. Jarrett clears up common misunderstandings, e.g., about what constitutes scandal and about the difference between temperament and character. And some of his meditations are real gems, as when he elaborates on the theme of the Eucharist as food for our journey by examining the story of the prophet Elijah to whom the angel brought food.

(Review by Marie George)

Classic Catholic Meditations: to enrich your faith & help you to pray by Fr. Bede Jarrett, OP

Bede Jarrett was an English Dominican, who combined gifts of scholarship, spiritual acumen, and administrative skill. He was elected to the Provincialate of his order at an early age, and spent much of his time travelling and fundraising as he established priories in England and South Africa until exhaustion hastened his death in 1934 at the age of fifty-two. He had trained as a medieval historian at Oxford, but was equally imbued with Thomistic philosophy and with a compelling understanding of human nature that came from his wide interactions with so many people in his ministry.

No habitué of the cloister, he valued the lay life profoundly, and in 1915 wrote a book specifically for those whose vocation is in the world, which he called *Meditations for Layfolk*. It has been reissued in the present century under the title *Classic Catholic Meditations*, and consists of over 140 meditations, each occupying three pages of text, that treat of faith, the sacraments, the Church, and how to live one's life in accordance with God's will. Each meditation has a sufficiently long expository title (e.g., "God does not desire your perfection, but your attempts to attain perfection" or "Trust in God when you face the death of loved ones") that it is easy for the reader to find a given topic of interest, despite the lack of an index.

The style is colloquial, with few quotations from sources that would betray Jarrett's erudition. But occasionally, such instances occur that add to the trenchancy of his meditations. For example, when discussing the eternal salvific nature of the crucifixion, he invokes Florentine art of the cinquecento, in which the background to Calvary is peopled with figures and buildings representative of the artist's era. The juxtaposition cannot be the result of naïveté about Palestinian culture, because the Italian city-states had been involved in the Levant since the crusades and were better positioned to depict their features than moderns are. "But it was a deliberate attempt to make the life and death of Christ an ever-living event of eternity rather than of time." To God, unfettered by time, the sacrifice of Christ is not something that happened 2000 years ago, but is a perpetual act pouring out grace on our behalf.

Like other shrewd spiritual directors, Jarrett reminds his readers that perfection is unattainable in this life, and that God's love is always available to sinners. Hence the greater danger even than sin is the despondency that can come in its wake, which causes people to give up trying to overcome faults. At the same time, we ought never to presume that we have totally defeated any given sin or temptation, or that life's journey will become easier with age. Nor ought we to be upset by distractions at prayer, lack of fervent feelings when receiving Communion, or the unceasing sameness of sins recited in the confessional. He recommends patience here, reinforced by faith—the perception that everything around us is part of God's overarching scheme for our lives. He also calls our attention to our uniqueness. We may seem to ourselves to be serving no purpose with our lives, but that is not true. "God gets from me a peculiar glory that no other work of His hands can show, and therefore in me alone is some fragment of His splendor reflected."

Fr. Jarrett intended this book to be read in small installations, one meditation being sufficient for a day. But one leads to another, and the reader, captivated by his timeless style and intense desire to kindle a fire in the spiritual lives of lay folk, will probably benefit from reading three or more meditations at a time from one of the fifteen groupings into which the book is divided. They challenge our complacency, and invite us to greater intimacy with God.

(Review by David Rooney)

Other works by Bede Jarrett include *The Little Book of the Holy Spirit* and *Little Book of the Blessed Virgin Mary*.

Divine Intimacy: Meditations on the Interior Life for Every Day of the Liturgical Year by Fr. Gabriel of St. Mary Magdalen, OCD

Fr. Gabriel's *Divine Intimacy* presents meditations on the interior life for every day of the liturgical year. It gradually builds from basic aspects of spirituality to the purgative, illuminative, and unitive ways of spiritual life and the interplay of the virtues and gifts of the Holy Spirit in reaching the life of the Beatitudes.

Divine Intimacy is structured around the Teresian method of prayer. The first step is the presence of God, i.e., an "appropriate thought which brings us into contact with our Creator and orientates us toward Him." Each meditation in *Divine Intimacy* starts with a one- or two-sentence statement placing us in the presence of God. We then have the reading that provides the subject for meditation. *Divine Intimacy* provides a three-page reading for every day, but any appropriate reading may be used—Scripture, books about Jesus or Mary, or the lives of the saints.

After the reading, we come to the two essential steps in Teresian prayer—meditation and the (loving) colloquy. In the meditation, we reflect on the text read and realize the love that God has for us, as disclosed in the subject of the reading and meditation. We then come to the colloquy, which is at the heart of the Teresian concept of prayer. Here we respond to God's love for us, as discerned in the meditation, with our own expressions of love for God. The colloquy may be extended by the three "optional" steps: thanksgiving, offering some good resolution to God, and asking God's help for our weaknesses.

A major feature of *Divine Intimacy* is its vast array of sources, ranging from Scripture to the latest papal encyclicals (at the time Pius XII) and everything in between. Included are writings of the saints, the *Summa Theologica*, the Liturgy, the *Imitation of Christ*, and a great variety of Catholic doctrines, practices, and traditions. Many of the saintly writings, not surprisingly, are Carmelite—St. Teresa of Jesus, St. Teresa Margaret of the Heart of Jesus, etc.

By around Corpus Christi, *Divine Intimacy* begins discussing the virtues. By the Tenth Sunday after Pentecost, charity is discussed in great detail. Then the moral virtues follow, along with other virtues related to them. During the Fifteenth and Sixteenth weeks after Pentecost, Fr. Gabriel notes that intense practice of the virtues ordinarily results in God activating the Gifts of the Holy Spirit. At that point, we may begin to become men and women of the Beatitudes: "When we cooperate with the action of the gifts of the Holy Spirit, they produce in us fruits of virtue so exquisite that they give us a foretaste of the eternal beatitude of which they are a pledge. For this reason, we call them *beatitudes*."

Gradually, Gabriel matches the virtues and gifts to their beatitudes. He concludes that the highest Gift of the Spirit is wisdom, which comes from practicing the virtue of charity and corresponds to the beatitude of "Blessed are the peacemakers" (Mt. 5:9). They are peacemakers not in the sense of diplomacy or conflict resolution, but in the sense that "one who possesses peace, disseminates peace." It is at this point that the soul is ready to move toward complete union with God, culminating in divine intimacy.

Beginners, both older and younger, who are informed about the faith and have done some spiritual reading, would find the book suitable and understandable. Those who are more familiar with the contemplative life would enjoy the book as a systematic program for growth in the spiritual life.

(Review by Robert F. Cuervo)

EDITOR'S NOTE: There are two versions of *Divine Intimacy*: the original that uses the liturgical calendar used in the 1962 Missal and a newer one by Ignatius Press that uses the contemporary calendar. Readers are divided over which is better. There is a significant difference in the content of the two versions. A considerable number of readers are of the decided opinion that the content of the original is much richer. The new version, however, in addition to being in sync with the current calendar, has a much better system of citation and indexing.

Divine Intimacy by Fr. Gabriel of St. Mary Magdalene, OCD

According to the Foreword, written by a high-ranking confrère of the author, *Divine Intimacy* proposes to "introduce souls to intimate prayer" in order to meet the spiritual needs of the modern world. To achieve this objective, Fr. Gabriel unpacks Carmelite spirituality according to the pre-Vatican II liturgical cycle. Make no mistake, this text will be daunting to some, even those most seasoned in spiritual reading. It is well more than one thousand pages, and the pre-Vatican II liturgical year can be confusing. Such obstacles notwithstanding, this book makes good on the promise borne in the title.

To achieve his objective, Fr. Gabriel employs St. Teresa of Avila's method of mental prayer, which relies on the classical Catholic understanding of the human soul's faculties. In his Preface, the Carmelite priest clearly identifies that the intellect guides the will throughout the subsequent meditations: "the intellect seeks to convince the soul that God loves her and wishes to be loved by her; the will, responding to the divine invitation, loves. That is all." Thus, the basic guiding principle for the entire text is that a person cannot love what she does not know, and that she will act according to what she loves.

This method, as Cardinal Richard Cushing notes in the introduction, is quite fruitful. "Faithful to these meditations from day to day," he writes, "we shall know Christ and live Christ, absorb His teachings more fully and become more dedicated to His service." The daily reflections and prayers move with the liturgical seasons allowing for stability and variety. Through them the reader's mind receives the Divine Light, while his will is purified, and he comes to love God more, and he begins to understand the place of holy and zealous action in his life.

With the method made clear in the beginning of the text, the author begins to move the reader toward the intimacy that he seeks. To capture the essence of the ultimate end of prayer, Fr. Gabriel quotes another well-known Carmelite mystic and Doctor of the Church, St. John of the Cross, who teaches: "And this [divine intimacy] comes to pass, when the understanding [i.e., the intellect] is divinely illuminated in the Wisdom of the Son, and the will is made glad in the Holy Spirit, and the Father, with His power and strength, absorbs the soul in the embrace and abyss of His sweetness." From beginning to end, the meditations laid out by Fr. Gabriel foster a certitude in him who reads and prays through this book: he knows the delectable truth that he is infinitely loved by a providential Father.

Even while the content of *Divine Intimacy* fills the mind and heart with wonderful things, it is necessary to offer one note of caution. Anyone who takes up this book might feel overwhelmed or quickly burned out if he does not have a significant amount of time to read and ponder. Single sentences drawn from the Carmelite saints, as well as Fr. Gabriel's own spiritual insights, are worthy of much reflection. Yet, each day's text spans three typewritten pages. The reader ought not to think that these rich meditations will be digested in full, and quickly, on a daily basis. Because of that, *Divine Intimacy* is a prayer text that is most beneficial for those who are willing to sit patiently and unpack spiritual wisdom slowly. Anyone who approaches in this manner certainly will receive a nearly inexhaustible treasury of spiritual jewels directly from God's hand.

(Review by Derek Rotty)

Everyday Meditations by Bl. John Henry Newman

Everyday Meditations is a section of Bl. John Henry Newman's *Meditations and Devotions*, a collected work of devotional papers written toward the end of Newman's life. The fifty devotions each run between two to four pages in length. They take the form of a prayer. Fervent and refreshingly down to earth, I find them to readily fuel my own prayer. Newman's prayers are those of an avowed sinner who is weak and can do nothing without God's help. Here is a typical example: "You will never forsake me. I earnestly trust so—never, certainly, without fearful provocation on my part. Yet I trust and pray that you will keep me from that provocation. Oh, keep me from the provocation of lukewarmness and sloth." Newman covers many of the classic subjects of meditations in an ever so lively way: Our Lord's sacred humanity, the Holy Spirit, Holy Communion, the evil of sin, and Divine Providence. He also deals with subjects that receive less frequent mention. For example, with simple direct-ness, Newman faces up to the reality that not all are predestined to heaven. He also reflects on how one of the sorrows of Mary includes the absence of Jesus from her life both during his public mission, as well as during the period that she remained on earth after Christ's Ascension. His meditation on "Behold the Man" is striking, and I resist the urge to quote part of it, lest I spoil it for the reader. This work by Newman can be used with profit by just about anyone, and would be especially helpful for those who are trying to develop a prayer life, but are short on time.

(Review by Marie George)

Everyday Meditations by Bl. John Henry Newman

Everyday Meditations is a small book of brief meditative passages, excerpted from a longer posthumous collection of Bl. Newman's devotional writings, *Meditations and Devotions of the Late Cardinal Newman*. Newman, the great 19th-century scholar and cleric, was a famous Anglican divine before becoming Catholic (a spiritual jour-ney recounted in his more famous work, *Apologia Pro Vita Sua*), who brought the Oratorian religious life to England and died a Car-dinal of the Church. For a reader—like this reviewer—first intro-duced to Newman through his more formal works (e.g., *The Idea of a University*) that are both impressive and dry, the present volume will appear a shocking departure, for in this diminutive volume we find a Newman of passion and emotion, conversing familiarly and intensely with God.

The content of the meditations varies widely, from the inspira-tional—"God has created me to do Him some definite service; He has committed some work to me which He has not committed to another. . . . He has not created me for naught"—to the contrite, "My God, I have had experience enough what a dreadful bondage sin is. If Thou art away, I find I cannot keep myself, however I wish it—and am in the hands of my own self-will, pride, sensuality, and selfishness." The unifying theme is, as the title suggests, meditation on God and His ways, and on the proper (and improper) response to God that we humans experience.

The length of the various meditations makes them ideally suited to daily perusal, with a typical meditation covering two or three small pages in four or five tight paragraphs. In contrast with much of Bl. Newman's other work, the content is much more affective than explanatory, and is thus best thought of as an inducement to further private meditation and prayer than as a guide for study. Indeed, a prospective reader should not worry that this book will prove impenetrable or recondite; it is, instead, a remarkable case of a first rate mind and great prose stylist exercising that craft on a humble and human scale, with the clear intention of leaving the focus entirely on God, with as little attention drawn to the writer as he could contrive.

Despite my admiration for this book and its author, which I hope is clear from what has preceded, I found this book hard to love as a work of devotional reading. After wrestling with this conclusion for some time, I suspect it arises from the fact that most of these meditations are suggestive and allusive—they do not bring thoughts to a decisive conclusion, nor do they develop arguments; instead, they dwell more heavily on the emotions. Indeed, one finds more ejaculations and exclamation points in this work than in the widely—if lovingly!—teased-for-its-emotion *Story of a Soul* of St. Thérèse. Prospective readers who have found Newman's other works too intellectual may find a surprising contrast here. Those, like myself, who love Newman in his more intellectual mode (as in his sermons, for instance), may be less taken with this side of Newman. All told, however, this book is an excellent brief collection of spiritual meditations which—with proper expectations set—I can recommend to any reader.

(Review by Mark Wyman)

An Ignatian Introduction to Prayer: Scriptural Reflections According to the "Spiritual Exercises" by Fr. Timothy M. Gallagher, OMV

If one is looking for a guide to Ignatius's method for praying with Scripture, one is liable to be disappointed by this book, as it does not explain the different steps (although it does lead one through them). As Fr. Gallagher notes in his brief foreword, this book is not about prayer, it "is a book to be used for prayer." Gallagher presents us with meditations on forty selections from Scripture. Each meditation incorporates the various elements of the Ignatian approach: putting oneself in the presence of the Lord, prayerfully reading a passage, imagining it, reflecting on it, conversing with our Lord (and with the other Persons of the Trinity, or with Mary or the saints, as is appropriate), and then mentally going over what has transpired to fix in mind lights and graces received. The book does not presuppose familiarity with the *Spiritual Exercises*. It is a wonderful introduction to *lectio divina* for the beginner, and it also provides assistance to those who are trying to pray with Scripture, but for whatever reason are having a hard time doing so. One caveat, however, is that some readers may find using their imaginations to engage with Scripture passages more of an obstacle than a help, especially those who have a poor imagination or who feel called to higher forms of prayer.

(Review by Marie George)

An Ignatian Introduction to Prayer: Scriptural Reflections According to the "Spiritual Exercises" by Fr. Timothy M. Gallagher, OMV

An Ignatian Introduction to Prayer by Fr. Timothy M. Gallagher, OMV is a set of forty guided prayer sessions based on the *Spiritual Exercises* of St. Ignatius of Loyola.

Closely following the outline of the *Exercises*, it presents the reader with guided meditations on scripture passages in order to cultivate an intimate knowledge of Christ. Ignatian prayer involves calling a scene from Scripture to mind using the senses and imagination, allowing the reader to experience its story as if he were part of it. This leads in turn to conversation with Our Lord.

There are no chapters devoted to instructing the reader on how to pray as Ignatius did. However, the format of each prayer session is the same, and so after doing a couple, one readily picks up the steps involved. After the title and a reference to the scripture reading for that session, a call to awareness is presented—identical in every case—and an invitation to read the scripture passage referenced. The reader will have to have a Bible at hand, as Gallagher does not include the passage itself. I was pleased by this, for I found it encouraged a regular use of the Bible itself: after finishing Gallagher's book I had the habit in place for turning to the Bible myself and praying with the scripture on my own.

After this follows the meditation, which makes up the bulk of each section. Following the events of the scripture just read, the reader is guided by Gallagher in a journey of the imagination. At one time he is encouraged to view the events as an onlooker, at another to participate in them, still at another time to see it through the eyes of one or another of the characters he has just read about. The writing style is simple and intimate, and encourages many opportunities of pausing for a moment of silence, reflection, and conversation with Our Lord by the use of ellipses which appear throughout.

At the end of the meditation are closing questions; they are the same in every instance. They succinctly bring the elements of the prayer together by addressing each time the reader's impression of the scripture, of his own heart, and of Our Lord's word in his life. Those searching for an instruction book or commentary will have to look elsewhere.

An Ignatian Introduction to Prayer is a kind of prayer book itself, its uniqueness being that the prayer originates not from the recitation of printed words but from within the reader's heart with the aid of the imagination.

This book will be best put to use in group settings. Owing to the fact that the meditations are written down, they naturally lead along an already fixed path, which sometimes hindered me from following spontaneous reflections that were carrying me in a different direction. However, I believe it will prove to be a wonderful guide for parish groups, circles of friends, or those leading retreats. One or several in a group can lead the session by the prayerful reading of an entire section along with the scripture it is built around. Here is where the written meditation is brilliant: all those in the group will be guided in the same way but will naturally be able to provide a richness of different reflections for the closing questions at the end.

This book provides a simple outline for achieving the synthesis of spirituality and one of our most powerful God-given tools: the imagination. Being led through the forty sessions of Ignatian prayer, readers will find themselves growing accustomed to praying in a deeply participatory way with Sacred Scripture.

(Review by Elizabeth Lademan)

Other works by Gallagher include *Discerning the Will of God: An Ignatian Guide to Christian Decision Making*, and *The Examen Prayer: Ignatian Wisdom for Our Lives Today* (reviewed in this volume).

Meditations for Lent by Bishop Jacques-Bénigne Bossuet

Meditations for Lent consists of selections drawn from several works by Bossuet, arranged so as to provide a reflection a day for each day in Lent and Holy Week, plus two for the Solemnities of St. Joseph and the Annunciation. The book is far more substantive than the free booklets parishes sometimes distribute during Lent, while still being suited to the reader who is short on time, as the reflections average four or five pages in length. Although intended for use during Lent, one could use this book at any time of the year, partly because some of the topics treated are not specifically Lenten (e.g., Christ's temptation in the desert), and partly because the Passion of Christ and topics related to it are appropriately meditated on at any time of the year. Bossuet is doctrinally solid and makes good use of Scripture. The average devout Catholic is liable to draw profit from his work; the less than devout, especially those who are young, however, might not find it engaging. I have to say that Bossuet less often touches me to the quick the way that Bl. Newman and certain other authors do.

The selections I appreciated the most covered the topics of forgiving others, being a good example without seeking to garner people's praise, our inability to do anything without Our Lord, the dangers posed by venial sin, Christ's teaching concerning the Eucharist, and our convenient deafness (like that of the Pharisees) to hearing anything that requires mortifying our will or passions.

The reflections on Christ's anointing with the costly oil and on his betrayal are moving, and the one on the brevity of life is rhetorically brilliant.

It is hard to give a representative excerpt from this work because the force of most of the reflections, similar to epic poetry, depends on the over-all build-up of thoughts offered. Here are two examples, however. The first is from "The Anointing": "To anoint Jesus with a fragrant balm is to praise him. To anoint his head is to praise and adore his divinity, for 'the head of Christ,' as St. Paul says, 'is God' (1 Cor. 11:3). To anoint his feet is to adore his humanity and its weakness. To wipe his feet with her hair was to place all her beauty and vanity beneath his feet. Thus did she sacrifice all to Jesus. Him alone she wished to please." The second is from the reflection on the humility of God, which is offered for the Annunciation: "Man can never become independent. In order to satisfy him God becomes submissive. His sovereign grandeur will not allow itself to be abased while remaining in himself, but this infinitely abundant nature does not refuse to go borrowing in order to enrich itself by humility, so that, as St. Augustine says, 'the man who disdains humility, who calls it simplicity and baseness when he sees it in other men, will not disdain to practice it, seeing it in God.'"

(Review by Marie George)

Meditations for Lent by Bishop Jacques-Bénigne Bossuet

According to the meditation on "Christian Righteousness," the Pharisee "*boasts only about the exterior. Those Christians who are attached only to exterior observances resemble him. To say one's breviary, to attend church, to go to Mass and Vespers, to take holy water, to kneel... It is a false righteousness. But what shall we say about those who do not have even this exterior precision, unless that they are worse than the Pharisees?*"

This line struck me with particular force, possibly because I so often hear the opposite truth emphasized, namely, that any number of good acts—no matter how holy—done without the right intention are so much wasted time and effort. Often the unspoken take-away is that it is necessary to have perfected one's intention (or at least have a very solidly good one) before making too much effort jumping through these holy hoops. A daily Rosary, or Mass? But are you doing it to "feel holy" more than you are to converse with God? If so, probably safer to skip it until you can get that desire a bit more purified. If we (many of my friends and I) do not vocalize this perception, we nevertheless often act on it. This meditation pulls a single thread in our reasoning and causes the whole to unravel. For, of course, doing good ought to be done with the right intention; but even if our intention remains imperfect and halting, how else will we go about perfecting it than through constant practice? To think that even the uniformly loathed Pharisees were likely faring better than myself when I opt to act "more honestly" than they — is there anything more galling? It is impossible to simply shrug and turn away. The matter compels a closer inspection and some (perhaps vaguely miffed but still beneficial) soul-searching.

I read these *Meditations* during Lent. They are vigorous, compelling, peacefully urgent, and rich with the wisdom of the Scriptures and holy men and women. Each Meditation is no more than a few pages long, which is wise since they all deal with the weighty matter of salvation. Each facilitates a closer look into some aspect of our Christian Journey. They are overwhelmingly encouraging, empowering. However the tone is not gentle. God's mercy is constantly recalled to mind, but so are our limitations, our wretchedness, and our continuing abject failures. This because the former, mercy, is in danger of becoming a rather abstract, bloodless talking point without the aid of some gut-twisting reflection upon the latter.

I know some (beginning with myself) for whom an uncompromising tone and sudden immersion in the live-or-die reality of the spiritual life can be unhelpful, usually because they are prone to scrupulosity, discouragement, anger, anxiety, boredom with anything not immediately relatable and supportive, or similar things. But truly, couldn't we all do with a less robust sense of self-defense and a good deal more humble humor in this area? If a truth of the Gospel can all but extinguish my light, when God promised a smoldering wick never to quench (Mt. 12:20), I must be doing something wrong. The treatments in these *Meditations* are balanced, beautiful, and true. If we, through some inherent wiring or even demons like acedia and pride, too often give more weight to the demanding than the graceful, it is no fault in the book itself. Rather it is a deeply interior fight we must hope to win someday, baby step by baby step if necessary. This book is an excellent sparring ground in which to cultivate the virtues of fortitude, hope, meekness, faith, and humility for people in all walks of life and of all temperaments, from early teenage years upward.

(Review by Angela Furhman)

Other works by Bossuet include *Meditations for Advent* and *Meditations on Mary.*

Treatise on Prayer and Meditation by St. Peter of Alcántara

After a short summary of the benefits of prayer, St. Peter of Alcántara presents us with a meditation for every day of the week on the topics he identifies as apt to help a person, at the beginning of his conversion to God, acquire love and fear of God; the topics include sin, the miseries of this life, death, the last judgment, hell, heaven, and the benefits of God. These classic topics of meditations are overall well-developed for the benefit of the beginner. (I say overall because he can be unduly negative, e.g., speaks as if the sins we've repented of should still elicit terror in us in contrast to St. Catherine of Siena who reassures us that God does not, so to speak, remember our forgiven sins.) St. Peter then presents us with seven beginner-friendly meditations on our Lord's sacred passion, followed by advice as how to best profit from one's meditations. He outlines six acts, initially alerting us that the list is not meant to be slavishly followed. The six acts include: preparation for prayer (putting oneself in the presence of God, etc.), reading (here he notes that if one is distracted, one should linger longer over the reading, as it will help one stay focused), the meditation itself (which in some cases is aided by imagining the scenes, in other cases not), thanksgiving, the offering (both of oneself and of the merits of Christ to the Father), and lastly prayer for various intentions (e.g., that all peoples come to worship God, for the hierarchy, etc.). St. Peter then adds eight counsels, the first of which is not to get fixated on any suggested schema, the second to avoid lapsing into study rather than prayer, the third to avoid forcing an emotional response, the fourth to avoid both lax and strained attention, the fifth to not be dismayed or give up prayer because one finds no sweetness in it, the sixth to spend as long a time as possible at prayer (anything less than an hour and a half is too short, according to St. Peter, granted one's duties do not always allow for this), the seventh not to neglect profiting from special visits from our Lord that occur outside the designated times of prayer, and the eighth to recognize that when inflamed to contemplation, one should set aside meditation, as the former is the greater good. The second part of the book is on devotion. He begins by giving part of St. Thomas's definition of devotion: "a virtue which makes a man prompt and ready for every good work, which urges him forwards and facilitates well-doing," but develops the topic differently. His advice here includes how to avoid temptation and deal with desolation.

I'm not sure who would best profit from this work meant for beginners. The average young adult, I think, would find it a bit formidable and seems better off following the path St. Peter of Alcántara recommends as it is traced in the exercises of St. Ignatius of Loyola. Perhaps it would work for young adults who are of a pious bent and/or have been homeschooled. As a person who is older, but still a beginner, I found both the meditations and the description of the acts helpful; indeed when I'm at a loss for a meditation topic, I not infrequently turn to this book.

(Review by Marie George)

Treatise on Prayer and Meditation by St. Peter of Alcántara

St. Peter of Alcántara, a sixteenth-century Franciscan friar and spiritual director, provides for posterity a handbook on the "art of mental prayer." In the first paragraph, the saint identifies the purpose of his treatise: he hopes to offer a resource by which the faithful might apply themselves to prayer "with a more joyous heart." From that opening paragraph, Alcántara achieves his objective with crisp writing that is both accessible to beginners and challenging for those who might be considered experts at prayer. More than that, the joy of this saintly director exudes through the ink and paper, and into the heart of the reader. There can be little doubt why this text has retained enduring value over the centuries.

The text is divided cleanly into two parts. Part I presents the subject matter for meditation. This section, in large part, consists of two seven-part meditations on the mysteries of the Catholic faith, which are meant to serve as guides for prayer in the morning and evening of each day for a week. In this part of the text, the author provides plenty of material on which even beginners can meditate fruitfully. Beyond these fourteen meditations, Alcántara also offers counsels that will lead one through meditation toward contemplation, which he knows and states explicitly is the goal toward which prayer is directed. The climactic pages of this section are the "Special Prayer for the Love of God," in which a soul asks God to make ready "a pleasing dwelling place within me."

Part II deals with devotion, which ought to proceed naturally from meditation, says the author. "This deep meditation and thought [the subject matter of Part I] does in fact engender that affection and sentiment in the will which we call devotion, and this incites and urges us on to well-doing." The brief chapters of this second part identify the dispositions and actions that build up "the ladder whence we may lay hold the fruit of happiness," as well as those habits that hinder devotion. This helps Christians, whether novices or well-seasoned in prayer, to gain dexterity in this "art of arts." Simply and accurately, each of these counsels reveals the steps to take, and those to avoid, on the journey toward the heights of the spiritual life.

At this point in the text, Alcántara identifies what he esteems to be those heights of the spiritual life and he lays out what he understands is the real measure of fruitful prayer. St. Peter writes that "the true touchstone for a man is not the relish he may experience in prayer, but his patience in tribulation, self-abnegation and the doing of the Will of God, to which, of course, spiritual consolations may themselves undoubtedly contribute." In other words, growth in virtue is the unmistakable evidence that prayer has been directed rightly and had its proper effect. Even if his prayer is not accompanied by consolations, the man of virtue is attaining the spiritual heights.

Finally, it should be noted that the TAN edition contains the text of *Pax Animae* (Peace of the Soul), not written by Peter of Alcántara, which was appended to *Treatise* early in its publishing history. In the preface, the publisher recommends that a reader refrain from reading *Pax Animae* immediately after *Treatise*, so that the spirit and content of St. Peter's work is not neutralized or diluted.

(Review by Derek Rotty)

Union with God: Letters of Spiritual Direction by Blessed Columba Marmion, selected and annotated by Dom Raymond Thibaut

Bl. Columba Marmion delivers simple, but deep messages in letters written to the wide variety of people to whom he gave spiritual direction: children, single and married adults, religious of both sexes. While some of the missives are addressed to persons who are holier than the average Christian, even they are of help to ordinary Christians, inciting them to aspire to greater holiness. The letters have been sagaciously arranged around the central theme of union with God, and each is prefaced by a few lines of helpful commentary by Dom Raymond Thibaut. Two of the seven chapters touch on matters concerning the religious life, and so are of lesser interest to lay persons; still the book contains an ample amount of material of interest to a general audience. The letter format makes the book reader friendly, especially for those of us who have limited time for spiritual reading. Many of the letters provide ready starting points for meditation. Marmion at times sounds like Teresa of Avila, at times like Thérèse of Lisieux, and he makes use of a number of spiritual authors, including John of the Cross and Francis de Sales; he also makes frequent reference to Scripture. What is remarkable about Bl. Marmion is that he always goes to the heart of the matter with a warmth that inspires one to listen attentively to his counsel. Consider a few examples: "Examine thoroughly the intention with which you act. The love with which you act is a thousand times more important than the material exactitude of your actions." "I have a great longing to make of you a little saint, I see that Our Lord desires it. What He asks is that you do ALL FOR LOVE, quite simply. And don't be astonished if you are not always as perfect as you might wish." "Your thoughts about Jesus are too narrow. He isn't a bit like what you imagine. His Heart is as large as the ocean, a real human heart. He wept real salt tears when Lazarus died. 'See how much He loved him.' He does not expect you to be a specter or ghost. No, He wants you to be a thorough woman wanting love and giving it, and when you leave those you love, He wants you to feel it deeply." It comes as no surprise that this book was one of St. Teresa of Calcutta's favorites, and that Bl. Marmion was a favorite author of St. John Paul II. *Union with God* is indeed a treasure for anyone who is desirous of getting closer to God.

(Review by Marie George)[1]

Union with God: Letters of Spiritual Direction by Bl. Columba Marmion

I first encountered the writings of Bl. Columba Marmion (1858–1953) when a wise priest recommended him to a group I had joined —with some hesitation—at his suggestion. We were investigating the spirituality of Bl. Mother Teresa in preparation for possible admission to the lay movement associated with the Missionaries of Charity. And while Mother Teresa certainly inspired me, and the sisters were amazing creatures, the way the group went about its work made me jittery, as its meetings involved a mostly emotional sharing of "spiritual" experiences seemingly disconnected from any recognizable theological principles. There were lots of tears and hugs, but no real substance, at least in my mind.

So when Father suggested *Union with God* by Bl. Marmion, I was happy to have something to sink my teeth into. I took the book up as a task I had set for myself, with really no sense of anticipation or

1. This is a very slightly modified version of a review that appeared in the *Fellowship of Catholic Scholars Quarterly*, Vol. 30, No. 4, Winter 2007.

expectation. Nothing prepared me for what I encountered in this text.

Bl. Columba began his priestly life as a pastor, a chaplain, and seminary professor. Eventually, he was given permission to follow his desire to join the Benedictines in Marsedous, Belgium, finally serving as its Abbot until his death. His systematic theological works were well known and translated into seven languages; he was a sought after retreat master and spiritual director. But it is said that most of the Fathers who attended the Second Vatican Council would have brought two books with them: a bible and their copy of *Union with God*. Originally published in 1934, it turns out that this collection of letters of spiritual direction was also a favorite text of Mother Theresa. Having been forever changed by this encounter, I fully understand that. For in them we hear, without any doubt, the voice of a spiritual master.

From the moment I picked up the text, I was the recipient of instruction that spoke to me directly, as if I were known to the author himself. It is the best kind of spiritual direction, grounded in an astonishing depth of theological knowledge, spoken by someone who possesses a profound understanding of the human situation. His insights are practical without ever leaving a hidden aquifer of spiritual depth or meaning—for their locus is at the intersection of divinely inspired truth both understood and lived.

As the title implies, the main thrust of Bl. Columba's direction is toward a real union with God which, as he helps us to see, is more possible in this life than we may realize. What it requires, above all, is recognition of our absolute dependence upon Him. He reminds us again and again that God can only help if we turn toward him in our need, not just theoretically, but *actually*. Perhaps the fundamental lynchpin of his entire teaching is found in the following passage: "God's mercy is infinite like God Himself. If we lay open our soul to Him with all its infirmities and sins, His Divine gaze penetrates this abyss of which we cannot see the bottom. His gaze goes into the most hidden recesses and brings us strength and light."

I have been astonished to find that when, in the silence of my own heart, I admit to God, to Jesus, that I am weak, that I am unable to meet life's challenges on my own, His strength floods my being with a quiet energy that cannot be defeated or brought to despair. This is what I learned from Bl. Columba Marmion. For he tells me that I can be absolutely certain that the voices that speak to me of my confusion and inadequacies are not the voice of God; they are from the enemy and must be ignored. With such a disposition, I can follow (sometimes!) his instruction to smile kindly on everything that God sends my way, to never lose hope in the face of difficulty or disappointment, secure in the knowledge that I am held in existence by a God who loves me. For this is now real knowledge, grounded in my own lived experience.

(Review by Deborah Savage)

Miscellaneous

The End of the Present World and the Mysteries of the Future Life by Fr. Charles Arminjon

The endorsement by St. Thérèse notwithstanding, it took me a while to get into this series of conferences by Fr. Arminjon, a nineteenth-century French priest. I was continually irritated by the missing or inaccurate references for quotations, as well as by the uneven scholarship (e.g., Arminjon often quotes Aquinas, but on a couple of key issues misrepresents him or fails to draw upon him). Some of what Arminjon says is pure speculation, e.g., the location of purgatory, leaving me cold. Some of his reasoning is incorrect, e.g., he concludes the necessity of the resurrection of the body from the cycles in nature; in these cycles, however, new individuals of a species replace the old ones, rather than the same ones returning.

The book is about the last things. The first two conferences are on the end of the world. According to Arminjon, saints throughout the ages have seen signs in their day that the world was coming to an end. Arminjon saw signs of it in his own age, and we can see the same in ours: "governments . . . striving to banish Jesus Christ from the school, the army, the very abode of justice!" However, as he points out, the anti-Christ has not come, nor have the Jews converted. The third conference is on the resurrection of the dead and the general judgment. Arminjon, like many saints, advises us to reflect on the account we will have to give to God of all that we have done. Conference four is on the state and location of the just after the final judgment, the moral of the story being we should keep our eyes on heaven and not become attached to the passing goods of this world or be overly exercised by social strife.

Conference five, on purgatory, caught my attention. Arminjon asserts (without offering any references) that the pains of purgatory are held by Doctors of the Church to be more severe than any known on earth. What he goes on to observe does seem to support this. Those in purgatory suffer continuously while those on earth usually get some kind of break (they sleep, a friend visits, etc.); those in purgatory realize that their sufferings can gain them no merit, whereas we on earth can unite them to Christ; those in purgatory no longer have the distractions we have on earth, and consequently their longing for God is immeasurably increased and their separation from Him exceedingly afflictive. Conference six is on hell. Arminjon makes is plain that hell is real and tries to show that it is not contrary to God's mercy. Conference seven is on eternal life and the vision of God: "Words cannot describe heaven's glory." Conference seven is on the Eucharist, the means of Redemption; it contains useful reflections on the sacrifice of the Mass. Conference eight is on suffering; here Arminjon comments on a number of scripture passages relevant to suffering and his somewhat original commentary on Lazarus and Dives hit home with me.

Despite the book's shortcomings, Arminjon is to some extent successful in achieving his purpose, which is "to turn souls away from the limited concerns of time, and raise them up to the thought and desire of the good to come." Our sufferings can seem never ending at times, but they are not eternal.

(Review by Marie George)

The End of the Present World and the Mysteries of the Future Life by Fr. Charles Arminjon

Most authors would never even dream of the endorsement blurb printed by Sophia Institute Press on the front cover of *The End of the Present World*. In her famous autobiography, *Story of a Soul*, St. Thérèse of Lisieux wrote that "reading this [book] was one of the greatest graces of my life." Thérèse goes on to say: "all the great truths of religion, the mysteries of eternity, plunged my soul into a happiness not of this earth.... I experienced already what God reserves for those who love Him."

The End of the Present World, originally published in French in 1881, is a series of conferences given by Fr. Charles Arminjon, a priest who spent nearly the last twenty years of his life preaching throughout France. In the Foreword to this book, Arminjon expresses alarm that rationalism has led to an "absence of the sense of the supernatural and the profound neglect of the great truths of the future life.... The two causes of this terrifying indifference and profound universal lethargy are, obviously, ignorance and the unrestrained love of sensual pleasure that, by darkening the interior eye of the human soul, bring all its aspirations down to the narrow level of the present life, and cut it off from the vision of the beauties and rewards to come."

As attested by St. Thérèse's enthusiastic endorsement, Arminjon has given us the means to overcome our ignorance and to open our hearts and minds to the eternal realities. The book is replete with scripture quotes, together with explanations with which one may or may not agree. But in either case, they lead the reader to meditation on these scripture passages from the perspective of the Last Things and the End Times.

Some people will be inclined to read only the first part of the book, which focuses on the end of the world and the nail-biting prophecies about the Antichrist. As Arminjon points out, we don't know whether these events will happen during our lifetime—though, too many in our times make the dangerous assumption that they will not. But readers should not forego the latter part of the book, which is arguably more important, as it addresses topics that will certainly be of relevance to each one of us: hell, purgatory, and heaven.

I found the last two conferences to be particularly thought-provoking. In discussing "Christian Sacrifice, the Means of Redemption," Arminjon focuses on the Eucharist, and explains facets of this Christian sacrifice that can lead one to a greater reverence for and appreciation of this sacrament. Two that are particularly compelling are how the priest assumes the person of Jesus Christ in the Holy Sacrifice of the Mass, and how Christ, in the state of victim, instructs us and offers us the example of all the virtues.

The last conference on "The Mystery of Suffering in Its Relationship with the Future Life," assesses suffering from God's eternal perspective of whether we will be ready to encounter Him face-to-face when we die. Arminjon is able to make suffering not only sensible, but in a certain sense, even desirable (at least in the abstract!).

As with any book written in a different era, readers need to keep in mind that the book was written in the late 1800s. It is reasonable to believe that Fr. Arminjon would have written about certain topics differently in our own time, for example, with respect to children who die without baptism, and the Antichrist in relation to the Jews.

Those who are critical of all religious assertions, who need empirical proofs or at least a line of reasoning accessible to his/her intellectual capacity, probably should not bother reading this book. But the simple, child-like soul who, like St. Thérèse, is eager to learn from Sacred Scripture, the Fathers and Doctors of the Church, and others with extraordinary wisdom and understanding, will find much in Fr. Arminjon's conferences to marvel about and reflect upon, and will gain great graces thereby.

(Review by A. M. Desprit)

Caryll Houselander: Essential Writings edited by Wendy M. Wright

Caryll Houselander: eccentric, mystic, wood-carver, writer, poet, amateur therapist, and spiritual director, is put before the reader by Wendy M. Wright, who has selected what she considers to be essential writings along with a few of Houselander's illustrations. For this reason, though the book is not a step-by-step spiritual guide, I personally found much in it of spiritual value.

In the first two chapters, Houselander gives accounts of three mystical visions, all having in common the identification of Jesus Christ with the members of his Mystical Body, which became a recurring theme for her spiritual understanding. The third vision, that of Houselander's "seeing" Christ in *all* humanity, which in her vision consists of "all sorts of people jostled together" on an underground train, followed by the crowd of passers-by when she came up onto the street, struck me, because she not only saw the spiritually alive members of the Mystical Body, but also those dead in sin. She speaks of the reverence one must have for the spiritually dead because they are Christ's tombs, and therefore are potential places for Christ to rise again. She says that to the person we might suspect is lost in sin, we "must comfort Christ, who is suffering in him." This view gave me insight into praying for wandering family members and a sense of hope and a new communion with loved ones.

In the second chapter, too, Houselander mentions that she has always been obsessed with the "world's sorrow," and that during the suffering brought on by the bombing of London, others had been

118

brought to the same obsession. I found this poignant and identified with it. Whether by nurture or nature, I find myself inclined to melancholy. My English mother, a child during World War II, had to leave her family and was evacuated to Oxford during the Blitz. My Polish father lived through the Bolshevik Revolution in Eastern Poland, and then spent the entire duration of World War II in a German prisoner-of-war camp. I grew up with a deep sense and fear of the tragedy and suffering of life. When Houselander, who was also a fearful person, reminded me that this sorrow is "only the shadow cast by the spread arms of the crucified King to shelter us until the morning of the resurrection from the blaze of everlasting love," it gave me comfort.

Houselander's reflections from Chapter 6 also gave me food for contemplation. She speaks of how easy it would be to hate one's enemies during the War. She identifies two causes of hate: fear and indignation at the suffering of others. Both of these, fear and apprehension of the air raids and indignation at the ruined buildings and people, would lead to hate if not countered by love. This love could be shown by putting others before self in the bomb shelters or wherever one encountered them, praying for them and being concerned for their welfare. This thinking about others would lessen fear and lead to love. Houselander says that "instead of becoming hard and acid, we shall become gentle and sensitive; instead of inflicting yet another wound on the human race, we shall heal one." She calls us to follow Christ, who by dying made his enemies his friends.

As I was reading and praying over this, a comparison to our present time came to me. Although we are not engaged in a world war at this time, there is so much division and polarization in our world. I hear and read many sentiments of anger and hate brought on by fear of what is happening to the world and indignation at laws and actions that are unjust. Houselander's words are a message to us to hate no one, whether politician or member of Isis, but to work to put others before ourselves, and to pray for all, even our enemies, trusting in Jesus Christ to work out his suffering, death, and resurrection in each of us.

(Review by Barbara Doran)

Caryll Houselander: Essential Writings

If you are looking for everyday encouragement in the nitty-gritty of your daily walk with Christ, you might want to look somewhere else. If, on the other hand, you want to be entertained by the story of a remarkable life and/or feel like being challenged by insights into the meaning of Life, Truth, and Beauty by a soul of rare sensitivity, in the context of two World Wars, look no further. You've come to the right place!

Caryll Houselander was, I feel, reasonably confident in saying, not very much like you or me. Dubbed by her biographer "the Divine Eccentric," she was a mystic to whom God granted life-changing visions; she was also an inveterate practical jokester who considered it an act of charity to stick out her tongue at a total stranger on the bus, thinking with glee about how much fun her victim would later have, telling stories about "the madwoman on the bus."

She saw herself primarily as a wood carver, seeking to follow the example of Our Lord in Nazareth: "Had you gone to visit . . . you would have found him like other men, but giving a significance to ordinary things that others often fail to do." She developed this theme of finding significance in ordinary things into what she termed the "Christing" of the world—seeing and loving God in all people and things.

Recognizing that "to become a skilled craftsman means imposing upon oneself the discipline that forms character," and furthermore that, properly viewed, work can be a way of entering into and sharing the experience of God Himself, she devoted herself to learning the craft of woodworking with a methodical intensity. She could be mercurial and utterly impractical; at one point she set out to re-read the Gospels, "noticing everything." Needless to say, she soon realized the impossibility (she called it "the stupidity") of the task!

Her work with the Catholic Evidence Guild convinced her that the average Englishman's spirituality was in a parlous state. Many Catholics are eager to tell non-Catholics what the Church has taught them about God, she reasoned, so what could be simpler? But, she found, "talking about God is hard. It requires skill acquired only by constant effort, patience and humility, throughout a lifetime."

It seems that writing about her faith came more easily than speaking; certainly by the 1940s she was one of the most admired Catholic writers in the great flowering of the faith that preceded Vatican II in England. A daily communicant, she looked on life not as a problem to be solved, but a mystery to be plumbed. To her, the Liturgy was "the love song of Christ in man; the voice of the Mystical Body of Christ lifted up to God." At the same time, she humorously described her cat as her spiritual director: having narrowly escaped the clutches of a neighbor's cat that was "marked by the underworld," her tabby jumped into her lap, indicated that his ears needed scratching, and promptly fell asleep. Houselander envied him his total trust in her, wishing that she possessed a similar trust in God that would leave her unfazed by the war.

All these contrasts make Caryll Houselander as difficult to pin down as a wisp of smoke from one of her chain-smoked cigarettes. Wendy Wright has done a splendid job of making her accessible, giving us a chronological framework on which to hang her writings, her art, and her "rhythms" (non-metrical, non-rhyming poetical fragments), as well as her children's stories, personal journals, and letters.

I highly recommend this book.

(Review by Alison Bernhoft)

Other works by Houselander include *The Reed of God*, *The Way of the Cross*, and *A Rocking Horse Catholic.*

Holiness for Housewives: And Other Working Women by Dom Hubert Van Zeller (Abridged version of a work originally published in 1951, *Praying While You Work.*)

Holiness for Housewives, originally published in 1951, is as relevant today as it was back then. In a society where women are still struggling to reach the top in their field and are fueled by corporate status, it's nice to have a reminder that we stay-at-home moms and wives can still find happiness, respect, and holiness in the simpler (albeit just as difficult and stressful) vocations of mothers, homeschoolers, and wives. Although specifically geared toward stay-at-home mothers, this book is for women (and men) of any vocation. It reminds us to find peace and simplicity in every job we do, while developing a closer relationship with God and a deeper understanding of prayer.

As a stay-at-home mother, I often find myself questioning whether my duties are as meaningful as those of people who are in the workforce. I'm sure many mothers can relate to feelings resulting from carrying the extraordinary burdens involved in balancing a household, the overwhelming sense of despair, drudgery, and exhaustion in performing everyday chores, along with feelings of being under-appreciated for what is done in the home, not to mention doubt as to whether vacuuming, doing laundry and the dishes, etc. have any type of real worth. This book actually helped teach me how to pray when I have those feelings and to truly understand the importance and value of my job. The importance of raising children is generally understood, yes, but this book offers a validation on a deeper, more spiritual level. It specifically reminds mothers that holiness can be found even in the most tedious of chores and that, amazingly enough, through such tasks we can develop a deeper relationship with God! It also validates how important and necessary the job of a wife is; often forgotten as being an actual "vocation," the calling of a wife is just as important as that of a mother. If we remind ourselves of God's presence in every task, holiness, peace and a respect for our position can be the reward.

Van Zeller has an incredible way of capturing the exact emotions behind what goes into the everyday lives of mothers and wives. His sense of compassion and understanding resonates in each page and educates the reader on how to seek the spiritual depth they crave.

I found this book to be a very practical spiritual guide for mothers and housewives alike. Each page seems to offer a small pearl of wisdom that can be applied to everyday life. It's a great book to keep next to your bed to read daily as a reminder that by seeking God through prayer, you will learn the value and importance of any job you do.

(Review by Wendy Biondi)

Holiness for Housewives: And Other Working Women by Dom Hubert van Zeller

Dom Hubert van Zeller's Holiness *for Housewives and Other Working Women*, published in 1951 as *Praying While You Work*, offers three chapters about how to connect with God, and a fourth of prayers for women. The book is for "souls who are anchored in their God-given vocation, and who, nevertheless, are conscious of their parallel vocation to the interior life."

Written during post-war years when many women left home for jobs traditionally filled by men, the book meets needs of women today. Currently, working women's lives are regarded as more glamorous, vibrant, and desirable than life at home. The domestic vocation is viewed as insignificant, reserved for unfortunate, uneducated, unintelligent, or lazy women. This viewpoint is a source of psychological and spiritual disquiet for women, especially for women at home raising children. Addressing this, Chapter 1, "Your Special Vocation as a Housewife" explains that we serve God best through the particular circumstances of our lives, regardless of how humble. Souls seeking to escape present obligations attached to their state in life because they imagine they could serve God better by doing something else are mistaken. What is real and present is what matters, what is past or imaginable is not. "This is the first lesson for the Christian wife and mother today: to let go of what may once have been—and under other circumstances might be now—a recollected self, and take on, with both hands, the plan of God."

For embracing God's plan and growth in holiness "the first necessity is to find in your soul a respect for your vocation." Dom Hubert explains that once a woman (or man) is convinced that her state in life is God's will, she will learn to find happiness and peace in the fulfillment of the duties connected with this state. As he explains: "The greatest and most lasting pleasures are those that emerge out of life itself. They are those that come in virtue of the vocation, not in spite of it."

Chapter 2, "How to Pray Amidst Your Daily Duties" discusses prayer amidst constant flux and aggravations. Most housewives, immersed in the swirling sea of petty details and activities, find it difficult to reach union with God. Housewives must "find a way of communicating with God *by means of* and not *in spite of* the calls upon your time and energy and patience." Souls must develop prayerful attitudes, requiring initially forced deliberate acts of prayer which if sustained eventually become habitual.

Chapter 3, "How to Grow Holier Day by Day," speaks of temptations that deflect the search for holiness. Refreshing breaks from tiresome duties are important, but material escapes—movies, alcohol, vacations, cause the opposite effect. Instead of replenishment they cause self-disgust and emptiness. Weariness caused by daily work cannot be alleviated by means of material things, but rather through the immaterial and spiritual: "If living in the senses and for the senses has produced the civilization in which we exist, it seems peculiarly futile to turn for relief and escape to those very senses that have been at the bottom of all the trouble." Relaxation is better found by spending fifteen minutes in spiritual reading or in a weekend retreat. Dom Hubert also talks about the temptation to escape duty and about offering leisure time to God, who inspires you to use it in the way that pleases Him best. He advises to learn to pray simply by praying—and "in proportion as you draw near to Truth by prayer, you inevitably increase your own conformity to the true pattern of yourself as it exists in the mind of God."

Chapter 4 is a collection of prayers for all occasions, and a list of recommended texts for spiritual reading.

(Review by Jeannette Roberts)

Other works by Van Zeller include *Spirit of Penance, Path to God: How Acts of Penance Will Make Your Life Holier and Your Days Happier* and *Prayer and the Will of God* (reviewed in this volume).

Interior Freedom by Fr. Jacques Philippe

In this short book, consisting of five chapters, Fr. Philippe develops the theses that without interior freedom we are subject to being overwhelmed by life's difficulties and thus never enjoy authentic happiness, and that we acquire interior freedom in the same measure that our faith, hope, and charity increases. Fr. Philippe shows an acute understanding of unhealthy mentalities so widespread in our day, such as the victim mentality and the tendency to measure people's worth in terms of what they do or have, and he manifests both psychological and spiritual insight when he treats of suffering. In the opening chapter he speaks of misconceptions concerning freedom widespread nowadays that we may consciously or unconsciously endorse. He brings us to see that our lack of freedom is not primarily due to external circumstances, but comes from inside us, from our lack of love—we are imprisoned by our fears and selfishness. As he notes, there are three attitudes we can adopt in the face of events that we not have chosen: rebellion, resignation, or acceptance. He argues that freedom consists in accepting what we did not choose by examining three types of limitations we experience: (1) our personal limitations; (2) suffering in general; (3) suffering imposed by others. In regard to the first, he shows that the key to self-acceptance is the experience of the tender love that God has for us. In regard to suffering in general he astutely notes that our anxiety, resentment, and resistance to suffering is often a worse suffering than the suffering itself. We augment our suffering by rejecting that it can in some way be beneficial. We need to trust that God can bring good out of evil. What he says here about purifying the mind I found especially helpful. Our desire to know the reason for a given suffering is often motivated by a desire to be in control; we suffer from insecurity because we trust in ourselves, instead of trusting in God. Fr. Philippe further notes that not only can we put up with contrarieties, we can in a certain sense choose them. Every event can be given a positive meaning and can be an expression of love, or be transformed into abandonment, trust, hope, or offering. God can obtain some good out of every event. In regard to suffering inflicted by others, Fr. Philippe makes it plain that the sins of others ultimately do not deprive one of anything (at the spiritual level). We ourselves do so by choosing to let them affect us negatively. He also makes some brief, but helpful remarks on forgiving others. In Chapter 2, on the present moment, he shows that we should not fret over past or future, but rather recognize that the past is in the hands of the merciful God who can draw good from anything and the future is in the hands of a provident God who looks out for his children. Chapter 3 is devoted to explaining how living in accord with faith, hope, and love bring about interior freedom. Here he gives an insightful account of how Peter's fall allowed Peter to move from trust in himself to trust in God. In Chapter 4, Fr. Philippe develops the theme that a legalistic attitude kills love. Love consists in giving freely, and also in receiving freely. In the final chapter on spiritual poverty and freedom, Fr. Philippe notes, among other things, how identifying ourselves with the good we can do leads to spiritual pride where we more or less consciously consider ourselves the origin and author of this good. He shows how the dark night of the soul (and suffering in general) is an opportunity for one to learn one's true identity and that God's mercy is all. Fr. Philippe's understanding of the psychology of contemporary man makes this a good book to start with for those whose spiritual life has yet to take deep root, while at the same time it has a lot to offer to those of deeper faith.

(Review by Marie George)

Interior Freedom by Fr. Jacques Philippe

Interior Freedom is one of the best-known books by the popular author and retreat master Fr. Jacques Philippe. Few contemporary works on the spiritual life have merited the level of interest regularly shown toward this little tract. Weighing in at a mere 134 pages in the edition I read, Fr. Philippe's miniature masterpiece is as powerful as it is brief. The author modestly frames this work as a "commentary on the first beatitude: 'Blessed are the poor in spirit, for theirs is the kingdom of Heaven.'" Yet for Fr. Philippe, it is this first beatitude which unlocks the spiritual efficacy of the other seven, the portal through which one finds true freedom in the whole of the Christian life.

Part of Fr. Philippe's particular genius is his mastery of the contemporary idiom. Even in translation, his writing style is seamless, dense, free of pretense, and eminently quotable. Those who read spiritual works from centuries past can be tempted to suspect that certain of their insights lose relevance owing to the great distance between their cultural context and our own. Such readers will be heartened by Fr. Philippe who with just a few sentences evinces a keen grasp of the forces at work in contemporary culture.

Yet *Interior Freedom* is less concerned with cultural commentary than with spiritual direction. While Fr. Philippe is attentive to the disorienting effects of modernism on the interior dialectic of twenty-first century Christians, his work brims with optimism. He identifies our thirst for "freedom" as possibly the last remaining modern value about which all people still agree. Yet Fr. Philippe is not content simply to decry freedom's distortions and to affix them to a syllabus of modern errors. Rather, he sees our shared thirst as a potential springboard toward authentic restoration.

By a series of distinctions Fr. Philippe steers his readers past the pitfalls which often end in private despair or public totalitarianism. Is freedom primarily about claiming autonomy or accepting dependence? Is it won or bestowed? Is it something external or something internal? Each of these paradoxes is tackled with clarity and economy. To light our way, Fr. Philippe puts before us figures who have found true freedom in types of imprisonment. We hear from St. Thérèse of Lisieux—about whom he's written extensively elsewhere—as well as the surprising witnesses of Jacques Fesch, the murderer-turned-saint, and Etty Hillesum, the Auschwitz prisoner who upon finding total freedom behind bars declared: "I find life beautiful, and I feel free. The sky within me is as wide as the one stretching above my head." Adding to his deft curation of Scripture, Fr. Philippe brings to bear on his work important insights from such figures as St. Athanasius, St. Catherine of Siena, St. John of the Cross, Seraphim of Sarov, as well as from more contemporary authors, including Charles Péguy, St. Faustina, Georges Bernanos, St. John Paul II, and Matta El Meskeen.

Fr. Philippe is far from the first author to elucidate the three Theological Virtues of faith, hope, and love. After addressing each separately, Fr. Philippe takes up what he considers to be of vital importance: the *dynamism* between them. He shows us how the Holy Spirit is most active in free souls through what he calls the "dynamism of grace"—faith begetting hope begetting love. This dynamism is the efficacious remedy to their opposites, "the dynamism of sin"—doubt begetting distrust begetting sin. *Interior Free-*

dom charts a course for the spiritual life that is at once both encouraging and liberating, ultimately enabling us to say with Fr. Philippe "I am what I am in God's eyes: a poor child who possesses absolutely nothing, who receives everything, infinitely loved and totally free."

(Review by Christopher M. Candela

Other works by Fr. Philippe include *Searching for and Maintaining Peace, Called to Life,* and *The Way of Trust and Love—A Retreat Guided by St. Thérèse of Lisieux*

"Leaf by Niggle" by J. R. R. Tolkien (found in his book *Tree and Leaf* and in other places as well)

Tolkien's short story, "Leaf by Niggle," is a modern day parable on how preoccupation with our personal projects hinders us from loving our neighbor, which is what God means for us to be doing during our stay on earth. Though it may seem strange to suggest a work of fiction for spiritual reading, many will readily see themselves in the somewhat ridiculous character of Niggle who, though not a particularly good painter, is passionate about his art-work, and consequently regards the demands that others make on his time as interruptions to be dealt with as expeditiously as possible so that he can get back to his painting. Niggle eventually ends up in a purgatory of sorts, where he slowly starts realizing the true value of time and the importance of genuine love of neighbor. Those of us who are "driven" can benefit from this cautionary tale filled with hope.

(Review by Marie George)

The Saints, Humanly Speaking: The Personal Letters of the Saints, selected and arranged by Sr. Felicitas Corrigan, OSB

This is a fascinating collection of 114 letters by 47 different writers, all of whom have been beatified or canonized. The work, for obvious reasons, lacks the unity and sustained treatment that one finds in a work devoted to a specific theme. This is weakness, but also a strength, as the book ranges over a wide field of topics. The various themes have been grouped under five broad headings: the Christian in the world, in the home, in the church, in life, and in death. Each letter is short, and thus the book offers a friendly format for someone whose time for spiritual reading is limited. The book is successful in portraying the saints as people who are not all so different from us, from Bl. Perboyre who humorously recounts an Asian's fascination with his European nose to St. Louise de Marillac who is rebuked by St. Vincent for blaming herself for her son's behavior to St. Anselm who writes to pacify an overly demanding friend. The letters often make enjoyable reading because of the heart-felt concern one senses in them. For example, one can tell that St. Bernard cared about the recipients of his letters, both from the tender words he addressed to the parents of a future monk, as well as by the stern reprimand he sent to a layman who was trying to dissuade someone from his vocation. Although some of the letters did not strike any spiritual cord in me, most did. There are at least four sorts of spiritual benefit to be derived from these letters. Some letters gives us perspective. We tend to think that our society is off-the-charts corrupt and that nowadays the Church is going through particularly difficult times, but as these letters make clear, our situation is hardly unique. Some letters portray the saints as setting a good example for us; you think your life is difficult, read Isaac Jogues' letter about how he was tortured, and if you find your life tedious read the former nobleman St. Stanislaus's letter on how he found heaven amidst broom and saucepans as a novice in the Jesuits. Some letters contain accounts of the saints' human limitations and failings, and thus give us hope; for example, a heart-wrenching missive about priest's struggles to be a good Christian while living in the world (as opposed to in a monastery) turns out to have been penned by St. John Chrysostom! Lastly, many letters contain profound spiritual advice concerning suffering, death, family life, correcting others, and many other important topics. A nice addition to the volume are the short biographies at the end; they are both interesting in themselves and often help us better understand the saints' letters.

(Review by Marie George)

The Saints, Humanly Speaking: The Personal Letters of the Saints, selected and arranged by Sr. Felicitas Corrigan, OSB

This is a wonderful book. I would love to meet Sr. Felicitas who had the joy of compiling these letters and of thus allowing the saints to speak to us directly. Letter writing is becoming a lost art in today's high tech world of instant messaging across a variety of media. These beautifully written letters are concrete evidence of just how much we have lost. Most importantly, however, the letters show us how down-to-earth and human the saints are, and how they faced many of the very same issues and problems as we do. They become our friends.

"Christianity is a rough profession." "Christianity is warfare and Christians spiritual soldiers." So wrote St. Robert Southwell to his fellow Catholics in prison in 1584. Yet, a thousand years earlier, in 404, St. John Chrysostom also wrote about the storms that had rushed upon the Church: "fierce and threatening while the whole world is toppling over into ruin." These letters, and others in this book, remind us that living as a Christian has never been easy. The letters give us insights into the lives and times of our saints and how they fought their daily fight with grace, compassion, and humor. Given the harsher standards of living of their day and difficult modes of travel, many of these saints experienced adventures requiring a level of bravery that we moderns can scarcely imagine.

The letters of the Jesuit and other martyrs in Elizabethan England, in the New World of the Americas, in Japan and the East all contain pretty gripping material. Their experiences are riveting and we can only gasp at the extent of their suffering for Christ. Other letters respond to requests for guidance and these provide practical common sense and often humorous advice on a variety of subjects. We meet people who have dealt with the same problems we do and have conquered them. Thus, we get to see our favorite saints in a new light and meet new friends in saints we did not know. They come alive and are no longer "Plaster of Paris" figurines on the mantel. They show us how we too can follow Christ in the events of our own daily lives.

This is a great book for those just starting out on their spiritual journey. It contains much spiritual direction from the masters in a practical and highly readable form. It provides encouragement to see that others have encountered the same "bumps in the road" that we do and were able to persevere. It is also beneficial for those who have advanced further along the spiritual road by reminding them of the constant closeness of God in our lives.

(Review by Joan Lovett)

Sermons of the Curé of Ars by St. John Vianney

I'm not sure to whom I'd recommend *Sermons of the Curé d'Ars*. The Curé, in his concern that we avoid landing in hell, sometimes goes overboard; for example, he sees no room for mitigating factors involved in alcoholism, he comes down very hard on the cursing popular in his day, and goes so far as to label as damned a dying hardened sinner who does finally plead for God's mercy. I can see that his excesses would turn certain people off (e.g., if you do your penance in a position other than kneeling you need to confess it). He speaks mainly about the typical common sins your average Joe (or Jane) commits, sins that most people doing spiritual reading probably abandoned long ago. And yet, I have to say that he made me aware of my casual attitude regarding certain sins and he called me out in regard to some sins "where I know better." One does need a certain amount of discernment to see where he goes too far, and if one is looking for a "sensitive" approach to identifying and overcoming failings, the Curé is not the one to turn to. It is important to read the sermons in their entirety and to make an effort to understand where he is coming from and then to transpose his thoughts into our day and age. For example, the Curé speaks about people shopping around to find a confessor who will give them absolution; this should call to our attention the gravity of neglecting to make firm plans to amend our lives. For the reader motivated and able to exercise a little effort and discernment, there is goodly amount of sage advice to be derived from reading this work.

The Curé provides concrete, easy to recognize, descriptions of envious behavior, and then notes how envy is a sin that we often hide from ourselves, and that we must pray to the Holy Spirit to discover it in ourselves. His treatment of sins in speech is equally graphic. He wastes no time condemning licentious talk as outraging God, scandalizing our neighbor, and "to put it even more clearly, loose talk releases all the passions." Although he goes overboard in saying that it is a sin only second to sacrilege in gravity, he is doubtlessly right as to it being conducive to sins of impurity. He is insistent that parents keep a careful eye on teenage children as to the company they keep and as to not leaving them unattended with a member of the opposite sex. He is highly critical of allowing young people to go dancing. At one point he quotes saint after saint who opposed dancing. While we can be sure that he did not have a homeschoolers' swing dance in mind, some of what he says applies to it, and, *a fortiori*, to what goes on at most dances nowadays. He attacks the common sin of grumbling, noting that not only does it not make one's affairs any better, it results in the loss of merit one might have gained. He urges that we prepare ourselves before we go to Mass. This and other down-to-earth advice is to be found in the *Sermons of the Curé d'Ars.*

(Review by Marie George)

Sermons of the Curé of Ars by St. John Vianney

St. John Vianney directs these early sermons at "lukewarm" souls who can slowly fall into mortal sin rather than at hardened sinners or people who make bad confessions and sacrilegious communions for appearance's sake.

Today, when we think of serious sin, we dwell on family-related issues—abortion, cohabitation, same sex marriage—or we think of social injustices and "structures of sin." But St. John says that there are many serious and harmful sins that seldom cross the minds of 19th-century Frenchmen, and the same could be said of 21st-century Americans. These include envy, jealousy, gossip and scandal-mongering, anger, cursing, and blasphemy.

Vianney had a very harsh attitude toward dancing, regarding the tavern and the "cabaret" as sources of serious sins against chastity and marital fidelity. Today we would regard dancing and social drinking as relatively innocent, given technologies like internet pornography and chat rooms and a highly developed drug trade. But even today, there are plenty of news reports on bars, parties, and raves as the venue for sexual hook-ups, drug abuse, sexual assaults, fights, stabbings, and shootings.

Vianney also was very critical of his parishioners' behavior during worship. Given sacrilegious communions, deliberate distractions in prayer, immodestly dressed women and the men who leered at them, and the practice of fleeing from church after Mass as if being released from prison, he felt that some worshippers left Mass with thirty more mortal sins than they arrived with. Vianney's harsh tone and his emphasis on human sinfulness lead some to believe that he was a Jansenist heretic at heart. In the afterward of the book, Monsignor Francois Trochu says that St. John hated Jansenism, but that the textbooks used to train priests in his time still retained the language of Jansenist rigor. Also, Vianney is fully committed to God's mercy on sinners, but like all Catholic advocates of mercy, including Pope Francis, he says that the confessional is the place where mercy is found.

Vianney pastored a parish church in the years just after the French Revolution and Napoleon, a period that devastated Catholic life. He found that his people had lost all but the basics of their faith, especially in the areas of morality and worship. Vianney worked to restore these, though he constantly upbraided and scolded his flock to remind them of what they had lost during the revolutionary years. Someday, when legalized abortion is no more and government no longer imposes HHS mandates and other violations of conscience on Catholics, we may need a new St. John Vianney to preach the fullness of our faith to us.

(Review by Robert F. Cuervo)

There is a short compilation of various sayings of St. John Vianney entitled: *Thoughts of the Curé D'Ars*. The anonymous editor is to be congratulated on his astute selection from Vianney's works, for it allows the reader to appreciate why the Curé was such a successful preacher.

133

Spiritual Conferences by Fr. Frederick William Faber

Spiritual Conferences, perhaps Fr. Faber's most widely read work, consists of twelve essays on various aspect of the spiritual life, most of which can be read in one sitting. Faber vividly outlines various difficulties in the spiritual life and proposes no-nonsense remedies for them with the nuance to be expected from an experienced spiritual director who knows that one size does not fit all. I do not think that he is well-suited to someone who has just begun to do spiritual reading. He considers with almost brutal realism subjects that perhaps we'd rather not look at, e.g., wounded feelings, self-deception, taking scandal, weariness in well-doing, death, hell; granted, he does this in a way that is kindly and understanding of the limits of human nature. Faber is erudite, and can be a little hard to follow at times, especially when he's being paradoxical. Some may find his writing style heavy. It cannot be denied, though, that he has an uncanny ability to put human failings in sharp relief. One of the most telling portraits of many of us is found in "The Monotony of Piety," where Faber does a striking job of contrasting the zest, busyness, and self-satisfaction that surrounds our pursuit of worldly occupations with the apathy we feel in regard to prayer and mortification.

The essay on kindness alone is worth the price of the book. As Faber points out, people often fail to cultivate it as part of their spiritual life due to being more focused on self-inspection. People can be merciful and self-denying without being kind. "If they would add a little common kindness to their uncommon graces, they would convert ten where now they only abate the prejudices of one." The essay on death, unlike the essay on kindness, should not be read indiscriminately by all; some may find it too "scary," for want of a better word, whereas others will find it beneficially sobering. The essay on self-deceit is considered a classic. For example, Faber, showing his typical balance, advises: "Praise people as little as you can consistently with kindness; for you never run a greater risk of doing the devil's work for him than when you praise people. Nevertheless you must praise others sometimes. We cannot go on without it." In "Why So Little Comes of Frequent Confession" Faber points out the root of why our spiritual practices in general bear so little fruit: we do not put much love of God in them. In "Confidence the Only True Worship," Faber gives much sage advice concerning trust, e.g.: "If from confidence in God and not in self, we believed we should never commit the sin again, probably we should not commit it again. We have fallen for want of faith in grace." In "On a Taste for Reading in the Spiritual Life" Faber points out that suitable secular reading prevents us from using our time pursuing inappropriate activities, and makes us less judgmental by showing that goodness in people can take many forms. In "On Heaven and Hell" he observes that "We aim at disinterested love before we have half learned interested fear." In "All Men Have a Special Vocation" Faber notes how in times when our hearts are cold and God sends us special trials we are sometimes led "to suspect God and resolve to be cautious with him. . . . Yet we should be greatly surprised if he [God] was to put before us the hundreds, perhaps thousands of protestations . . . that we only wanted one thing—which was to love him more, and we did not care what it cost us. You see he has done no more than take us at our word." I feel that Faber has me pegged, and knows what I need to hear; and many others heartily agree with me.

(Review by Marie George)

Spiritual Conferences by Fr. Frederick William Faber

"But we must deal gently with the great multitude of those who are honestly trying to keep closer to God than a mere avoiding of sin implies." This quotation comes from Fr. Faber's essay "On the Monotony of Piety," and I think it characterizes his *Spiritual Conferences* aptly. It occurs to me as I write on this feast of St. Francis de Sales, that "gentleness with the seeking soul" is a characteristic of both this beloved saint and the author. If you were to cross St. Francis and Charles Dickens, I think you would come quite close to having the sense of Fr. Faber: his insight and his writing style. He takes the reader into his confidence and occasionally bursts forth with a lovely description of events in the spiritual life; for instance:

"Like a lantern in the night, grace gives light around our feet, a circle of light just wide enough to prevent our stumbling. But then we must look at our feet. If we strain our eyes into the gloom ahead of us, we shall stumble in spite of the lantern" ("All Men Have a Spiritual Vocation").

"[T]here falls from the veins of Jesus a shower of the precious blood . . . and bedews the sinners soul. . . . All heaven is stirred at the event. It is the special subject of an angelic jubilee. It is the immediate action of the Creator on the soul of his creature" ("Why So Little Comes from Frequent Confession").

Father Faber's *Spiritual Conferences* was published in 1858 and is a hefty 327 pages, consisting of a collection of his writings taken from notes made before and after speaking on the subjects of the chapters. The book is broken into three long parts: "Kindness," "On Death," "Self-Deceit," and nine shorter conferences on a variety of topics in the spiritual life. The collection is a good book to have around. You can delve into it for an hour and finish a shorter conference, or you can take several days at a time, as you deal with the three longer conferences.

I began this book several years ago, and as I look back over my notes in the margins, I am especially struck by how topical his subjects and treatments are even today even 150 years later.

- What better "anti-bullying plan" could a school hope for than that the students read and absorb Father's words on "Kindness"?
- Has anyone not questioned the seeming lack of efficacy of frequent confession? See: "All heaven is stirred at the event . . . an angelic jubilee."
- Is it time to shake up your spiritual life? Take a look at what Father has to say about "The Monotony of Piety," and how it doesn't really exist.

Perhaps the most pertinent chapter to those of you reading book reviews of spiritual works is a chapter that affirms your quest through literature as truly helpful and even necessary. When Faber takes up the subject of spiritual reading, he says that it is a "particular kind of prayer," quoting "the old masters" who say that reading holy works is the "oil in the lamp of prayer." While pointing out that reading in general gives us edifying topics for discussion, he somewhat humorously adds: "Our books are our neighbor's allies, by making it less necessary for us to discuss him." As a final note,

Faber has this to say, "[A taste for reading] raises us. It calls out our manhood. It makes us grave. It infuses an element of greatness into everything about us."

(Review by Ann Turner)

Other works by Faber include *Growth in Holiness: The Progress of the Spiritual Life* and *The Blessed Sacrament: The Works and Ways of God.*

Suffering: The Catholic Answer by Dom Hubert van Zeller

Having read van Zeller before and having appreciated his down-to-earth style, I picked up this book, looking for understanding as I watched a good friend suffer betrayal and loss, and felt the ripples it sent through her life and ours. I find myself returning to it now as I cope with elder care and its effects on our family and on my own spiritual life. The text seems to fit itself to the reader's need like the Mona Lisa watching from whatever direction she is approached.

Van Zeller (1905–1984), a monk at the famous Benedictine Abbey at Downside, England, begins with a brief prologue explaining his purpose, which is to deal with the questions, "why there has to be pain, how it justifies itself, what we are to do about it." Positing that our sufferings only makes sense in so far as we can unite them with those of our Lord, the book is a series of meditations on the Stations of the Cross, each short chapter devoted to one station. It is thus fine Lenten reading, even if neither you nor the ones you love are in crisis. I would have no qualms in giving this to teenagers, though I would think only the most mature would be engaged by it. Both van Zeller's style and his theme are nicely illustrated in the following quotation from the epilogue:

> Our thesis is that a whole surrender to Christ's passion gives us an understanding of the whole of life, and that an appreciation of part of Christ's passion gives us only a devotion. If you asked an actor what the play was like in which he was acting, and he replied, "I don't know, I haven't read it. When I have said my lines, I put on

my hat and go home," you would judge that the richness of his profession had escaped him.

The book is well grounded in Scripture and examples from everyday life. Van Zeller is much like St. Francis de Sales in his accessible profundity, as he writes for the readers, lay and religious, of the twentieth century.

(Review by Ann Turner)

Suffering: The Catholic Answer by Dom Hubert van Zeller

A friend with an inoperable brain tumor steadily declined to the point that he could no longer speak. When visiting him, I quickly realized how difficult it is for a person to retain the full powers of the mind, but be incapable of conversing. Upon detecting that he earnestly desired to convey something, I started a guessing game: I would guess at his thought and he would nod "yes" or "no." Well, I guessed everything I could think of, from "do you wish you could speak?" to "are you anxious over leaving your children?" To each inquiry he firmly shook his head "no." Finally I asked, "Are you trying to tell me you are accepting all that God is sending you?" Smiling happily, he emphatically nodded his head up and down to say "yes," and then sank back into his wheelchair at peace.

Would that we all arrive at so complete an acceptance of our cross! Hubert Van Zeller offers us help in doing so by having us follow Christ on his way to Calvary. Each chapter of *Suffering* takes up a station of the cross and shows us what Christ is teaching us by His example in that station. The book's writing style is concise. Each short chapter abounds with keen insights into the mystery of Christ's Passion, and what it means for us.

Van Zeller notes that suffering does not always purify the soul. Often times it embitters us. We ask, "why me?" Though God does not prefer to see us suffering rather than not suffering, Christ spoke about our picking up our crosses if we would follow him. This book shows us how Christ, when the cross was placed on his shoulders, became a "living model" for us. When Jesus is condemned, that suffering is unable to extinguish happiness conditioned by love. As

Jesus receives the cross we reflect that, "it is one thing to accept the doctrine and another to accept . . . the fact of the cross in our lives."

As Jesus meets his mother we ponder on what her example teaches us about compassion. We must not think of Mary as being above human emotion. Mary felt more, not less. The essence of compassion is the ability to co-suffer, "yielding to another's cross as though it were our own." Van Zeller makes the interesting observation that idle compassion, the emotion of pity allowed to remain sterile, evolves into such mean qualities as cynical indifference, preoccupation with our own small difficulties, quickness to blame, and more.

Van Zeller points out that very often it is our weakness that is the chief cross. "Given strength, the right mood, the sense of doing something big, the knowledge that we shall not have to keep this up forever . . . given conditions of our own choosing—any fool can manage it." The real weight of the cross comes from the weakness we feel as we toil through the troubles of each day.

I can think of no one who would not profit by reading this superb book. Van Zeller helps us forsake a superficial devotion to the symbols of the Passion, and instead he inspires us to "truly live the cross-bearing life." In so far as we are able to do this, we come to know joy through suffering. It is in wholly surrendering to Christ's Passion that we begin to have "an understanding of the whole of life." With this understanding we begin to see the "mind of Christ."

(Review by Mathilde Misko)

Van Zeller is author of a number of books, including *Prayer and the Will of God* and *Holiness for Housewives and Other Working Women* (both are reviewed in this volume).

Tuning in to Grace: The Quest for God by Fr. André Louf, OSCO

I read André Louf's *Grace Can Do More*, but decided not to review it because to my mind Louf relies far too heavily on Freudian psychology (for example, he speaks at length about transference in spiritual direction); I had the same problem with *The Cistercian*

Way. Tuning in to Grace only occasionally takes this tack. The book is not for beginners, and there are some parts that may be misconstrued. However, for those who have been seeking God for some time the work does helpfully "describe and illumine some of the most fundamental experiences that are part of an evangelical quest for God."

In Chapter 1, Louf points out that it is an "illusion to think that one has been converted once and for all"; indeed, the one who thinks this way has no need for Jesus. Louf terms such people the "hardened righteous"; they do not truly know God's love and mercy and they maintain their own self-image by their own strength. God often acts to break down this self-sufficiency in ways that cause distress. At such moments, we must be like the prodigal son who the "very same moment he was reconciled with the wreckage of his life ... was at home with his father." In Chapter 2, Louf speaks about idols we form of God. He considers how Job had an image of God as someone who would approve of his good deeds, and how when instead great sufferings befell him, he questioned God and accused God of attacking him. Louf says that when God breaks an image that we had made of him, we are faced with denying God's existence or wishing that we did not exist. A third option is that this experience will allow us, like Job, to know God no longer by hearsay, but with our own eyes: "it is he who wounds and it is he who heals" (Jb. 5:18). Louf's main point in Chapter 3 is that faith in not primarily affirming religious doctrines, but believing in Christ: "only say the word, and my soul shall be healed." In Chapter 4 Louf parses St. Paul's affirmation, "for it when I am weak that I am strong" (2 Co. 12:10). He maintains that: "[W]e even have to suffer shipwreck on the road of good intentions in order that we may experience our weakness, the weakness in which the power of God can unfold its strength." In Chapter 5 Louf speaks about how easy it is to act like the Pharisee who seeks to arrive at self-perfection largely according to his efforts. By contrast, the Publican represents "the way of repentance which humans can never discover by themselves but to which they are brought by God himself as the fruit of an undeserved election and as a miracle of grace." In Chapter 6 Louf elaborates further on theme of acknowledgement of weakness and repentance of sin as essential to knowing God's love and mercy, and ties in the theme of ascetic practice. In Chapter 7 Louf speaks at length about spiritual direction, or to use his expression, "spiritual companionship." He explains why we need it, and indicates pitfalls the companion might fall into. For example, he speaks about the ideal self-image we create for ourselves and how God continually seeks to shatter this obstacle to grace. Then he observes that in the distressing event that a person's self-image has been shattered, the spiritual companion must both show the individual loving understanding and must steer away from helping to reconstruct the image. The final chapters are on some of the fruits of the Spirit and on prayer.

The second reviewer ultimately declined writing a review. She could not recommend the book due to what Louf says concerning a variation on the "Jesus prayer" (Lord Jesus, Son of God, be merciful to me, a sinner). Louf begins by noting that this prayer, used in the East in medieval times, "has again found wide acceptance today." He goes on to say: "For some this love-filled repetition, the breathing-in-and-out of Jesus's name, will be amply sufficient. For them the name that is above every name ... expresses all sorts of feelings—repentance as well as love, confession of guilt as well as the most intimate union.... Eventually the repetition of the name Jesus takes on a dizzying quality. But the dizziness is no one other than God himself, secretly living in our heart." While I agree that the potential reviewer has reason for her concern, at the same time, depending on the intention with which the prayer is practiced and on the person praying it, it may have value. According to Joseph Cardinal Ratzinger, who was at the time prefect for Congregation for the Doctrine of the Faith, "Eastern Christian meditation has valued 'psychophysical symbolism,' often absent in western forms of prayer. It can range from a specific bodily posture to the basic life functions, such as breathing or the beating of the heart. The exercise of the 'Jesus Prayer,' for example, which adapts itself to the natural rhythm of breathing can, at least for a certain time, be of real help to many people. On the other hand, the eastern masters themselves have also noted that not everyone is equally suited to making use of this symbolism, since not everybody is able to pass from the material sign to the spiritual reality that is being sought. Understood in an inadequate and incorrect way, the symbolism can even become an idol and thus an obstacle to the raising up of the spirit to God."[2] The suggestion of using a single word to help one in prayer is not unique to Louf, but is also found in the *Cloud of Unknowing* and in Dom John Chapman's *Spiritual Letters*. I do not intend, however, to embark on what would be a lengthy examination of this matter. I conclude that while some are rendered understandably uneasy by what Louf says on the topic and will not be putting this work on their reading list, others may find that this is not an obstacle to deriving profit from his book, especially from Louf's exegesis of Job and his explanation of how it may apply to our lives.

(Review by Marie George)

The Way of the Disciple by Erasmo Leiva-Merikakis

Leiva-Merikakis, a former professor of Literature and Theology, presents the essentials of Christian discipleship largely by way of examining six gospel passages. Among other elements, he speaks of the need to let God purify us of our false self-constructed images of ourselves. We need to recognize our neediness and rely on God alone. We need to set aside our projects by which we attempt to achieve happiness by our own efforts in order to make ourselves available to God, listening attentively to God's word. Leiva-Merikakis points out in the call of the apostles recounted in Mark that the initiative comes from Jesus who chooses his disciples, and that he chooses them "that they might be with him," i.e., share his divine life with him. He observes that just as Christ went up into the hills with those he chose, so too it is he who calls us out of the world to be with him in solitude, "the shared solitude of daily companionship." He goes on to speak of the role of Scripture in helping us come into contact with the person of Jesus. We need to be like little child, "empty to receive what he wants to give," instead of being full of our own "ideas, projects, desires, anxieties, and prejudices." We need to let Jesus give us rest, a rest that is not a lull from everyday

2. Congregation for the Doctrine of the Faith: *Letter to the Bishops of the Catholic Church on Some Aspects of Christian Meditation*, October 15, 1989, no. 27.

activities, but a state of life obtained by trusting in God's loving care for us. Leiva-Merikakis further develops the theme of trust by examining the incident where a storm strikes up while the disciples were in a boat and Christ is sleeping through it: "Jesus gets his own cherished friends into straits so that they will learn what it means to believe and to trust." Leiva-Merikakis observes that we cannot learn to trust if everything goes well. Christ can set all things right with a word; we need to cease our efforts to be our own Lord. Leiva-Merikakis continues with this same theme in examining Jesus's healing of the blind beggar Bartimaeus: "We too have to recognize ourselves as truly needy in order then to expose ourselves in this way to God's transforming action in Jesus and to dare to persist against whatever obstacles may arise, coming from within ourselves or from others or from adverse circumstances." Leiva-Merikakis next examines the gospel passage where a woman of ill-repute anoints Jesus's feet, bringing out how recognition of our sinfulness and of God's great mercy in forgiving our sins is what gives rise to a desire to live for God and abandon our selfish pursuits. In the final chapter, he makes a case for the position that a disciple of Christ needs to be in constant communion with Christ's mother Mary.

The Way of the Disciple reiterates the same points, but in a way that reinforces what its author is trying to convey, rather than being repetitive. Though the book contains a certain amount of erudition, its short chapters combined with the reiteration of themes makes it accessible to the vast majority of readers. The *lectio divina* of six passages of scripture, which are at the heart of this book, is compelling, and both beginners in the spiritual life and the more advanced can draw profit from it.

(Review by Marie George)

The Way of the Disciple by Erasmo Leiva-Merikakis

This short book of spiritual reading offers thoughtful reflections on several scriptural passages that call us to be open to God's will as his disciples. Its author, Erasmo Leiva-Merikakis, is now Fr. Simeon, a Trappist monk living a contemplative life at St. Joseph's Abbey in Spencer, Massachusetts. In his former life, Leiva-Merikakis was a professor at the Ignatius Institute of the University of San Francisco. The book then is, as you might expect, very well written and reflects the author's deep understanding of scripture and its many levels of meaning. It also reflects the author's love of and appreciation for language.

I have often wondered if an author of a spiritual work can appreciate the challenges of the spiritual to one who lives in the world. However, I found this book to be very realistic and applicable to my life as a layman.

The book begins with a chapter on discipleship, what it means to be a true disciple of Jesus. Entitled *Becoming Wet Clay in His Hands*, this chapter is a beautiful, thoughtful, and even challenging reflection on our call to be disciples. This first chapter really sets the groundwork for the following chapters. In each of the next six chapters, Leiva-Merikakis takes a passage from scripture and reflects on its meaning, drawing out a message from each. The passages of scripture follow a roughly chronological order in Jesus's ministry from his calling of the disciples to time from His Ascension to the Pentecost. The last chapter, *The Disciple Contemplates the Mother*, is a beautiful reflection on the role of Mary as the mother of God, and model for all disciples.

The author prepares the reader before giving a carefully chosen scriptural passage for reflection. Leiva-Merikakis goes out of his way both to quote spiritual fathers on how to approach the scriptures and to give readers the context of the passage they are about to read. I found this to be an excellent preparation not just for the passage in the chapter, but also for how to approach other passages not contained in the book.

I really enjoyed the author's very evident love of and appreciation for language. There were several places where he reflected on not just the meaning of a particular word, such as the Latin word for yoke, *jugum*, but it connection to other words, in this instance, conjugal, literally meaning *yoked together*, as a reflection of the intimacy between Jesus and his disciple who bear their burdens together.

This little book provides a busy layman with several very important and worthwhile things. First, it reminds us that even as a layman we are called to be disciples, and it provides inspiration to take that seriously. Second, Leiva-Merikakis's observations and reflections on discipleship encourage us that this can be something real and attainable not just something to think about. Thirdly, the passages he chooses and the pearls of wisdom he extracts from them are worth re-reading many times. Lastly, his way of proceeding with the six passages he chose for this book is instructive in itself. We can learn a lot of how to approach other passages in scripture by following the example he sets for us.

(Review by Daniel Davidson)

Erasmo Leiva-Merikakis is the author of several other books including *Fire of Mercy* and *Love's Sacred Order.*

Way to Inner Peace by Archbishop Fulton J. Sheen

Bishop Sheen does not provide an overview for *Way to Inner Peace* and in fact rarely explicitly mentions this theme. The book is loosely structured according to nine headings (e.g., happiness, wisdom, external influences). Under each heading are a number of five to eight page essays. Sheen for the most part is simple, straightforward, and scriptural. He is fond of stories and homey comparisons, which depending on your sense of humor, you will find either corny or humorous or a mixture of both. He rambles at times. Some parts of the book are dated by concerns about the Soviet Union and communism. Sheen does touch on a lot of classic topics in the spiritual life, such as judging others, patience, silence, etc., and he make good points; however, he never develops them at any length. He makes some interesting reflections on certain currents in psychology that ignore the reality of sin. I do not find him hard-core like some authors whose every page makes you feel that your soul is being stripped bare, as in your heart of hearts you know it needs to be (for this reason he is more likely to appeal to those of the sanguine temperament). Sheen's frequent social critiques and criticisms of certain groups of people are too easily read as being addressed to people other than oneself. I think that the people most likely to appreciate this book are those who have received basic catechesis, but have not studied theology, especially if they also have a family and work hard and thus end their day with their mental energy depleted. The fact that so many of Archbishop Sheen's books are still in print even today witnesses to his general appeal.

(Review by Marie George)

Way to Inner Peace by Archbishop Fulton J. Sheen

In *Way to Inner Peace* American archbishop, author, and noted tele-vangelist Fulton J. Sheen concocts a spiritually healthy mixture of psychological insights, common sense, highly effective homespun metaphors, artfully constructed yet original gospel-like parables, not to mention his trademark humor, to lead us away from the darkness of sin and toward the light of salvation. While the spiritual truths he conveys are universal, a striking emphasis upon America and its people as a whole reinforces Sheen's unofficial title as America's priest. A titan of the twentieth century Church, Fulton Sheen is both generous and *sui generis* in that he digs deeply into the well-springs of his own personal humility in a confident yet recognizably singular way so as to lead us toward the promised land of inner peace.

The book is divided into nine sections and consists of fifty-nine brief chapters. For those familiar with and fond of Christian symbolism the nine sections might remind one of the nine circles of Dante's Inferno, and could thus be interpreted as highlighting Sheen's efforts to marshal the resources of virtue in the battle against sin; or the nine choirs of angels identified by the Pseudo-Dionysius and St. Thomas Aquinas, which can signify the spiritual steps upon the way to the One who is the Way, the Truth, and the Life—Jesus Christ. To derive maximum pleasure and profit from the book it is not necessary to read it in sequence from start to finish. Just go to whatever topic strikes your immediate fancy and read. The chapters average about three to four pages, or less than ten minutes of reading time.

The pilgrimage is a time honored and traditional "way" that symbolizes and actualizes a movement of the body and the soul toward God. By "inner" Sheen refers to the inner life of the soul that is surrounded by a sea of external and worldly distractions. By "peace" he refers to the fulfillment experienced by the person when his or her soul, like a violin string, is in perfect attunement with the will of the Creator. Hence the words of Sheen's title echo those from Book I of Saint Augustine's *Confessions.* The soul cannot come to rest until it rests in God.

Sheen wrestles with virtue and vice as two sides of the same coin, which is the human person minted in the image of God. He offers sage advice on how to strengthen our natural inclination toward virtue and undermine our temptation to surrender to vice. In this vein the twin centerpieces of his reflections revolve around the virtue of humility and the vice of pride.

Philosophy distinguishes between "saying" (*sagen*) and "showing" (*zeigen*) as two ways of communicating meaning. Like the foretaste of heaven experienced by the holy during their earthly lives, let us end with a foretaste of the book's content by showcasing a vintage Sheen quote: "Humility is truth about ourselves; it is a virtue by which one does not esteem himself to be more than he really is.... The real self is what we are before God in an examination of conscience." Sheen teaches us that humility is not the result of an inferiority complex, but a profound faith-inspired recognition that we are superior when we know our place in relation to God. Oscar Wilde once quipped that he could resist anything except temptation. Fulton Sheen gives us a diet of spiritual nourishment so that we will be better equipped to avoid even that lone exception.

(Review by Glenn Statile)

Sheen is author of numerous works, including *Life is Worth Living*, *The World's First Love* (reviewed in this volume), and *The Way to Inner Peace* (reviewed in this volume).

The Mystics

The Cloud of Unknowing and the Book of Privy Counseling by Anonymous, edited by William Johnston

I am not able to judge works on the form of contemplative prayer sometimes called the prayer of quiet, except in a relatively superficial way. Adding to this reservation about reviewing *The Cloud* are the numerous warnings its anonymous author enjoins on the reader: the book should not be read out of curiosity, that it can easily be misunderstood if not read slowly and in its entirety (which is indeed true), and that only certain people can benefit from it (namely those who have been faithful to God in the active life and who are drawn to a contemplative love of God). So I shall provide but the roughest of sketches here of a book that certain people may profit from.

Essential to this form of prayer is the lifting of one's heart to God "with a gentle stirring of love desiring him for his own sake and not for his gifts." To this end one must fashion a "cloud of forgetting" between oneself and every created thing, both material and spiritual, for thinking about these things becomes an obstacle to union with God. One must even put aside the holy thoughts that are necessary and beneficial earlier on in the spiritual life, such as meditating on the Passion of Christ and the attributes of God. Why? "Just as it is wrong for a person who sits in meditation to be thinking about the things he has done or will do regardless how good and worthwhile they may be in themselves, likewise it is wrong for a person who ought to be busy with the contemplative work in the darkness of the cloud of unknowing to let ideas about God, his wonderful gifts, his kindness, or his works distract him from attentiveness to God himself." The cloud of unknowing that is spoken of refers to our inability to know God in himself; contemplative prayer consists in piercing this cloud of incomprehension with the dart of loving desire. Contemplative prayer is a gift of God. One who aspires to it should study and reflect on Scripture. Scripture is like a mirror for detecting one's spiritual blemishes; one should then go to Confession. Once free of sin, one prepares oneself for contemplation by banishing distracting thoughts and restraining them under the cloud of forgetting. Two techniques for dealing with distractions are to look beyond them as if they were not there, and to acknowledge that one is defeated by them and to cry to God for help. For contemplation, the author counsels that one set aside reasoning, as it is unhelpful, and that one avoid the use of words, focusing on a single word or a few at most. He urges those drawn to contemplation to work faithfully and with perseverance in "beating upon" the cloud of unknowing, for then God may "sometimes work in your spirit all by himself . . . for as long as seems best to him." To some God sends a ray piercing through the cloud of unknowing that stands between him and oneself; this is an ineffable experience.

Some of the author's advice strikes me as odd; I cannot figure who it could be directed to, e.g., he devotes a chapter to describing the mannerisms of pseudo-contemplatives, and another chapter to warning one not to take expressions such as "up"—as in "lift up your hearts to the Lord"—to mean something physical. Also, the way in which he divides and describes the faculties of the soul are in some cases dubious. What he says about contemplative prayer corresponds roughly with what other mystics say. One noteworthy exception, however, concerns the role that Christ's humanity should play in our prayer. Contrary to what *The Cloud* advises, Teresa of Avila, in her autobiography, maintains that it is misguided to endeavor to *not* keep Christ's Sacred Humanity before us (see Chap. 22).

In the *Book of Privy Counseling* the same author clarifies a number of points. He notes that not all are called by God to the type of non-discursive prayer he refers to as contemplation. He says that people need to begin their spiritual life not with contemplation, but with meditation, using their faculties of imagination and reason in regard to subjects such as the attributes of God and Passion of Christ who suffered and died for their sins. God wills that some achieve their salvation by remaining in the state of meditation, whereas to other He offers the gift of contemplation. The author also gives two signs by which one can recognize that one is called to contemplation. One is a "growing desire for contemplation constantly intruding in your daily devotions," as opposed to a "blind longing of the spirit" that passes. The second is a repeated and persistent joyful enthusiasm that wells up inside one whenever one hears or reads about contemplation. Also useful is his brief description of a state in between meditation and contemplation, where one is no longer able to meditate, and yet God does not yet give one the ability to contemplate. The opening part of the work about resting in a "naked, stark, elemental awareness that you are as you are" is lost on me, as is true of many other things the author says. The only things I find questionable in this work are several statements of this sort: "For your God is the glorious being of himself and you, in the naked starkness of his being." God is not our being, but rather the cause of our being.

(Review by Marie George)

The Cloud of Unknowing, edited by James Walsh, SJ

In our era, in which popular understandings of spirituality are generally synonymous with self-improvement, *The Cloud of Unknowing* is a classic that stands apart. Written in the fourteenth century by an anonymous English author who was probably a Carthusian priest, *The Cloud* draws upon a centuries-old tradition of apophatic spirituality in which spiritual ascent to God correlates with leaving behind all finite attachments and mental conceptions. *The Cloud* is not for everyone; in the prologue the author identifies his audience as those cleansed from sin who are prepared to leave behind the active life for that of the solitary contemplative. Traditional monastic practices of meditative reading and prayer are prerequisites for the prescribed regimen. The author promotes no spiritual techniques besides urging the reader to enter a "cloud of forgetting" in which ties to other creatures are deliberately severed. Such forgetting is not to be undertaken out of pride or superiority, and *The Cloud* employs the traditional contrast between Jesus's disciples Martha and Mary. In Luke 10 Martha is worried about serving Jesus, while her sister Mary chooses the better part, which is to sit and listen to Jesus's teaching. Martha and Mary represent the active and the contemplative vocations in *The Cloud of Unknowing*, and while the author praises the active life and charitable works he grants the latter path a higher dignity.

At the beginning of his seventy-five chapters, *The Cloud* author distinguishes his approach from academic achievement and imaginative meditation, claiming that his "exercise" is the briefest one possible, actually indivisible in duration. He offers no apologetic defense of Christianity. Loving Jesus requires forgetting creatures, possibly with the help of a brief word such as "God" or "love" that can be used to quiet extraneous thoughts separating one from the divine. For his purposes these superfluous conceptions include traditional impulses toward contrition for one's sins; our author is less concerned with introspective penances than he is with cultivating the virtue that is composed of a person's affection for God. This is not to say that entering the cloud of unknowing is easy, for forgetting all creatures including oneself is difficult at first, although grace makes this less difficult as one grows closer to God. Chapter 32 exhorts the reader to recognize that one is worse than nothing, but such recognition should deepen one's attachment to God rather than prompt one to ascetic exertions. *The Cloud's* author shuns lengthy complicated prayers in favor of one-syllable interjections that encapsulate the entire will of the contemplative. All other activities in the life of the solitary are to be relativized in preference to this devotion, although one should guard one's health to the extent necessary to make this contemplation possible. Those following the advice of the author are not to expect sensible consolations, for God is spirit and such consolations are mere accidents that are not essential to experience the union of God and self.

For many modern Christians seeking to correlate the love of God and the love of the world, the spirituality exemplified by *The Cloud of Unknowing* can seem unduly detached and unworldly, but the author would hardly be moved by such criticism. He has carefully considered the implications of what loving God entails and is willing to sacrifice all other attachments to this end. Like other ancient and medieval Christians—including the so-called Pseudo-Dionysius, Meister Eckhart, and Thomas à Kempis—this nameless disciple judges that while one can do many things to serve God only one thing is ultimately necessary. Like Mary of Bethany he simply chooses to be in the presence of the Master.

(Review by Christopher Denny)

Come Be My Light: The Private Writings of the "Saint of Calcutta" by St. Teresa of Calcutta, edited by Brian Kolodiejchuk, MC

"Come be My light" was the personal request that Jesus made to Mother Teresa to carry Him and His love to the poorest of the poor in the slums. This book, an edited commentary of her private correspondence with her religious superiors, follows Mother's journey from her vocation as a Sister of Loreto teaching in Calcutta, India, to the founder of a new religious congregation, The Missionaries of Charity. The book focuses on Mother's interior life and the depth of her relationship with God.

The image many of us have seen of Mother Teresa shows her soft smile. Those who worked with and for her can testify to the iron strength beneath that smile. In terms of her spiritual life, she was truly a fierce commander in God's army—one of His "Green Berets." The depth of her love for God was revealed in a private vow she made in 1942, binding under pain of mortal sin, to give God anything He might ask—not to refuse Him anything. "We must allow him to possess our soul." This vow, one of her greatest secrets, was evidence of her total confidence in God and the source of her joy. "When I see someone sad," she would say, "I always think she is refusing something to Jesus." God loves a cheerful giver!

In 1946 Mother received the "call within the call" to leave Loreto and to go into the streets to serve the poorest of the poor—to follow Christ into the slums. The congregation she founded aimed to satiate his thirst for souls by living according to the four vows of absolute poverty, chastity, obedience, and charity toward the poor. The sisters' work was to bring Christ into the lives of the marginalized. Given the circumstances in post-war India and the still rigid caste system, she and her sisters were at times in real physical danger.

Mother's mission of "lighting the light of those in darkness" was especially heroic since she herself had "darkness" as her frequent companion (profound interior suffering caused by the apparent absence of God in her life and strong desire for Him: "the dark night of the soul" experienced by some great saints). She persevered in this suffering, unknown to all. Her focus was on Christ crucified and His thirst on Calvary. She read this thirst as a thirst for souls that her Missionaries would slake.

This book focuses on Mother's intense spiritual life and is so rich in insights for deepening our love and service to God. That said, I think it would be most beneficial for those readers who have already started to seriously consider what needs deeper focus in their own spiritual journey. Parts of it are a little heavy for someone just starting out (and the book is long). Yet four simple lessons do stand out: (1) Do small things with great love; (2) Seek God in everyone and everything; (3) Love of God requires love of neighbor; (4) Permit yourself to let God's love into your life.

(Review by Joan Lovett)

Come Be My Light: The Private Writings of the "Saint of Calcutta" by St. Teresa of Calcutta

After her death Mother Teresa's friend and postulator, the chief Vatican advocate for her canonization, compiled and commented on her private letters to her spiritual directors over the course of her life. What resulted was a unique revelation not only of the soul of a contemporary saint, but particularly her decades-long internal struggles with a kind of dark night of the soul. Unfortunately, but unsurprisingly, the media pounced on it when the compilation was published: "You see, she knew her Catholic faith was hokum." Such a take-away, however, is a misreading of the letters.

Reading these writings fairly paints a picture of a woman so in love with Christ, so desirous of being like him and sharing his burdens, that she asks to suffer spiritually and psychologically both what he suffered on the cross and what the poorest of the poor suffer in their despair. This meant asking to suffer his very abandonment by those he loved most, his people, his friends, and even in a sense by God. Since Christ had become her spiritual bridegroom, and he had become on Calvary the poorest of the poor, her plea meant a loss of the spiritual sense of her spouse. For decades she felt cold—about the work of the Missionaries of Charity, about the faith, about God's presence—yet, she never lost confidence in these things. She knew that God was guiding her work, that He was loving her from a distance, and that this spiritual desolation was from Him, and in fact was bringing her closer to Him. But the pain remained, and joy was elusive.

Still, this darkness had the effect not only of deepening her longing for Christ, but even of motivating her to throw herself more deeply into the service of the poor, whom she sees as clearly suffering this same torment of isolation. Her suffering, then, is in an important way not unique. Whereas some saints suffer a dark night of abandonment from God, the poorest of the poor suffer a dark night of abandonment by all of humanity.

What is perhaps most striking about this work, as spiritual reading and as biography, is its monotony. Mother Teresa never "gets out" of her spiritual darkness, although she speaks about it less and less as the years go by. She grows to accept it, to recognize it as her greatest cross. She is occasionally, in the first years, tempted to throw it off, but these moments pass, and she never gives her Spouse a deadline—"I will endure this for another year or so, but then. . . ." She takes the path of the secret hero, the one whose martyrdom spans an entire lifetime, while other people are oblivious to it. Thus, this book should not be read as a mining expedition for quotations to be taken out of context (as the mainstream media did upon its publication); the point of the book in a way is its length, her embodiment of Christ's unrelenting lifelong fidelity and love even when we withhold reciprocation. The perfection of Mother Teresa's love is revealed not so much in her service to the poor, but in her service while feeling no satisfaction. She never grows to despise her work, or anyone around her; her love is as constant as her smile.

I found the book edifying, and would recommend it especially to a believer undergoing a period—especially a long period—of spiritual dryness or a sense of hopelessness about his or her situation, provided he or she doesn't also struggle with deep doubts about the faith. Some of her cries to Christ can be shocking to the neophyte, especially when taken in isolation from her pilgrimage as a whole, and if one has never tried to take seriously Christ's own grief, "My God, my God, why have you forsaken me."

(Review by Christopher Decaen)

The Complete Works: General Introduction; Major Spiritual Writings by St. Elizabeth of the Trinity (Vol. 1)

This book contains a lot of scholarly apparatus (and it's not always there when you want it; for example, St. Elizabeth's lengthy quotation of St. Angela di Foligno is omitted). The portion of the book that is by Elizabeth herself is about thirty-eight pages, consisting of two sets of notes made while on retreat, a letter to a nineteen-year-old friend, another to her prioress, and a prayer to the Trinity. The retreat notes consist of a page or two of reflections for each day, making them suitable for meditation.

Elizabeth read and was influenced by Ruysbroeck who was said to have pantheistic tendencies, and at times this is reflected in her choice of words. For example, she quotes with approval Fr. Lacordaire's statement: "He [your Master] is your soul and your soul is He." Still, it is not unusual for saints to speak in such a manner about union with God. St. Athanasius famously said that the "Son of God became man so that we might become God." Elizabeth's letter to her prioress is odd in many ways; for example, Elizabeth refers to her as "my Holy Priest" and says that she will "spend her Heaven in the depths of her [the Prioress's] soul." For the most part, however, Elizabeth treatment of classic spiritual themes is quite traditional.

Elizabeth's text is dense and her message is stripped down to the bare essentials. This can make her words seem deceptively simple on the one hand, yet hard to digest by a beginner in the spiritual life on the other. She often quotes St. Paul. Many of her chosen texts match those that I have come to appreciate most, such as "I live in the faith of the Son of God, who loved me and gave himself up for me" (Ga. 2:20) and "the Spirit himself gives witness with our spirit that we are children of God" (Rm. 8:16).

The themes Elizabeth returns to again and again include: loving God, which means striving to do His will and not ours. This requires us to detach ourselves from all that is not God, including our very selves: "I decrease, I renounce self more each day so that Christ may increase in me.... I see 'my nothingness, my misery, my weakness.... I see the multitude of my shortcomings, my defects....' 'I fall down in my misery, confessing my distress, and I display it before the mercy' of my Master. 'Quotidie morior.' I place the joy of my soul (as to the will, not sensible feelings) in everything that can immolate, destroy, or humble me, for I want to make room for my Master. I live no longer I, but He lives in me." A related theme is simplicity of intention whereby a person "seeks only God and refers all things to Him." To this end we must "remain silently in God's presence." Yet another related theme is suffering: "If sometime His will is more crucifying, we can doubtless say with our adored Master: 'Father, if it is possible, let this cup pass me by,' but we will add immediately: 'Yet not as I will, but as You will'; and in strength and serenity, with the divine Crucified, we will also climb our calvary singing in the depths of our hearts."

(Review by Marie George)

The Complete Works: General Introduction; Major Spiritual Writings by St. Elizabeth of the Trinity (Vol. 1)

Although this book has 191 pages, only about fifty of those pages contain the actual writings of the recently canonized Elizabeth of the Trinity. For those who are interested in the details of St. Elizabeth's life and how it was that her writings came about and the technicalities of the translation, the first half of the book will be very satisfying. Replete with scholarly research and commentary by Conrad De Meester, OCD, this "critical" work is not meant simply for those who are interested in it for solely spiritual reading.

This volume contains four of Elizabeth's works: *Heaven in Faith* (in the form of a ten-day retreat), *The Greatness of Our Vocation* (a letter to a young girl), *Last Retreat* (a sixteen-day retreat), and *Let Yourself Be Loved* (in the form of a letter or notes to her Prioress shortly before Elizabeth's own death). Elizabeth herself did not appear to have left any formal titles for these works. Fittingly, De Meester places Elizabeth's brief prayer *O My God, Trinity Whom I Adore* at the end of the volume.

St. Elizabeth's writings are most suitable for those who like to read slowly and savor what they read. Her thought is rich and intense—perfect reading for the entirety of the Lenten season. She opened my eyes to many of the more mysterious passages in the psalms, teaching me that the psalmist invites us to seek God in the "abyss." Elizabeth's insight concerning Psalm 42 ("Abyss calls to Abyss") runs throughout her works. "The Kingdom of God is within you" and we must "hurry and come down," that is, we must strive to descend and find God who is at the very center of our hearts. For those who are accustomed to think about the progress toward holiness as an upwards path, Elizabeth reverses that tendency. This insight has given me an entirely new view concerning the spiritual life that also appeals to my more philosophical side. Elizabeth's insight that we should seek God at the core of our being opens up an understanding of the scriptures that I had never imagined. For example, Elizabeth says, quoting St. John, "There is one in the midst of you, in you, whom you do not know" (Jn. 1:26). By "in the midst of you," I never thought that was really in the midst of me . . . at the depth of my soul!

Elizabeth is well known for her interpretation of St. Paul when he says in his letter to the Ephesians, "We have been predestined by the decree of Him who works all things . . . so that we may be the praise of His Glory" (Ep. 1:11–12). Elizabeth says, "A praise of Glory is a soul of silence that remains like a lyre under the mysterious touch of the Holy Spirit so that He may draw from it divine harmonies." Again, one cannot read St. Elizabeth's writings without enriching one's own understanding of the psalms. When the psalmist cries "Give praise to the Lord on the harp; sing to him with the psaltery, the instrument of ten strings" (Ps. 33:2), Elizabeth makes it clear that our own soul is the harp or the lyre that might be attuned to the hand of God, the Divine Musician, through a descent to Him at the very center of our souls.

In view of St. Elizabeth's recent enrollment in the official canon of saints, I can't help but think that perhaps her model of holiness is especially worthy of emulation by the twenty-first century Christian. One easily may be duped into thinking that he must be busily bringing about the Kingdom of God, energetically transforming the world around us. While that may be true, Elizabeth gently reminds us that we do not need to go outside of ourselves to find God and His Kingdom for "the Kingdom of God is within."

(Review by Mark Langley)

160

Dark Night of the Soul by St. John of the Cross

Known as the mystic's mystic, St. John of the Cross (1542–1591) ranks among the greatest spiritual writers of the Christian tradition. A contemporary of St. Ignatius of Loyola, the ministry of St. John of the Cross was closely connected to that other great saint of the Counter Reformation period in Spain, St. Teresa of Avila. In tandem with Teresa he restored the rigor of the original Carmelite Rule and cofounded the Discalced Carmelites. The author of splendid mystical poetry, he is also known for four prose masterpieces that analyze, with philosophical precision, the mystical gauntlet that the soul must traverse on the way toward union with God. Along with *The Dark Night of the Soul,* these works include *The Ascent of Mount Carmel, The Spiritual Canticle,* and *The Living Flame of Love.* St. John of the Cross was canonized by Pope Benedict XIII in 1726 and declared a Doctor of the Church by Pope Pius XI in 1926.

The Dark Night of the Soul (1584–1585) is a theological treatise on a poem entitled *En una noche oscura,* and is a continuation of *The Ascent of Mount* Carmel (1578–1579). Preceded by a Prologue, the treatise is divided into two books, which provide an exposition of the first two stanzas of the poem, and ends with but a cursory segue into the third stanza. The Dark Night is a metaphor for the ordeals that the soul must undergo. By purifying the dross of a sinful human nature—as described by reference to the Seven Deadly Sins (Book 1, chaps. 2–7), into its golden potential—as described via a vivid fire analogy (Book 2, Chap. 10); the soul can advance, through a progressive, though painful, dialectic of purgation and illumination, to nothing less than the union of a spiritual marriage with God. A poetic précis of this spiritual ascent is presented in relation to the mystic ladder of divine love (Book 2, chaps. 19–20). The spiritual ladder is a metaphorical type whose pedigree dates back at least as far as Jacob's ladder in the Old Testament (Genesis 28:10–19) and Diotima's discourse on love in Plato's *Symposium.*

With uncompromising logic applied to his own mystical experience, St. John of the Cross reveals that a partially illumined contemplative soul must still pass through two additional stages of purgation, or dark nights. The first involves a purification of the senses (Book 1, chaps. 8–14; Book 2, chaps. 1–14) and the second a purgation of the spirit (Book 2, chaps. 15–24). "This night ... produces in spiritual persons two kinds of darkness or purgation, corresponding to the two parts of man's nature—namely, the sensual and the spiritual" (Book 1, Chap. 8). To successfully progress through these nights of extreme desolation and despair the soul must remain passive and acquiesce to a stream of loving solicitations from God consisting of "the delectable effects which this dark night of contemplation works in the soul" (Book 2, Chap. 13).

For those who might be described as novices in the field of spiritual reading the afflictions presented so graphically in *The Dark Night of the Soul* can appear repellent. This inadequate, although understandable, response occurs because "it calls one to go out from God-given light into a black and unknown darkness" (F. C. Happold, *Mysticism*, 355). On the balance sheet of the spiritual life, however, the credits gained from reading *The Dark Night of the Soul* far outweigh the debits. Both St. Thérèse of Lisieux and St. Teresa of Calcutta testified to being plunged into dark nights of the soul. Such a revelation came as a surprise to those who knew and were intimate with both. The theme of the dark night has also provided a fertile ground for the literary imagination, as attested to by the *Four Quartets* of T. S. Eliot. It has been said that the purpose of a good sermon is to comfort the afflicted and afflict the comfortable. As *The Dark Night of the Soul* aptly details, it is no less true that the itinerary of the contemplative soul on its journey toward union with God includes both terrible afflictions and divine comforts.

(Review by Glenn Statile)

The Dark Night of the Soul by St. John of the Cross, translated and edited by E. Allison Peers

In spite of the venerable tradition of its title, St. John of the Cross's *Dark Night of the Soul* is in one sense just part of a much larger work (the *Ascent of Mount Carmel*), and in another sense two short books stitched together (the Night of the Sense and the Night of the Spirit). The work is a unity almost exclusively because it is the beginning of an exposition St. John had been requested to write on a one-page poem he'd composed called "Stanzas of the Soul." As John puts it in his Prologue, the poem is about "the way and manner which the soul follows upon the road of the union of love with God," though, he adds, written from the perspective of one who has already finished the course and reached the union for the sake of which the spiritual darkness of the two nights descend upon the soul advancing to her Beloved.

The poem, though brief, is itself of striking beauty, even in the judgment of unbelievers. It is a love poem in which, by night, the soul seeks and then finds her Lover and rests with Him. Most significantly, the poem sings in praise of the darkness, which normally one would think to be the root of confusion and despair; for this night not only made this union with the Beloved possible, it even became the guide to it.

As one would expect, the explanation of a poem takes many more words than does the poem itself. In this case, almost 200 pages more, and it covers only the first three of the eight stanzas. (It is unclear why St. John never finished it.) Nor does one part of the poem refer to one of the dark Nights and another part to the other; like Scripture itself, each line of the poem has many senses; the same lines, understood in different ways, refer now to the Night of the Sense, now to the Night of the Spirit. As a result, the reader can think John has adequately explained a stanza, expecting him to move on to the next, and yet finding him backing up to the beginning of the poem. But if one is ready for this, the repeated circular movement is meditative and rhythmic.

An impediment for a reader of this work can arise from a lack of firsthand experience with the two dark Nights about which John is writing. Suffering is not the same thing as even the dark Night of Sense. The first Night might be approximately described as a total lack of the emotional or imaginary warmth one often receives upon spiritual exercises, whether participation in the liturgy or prayers; the second Night is a deeper darkness of the mind in which, though without any loss of faith, the soul possesses not even intellectual consolations. Both of these trials are graces that tend to be given to few and apparently only to those well advanced in spiritual growth. Whence, most readers, while benefiting from the contemplation of these Nights, may only see in them how far he has yet to climb up Mount Carmel.

(Review by Christopher Decaen)

Other works by St. John of the Cross include *Ascent of Mount Carmel* and *A Spiritual Canticle.*

The Dialogue by St. Catherine of Siena, translated by Algar Thorold (This is an abridged edition.)

The Dialogue is a conversation between God the Father and St. Catherine; it was dictated by her while in the state of ecstasy. I confess I often find it difficult to read for a number of reasons. While at times it is tightly written like an article out of Aquinas's *Summa Theologiae*, at other times it seems diffuse. Sometimes it seems what is said is incorrect, e.g., "every sin done against Me, is done through the medium of the neighbor." Sometimes St. Catherine's high degree of holiness makes what is said far beyond me, e.g., she asked God that he "punish the faults of others" in her. And often the *Dialogue* recommends things that seem only for the saintly, e.g.: "Humility is not alone but has the handmaid of contempt of self and of the world, which causes the soul to hold herself vile, and not to desire honour but shame." It is not a short work, being over 300 pages long. Perhaps *The Dialogue* is best read when one is more advanced in the spiritual life. This being said it, there is a reason St. Catherine is a Doctor of the Church, and there is much profit to be drawn from *The Dialogue.*

In the first section, on Divine Providence, God speaks to Catherine about the various means He employs in order to elicit love from human individuals and of His concern to lead those who have strayed back to grace, as well as about how we are to help Him in doing so by word, example, sacrifice, and good counsel (counsel that is to be "without any passion of self-love"). This section speaks eloquently of God's mercy. The second part, a Treatise of Discretion, tells us that indiscretion is founded on pride and robs God of his due honor by attributing to self what is due to God, whereas discretion is founded on humility (and humility proceeds from self-knowledge). It speaks of three states of the soul advancing toward God, the first of which is to free oneself from vice, the second to fill oneself with love and virtue, and the last to attain union with God as with a dear friend. This section outlines various impurities that may be present in our love of God and neighbor. The third part, on prayer, contains the sort of advice we find in other great spiritual works. For example, it advises us not to examine our conscience without also remembering the wideness of God's mercy. It also enlarges on the unitive state, as well as on the gift of tears, and talks about the trap of passing judgment on others' souls. It speaks at length about the dignity of priests and of the importance of praying for them, especially those who are bad. The fourth part, a treatise on obedience, speaks of the importance of general obedience to God's laws and of the special obedience required of religious.

(Review by Marie George)

The Dialogue by St. Catherine of Siena

St. Catherine of Sienna was a 14th century Third Order Dominican who appeared before the Pope, residing in Avignon, to all but demand that he return the See of St. Peter to Rome. She is well known for a several hundred page work, one of the first to be printed throughout Europe, which eventually acquired the name "the Dialogue." This work is a record she made of the mystical converse she had with God the Father in which He explains to her the nature of sin, both in general and in particular, the way He wants us to be healed from it, and how His Son is that way, the bridge to the Father. The Father counsels her on the benefits (and dangers) of penance, and of suffering in general, how providence works, and what the blessings of heaven consist in.

Though Catherine had no formal education, the *Dialogue* is remarkable for its theological and philosophical precision; one often has the sense that he is reading the words of what the medievals called a "master of Theology." It is no coincidence that she was one of the first women granted the title Doctor of the Church; were St. Thomas Aquinas to write mystical theology, it would sound like this.

That said, the *Dialogue* is not written in the often abstract or extremely subtle language of the scholastics, nor does it proceed with methodical and systematic rigor. As a conversation always does, the *Dialogue* often returns to the same theme several times (though without redundancy). It is written—no doubt as the conversation itself played out—in a mystical style, full of fertile and provocative images. The tone, and occasionally even the matter itself, is very personal; details and references are often impenetrable. But the essence of the Father's counsels and encouragements are too universal to be opaque.

Some spiritual works should be read very slowly, a few pages at a time for many months, and others need to be read at a quicker clip so as to see the forest in the trees. It is a rare work that can be read either way, but this one can. The *Dialogue* is best appreciated by those somewhat advanced in the spiritual life.

(Review by Chris Decaen)

Revelations of Divine Love by Julian of Norwich

The main reason I included *Revelations of Divine Love* in this guide is because the *Catechism of the Catholic Church* (nos. 313–14) quotes it:

> "We know that in everything God works for good for those who love him" (Rom. 8:28). The constant witness of the saints [i.e., St. Catherine of Siena and St. Thomas More] confirms this truth. . . . Dame Julian of Norwich [said]: "Here I was taught by the grace of God that I should steadfastly keep me in the faith . . . and that at the same time I should take my stand on and earnestly believe in what our Lord shewed in this time—that 'all manner [of] thing shall be well.'" We firmly believe that God is master of the world and of its history. But the ways of his providence are often unknown to us. Only at the end, when our partial knowledge ceases, when we see God "face to face," will we fully know the ways by which—even through the dramas of evil and sin—God has guided his creation to that definitive sabbath rest for which he created heaven and earth.

The postscript of Julian's scribe says the book is intended for those who "are willing to submit to the Faith of the Holy Church," and Julian frequently alludes to the need to do the latter. The scribe also warns us against reading the book selectively. Nonetheless, while it is true that an integral reading shows the book to be more balanced than appears if one reads it selectively, some of the things Julian says, if not out-and-out contrary to the faith, are liable to appear as such, and thus may lead the unwitting reader astray, especially since the affirmations in question are interspersed with reflections that are in keeping with Church teaching. Ultimately I had a hard time profiting from the book due to its steady stream of dubious and poorly worded statements.

The book is a series of sixteen revelations that Julian received while she was suffering from an illness (one that she had asked God for); she was seemingly on the verge of death. The revelations consist mostly in visions accompanied by interior illuminations. Some of the visions are typical, e.g., of Christ wearing the crown of thorns, and some of them are quite unusual, as when she sees her soul "as large as if it were an eternal world . . . a most glorious city . . . in the midst of it sat Our Lord" (reminiscent of Aquinas's exposition of the Our Father in which "heaven" is construed as the saints in whom God dwells).

I am going to restrict my comments primarily to three themes that frequently recur, the first of which are Christ's words to her: "everything is going to be alright." This theme is shrouded in ambiguity, as while at times Julian acknowledges that the devil and unrepentant sinners are damned, at other times she speaks of a great secret that God will reveal at the end of time, a secret that she describes in ways that make it sound like every rational being will ultimately be saved. There is, however, at least one aspect of the "everything is going to be alright" theme that offers legitimate consolation to those who are prone despair because of the gravity and/ or frequency of their sins:

> In this vision my mind was lifted up to heaven, and God cheered me by reminding me of David and countless others in the Old Testament, and of Mary Magdalen. . . . He reminded me how the church on earth knew them to have been sinners, yet they are not despised for that reason, but rather these things have in some way turned in their honor. . . . God allowed him [St. John of Beverley]

to fall, though in his mercy he kept him from perishing, and from losing ground. Afterwards God raised him to much greater grace, and because of his humility and contrition of his life, in heaven God has given him many joys, greater even than those he would have had had he never fallen.

Julian makes clear that despite the comforting truth that even our sins can bring us closer to God, we should not think "it is a good thing to sin because the rewards will be greater," but rather "we should hate sin for Love's sake alone." It is unfortunate, though, that when she speaks of how God brings good out of evil, she says things such as: "it [sin] is blessedly made good by God's surpassing worth." The *Catechism* clearly states, "evil never becomes a good" (no. 312). Also, her notion that the souls of the elect are never separated from God is incorrect, that is, unless she is talking about the presence of God that sustains the soul in existence (in this manner, God is present even to the souls of the damned). Mortal sin destroys God's presence in the soul through grace, and saints have committed mortal sins.

A second theme is blame, about which Julian says the following:

"Good Lord . . . I know too that we sin, indeed grievously every day, and are most blameworthy. I can never hide from you the truth about myself, and yet I never see you blame us. How is this?" The normal teaching of the Holy Church and, indeed, my own experience, told me of the blame of sin which has been hanging over us, from the time of Adam until we reach heaven. It was the more surprising that I should see the Lord God regard us with no more blame than if we had been pure and holy as his angels in heaven. Between these two opposites I was extremely perplexed.

She recounts Christ giving her a solution by way of a story of a servant "running with all speed, in his love to do what the master wanted. And without warning he falls headlong into a deep ditch and injures himself badly." Of course, the case is not at all the same when Adam sinned and when we sin, as Julian herself notes. Ultimately, her conclusion about the story is that the Second Person became incarnate to excuse Adam from blame. One might take this to mean that Christ came for the forgiveness of sins, and once a sin is forgiven one is no longer blamed for it. However, before one repents, God does blame one for one's sin, whence it is misleading to say, as Julian does: "It would be most improper of me therefore to blame or criticize God for my sin, since he does not blame me for it." At times she even denies that sin is in need of forgiveness in God's sight.

A third recurring theme is Julian's claim that Jesus is our Mother: "So we see that Jesus is the true Mother of our nature, for he made us. He is our Mother, too, by grace, because he took our created nature upon himself. All the lovely deeds and tender services that beloved motherhood implies are appropriate to the Second Person." "We know that our own mother's bearing of us was a bearing to pain and to death, but what does Jesus, our true mother do? Why, he, All-love, bears us to joy and eternal life!" While Jesus does say to the inhabitants of Jerusalem: "How often have I longed to gather your children, as a hen gathers her chicks under its wings, and you refused!" (Mt. 23:37–38), and while there are doubtlessly similarities between him and a mother, I do not see this as warranting calling him "Mother," and especially since he gave Mary to us to be our Mother.

There are many other problematic statements in this book, which I think to be a pity; for some of the earlier parts are apt to help us draw closer to our loving and merciful God and especially to Christ (who according to the Gospels was gracious to the Apostles after the Resurrection, despite their abandonment of him).

(Review by Marie George)

Fire Within: St. Teresa of Avila, St. John of the Cross, and the Gospel—on Prayer by Fr. Thomas Dubay, SM

The subtitle of *Fire Within* sums up the book's content, if one adds that the type of prayer Dubay is primarily talking about is contemplative prayer, which he defines thus: "Christic contemplation is nothing less than a deep love communion with the triune God. By depth here we mean a knowing loving that we cannot produce but only receive. It is not merely a mentally expressed 'I love You'. It is a wordless awareness and love that we ourselves cannot initiate or prolong."

The book, which is fairly long, contains a lot of argumentation about true and false concepts concerning contemplative prayer (including how Christian contemplative prayer differs from Eastern forms of meditation), and for this reason it may prove challenging to some readers. It is not the sort of spiritual reading that leads one directly into prayer—it exercises the head more than the heart. Similar to Fr. Green's book, *When the Well Runs Dry*, it provides a roadmap of where one should be heading in one's prayer life, doing so at greater length, while emphasizing that contemplation is meant for everyone. What Dubay says, at least in its general lines, is consistent with the teaching we find in the *Catechism of the Catholic Church*. I think that the bulk of Dubay's arguments and conclusions are correct. I note, however, that other writers on mysticism, such as Dom John Chapman, seem to disagree with some of his views.

The first chapter makes the case that contemplative prayer is for everyone, for everyone is called to be holy, and holiness is not possible without the transforming union with God that occurs in contemplative prayer. If in fact relatively few experience advanced infused prayer, it is not because God does not want this for them, but it is rather due to their lack of "humility, detachment and sound doctrine" or to the lack of proper spiritual direction.

Chapter 2 describes the character of St. Teresa and of St. John of the Cross.

Chapter 3 tries to describe somewhat the experience of God in contemplation; finally, though, such an experience is ineffable.

Chapter 4 speaks about meditation and its limitations due to its reliance on human effort, images, and concepts. Meditation "is only the introduction, the initiation into what should become a profound contemplative communion with the indwelling Trinity: we begin to pray in a human way and slowly are led by the Lord Himself into a divine way." I think that Dubay fails to sufficiently underline the importance of meditation in motivating us to the love of Christ and to the detachment generally requisite for receiving infused prayer.

Chapter 5 defines contemplation as "a wordless awareness and love that we ourselves cannot initiate or prolong."

Chapter 6 takes us through the seven mansions St. Teresa speaks about in *Interior Castle*. Dubay opens the chapter by giving reasons to consider stages in prayer, one of which is: "Those who do not recognize the normal delicate beginnings of infused prayer are almost certain to impede the gift through a misguided attachment to discursive methods." In the first three mansions the individual engages in discursive prayer; it is in the last four that they receive infused prayer.

The main reason why people never get to mansion four is because of their attachment to their will and to things of this world. For me this was the most helpful piece of knowledge in the entire book. The conditions for progress are further elaborated on in Chapters 7 and 8. A recurring point is that failure to progress in prayer is not due to the failure to employ the right technique, but rather in the failure to embrace our cross. Chapter 8 is devoted to detachment, which St. Teresa describes as "never indulging our own will and desire, even in small things."

Chapter 9 describes the two dark nights spoken of by John of the Cross. Dubay holds that ordinary sufferings do not constitute dark nights. The dark night of the senses concerns specifically one's prayer life; those who undergo it feel that "they have gone astray in their pursuit of God. They think their prayer is next to zero . . . they feel lazy and as though wasting time." Few who arrive at this night grow beyond it to the night of the spirit, which is characterized by feeling spiritually unclean, rejected by God, and not worthy of being received back by him.

Chapter 10 describes, so far as it is possible, the summit of prayer, along with characteristics that allow one to identify that one has reached it. Chapter 11 provides further reasons to think that all are called to contemplative prayer. Chapter 12 takes up the thorny problem of what role Christ's sacred humanity plays in infused prayer since the latter is without images or words. Chapter 13 is on discerning growth. Chapter 14 treats of locutions and visions. Chapter 15 speaks of the benefits of spiritual companions and the risks of worldly friendships. Chapter 16, on spiritual direction, points out the utility in having a good director when it comes to identifying delusions. Chapter 17 summarizes the author's theses.

(Review by Marie George)

Fire Within by Fr. Thomas Dubay

I had dabbled in the works of St. John of the Cross and those of St. Teresa of Avila before reading *Fire Within* by Fr. Thomas Dubay. My melancholic disposition has a tendency to overflow into scrupulosity, over-thinking, and generally mistaking flailing introspection for attempts at contemplative prayer. I first thought the two would be wonderful guides, only to withdraw in mild confusion. I was too young, or too immature. The sheer scale of the imageless interior world they opened up to me was overwhelming and so I retreated with the idea that their methods were good, helpful, and great . . . but not for everyone.

Fire Within seeks to correct precisely this notion, and I was convinced up to a point. It was a thought provoking, encouraging, and challenging read for me. Referring frequently to both Scripture and Vatican II's universal call to holiness, Dubay gives compelling arguments that we are all not only able to attain contemplative prayer in this life but destined for its fullness in eternal Beatitude. He then goes on to give us some idea of who our two guides truly were, so as to establish their credibility as common sense workers in our Lord's Vineyard, not given to emotional effusions or pious hysterics. This is more necessary than it may sound, for a large quantity of what St. John and St. Teresa communicate is an ineffable, imageless, spiritual journey.

Having reassured us that the saints too were human, Dubay turns to contemplation. There is a wide variety of ways to experience such a rich, complex reality but within this realm of possibilities, there are also reliable patterns and stages. Understanding these stages and movements are necessary if we wish to take this journey. Our own disposition is no less essential, however. We can do nothing to initiate, prolong, or affect infused prayer: it is a pure gift from God. We can do much to block it, since seed will not grow in rocky or weed-choked ground. Living the gospel to the best of our ability is a prerequisite that Dubay emphasizes in a particularly hard-hitting way. He shows why and how a life of humility, good works, detachment, etc. goes hand-in-hand with deep union with God (in prayer). In fact the one cannot exist without the other, and the two grow together, mutually nourishing each other. Roughly speaking, the first half of our journey is steely and untiring work to attain a certain kind of receptivity. The second half is growth in holiness and further purification brought about by God in our consenting soul.

Dubay fleshes out the conditions for growth, stages of purification, and their enduring benefits and consequences for the rest of the book. There is a great deal of food for thought here, as well as beautifully encouraging and demanding insights—that is, they demand that we give something. No force is possible, since we are free creatures, but the reality (whether we fully subscribe to Dubay's interpretations or not) is one that cannot just be enjoyed or acknowledged at a distance. One overarching theme of the spiritual life prevalent in this book is that even though God gives us everything, absolutely everything, and much of our greatest redemptive "work" is done via a holy receptivity, this passiveness is no sluggish or air-headed floating. "Nature would be torn apart," St. John says, were God not to impart strength. But He does impart strength, and this strength we are to use to the fullest. Dubay's breakdown of the multifaceted reality is illuminating, well-organized, and deeply rooted in its proper sources. It is for persons of any age from the unusually mature teenager on, of any temperament, and in any state of life.

(Review by Angela Fuhrman)

Other works by Dubay include *Happy Are You Poor: The Simple Life and Spiritual Freedom* and *Deep Conversion, Deep Prayer.*

Interior Castle by St. Teresa of Avila, edited and translated by E. Allison Peers

Interior Castle has truly earned its preeminent status as one of the most beloved and widely-read Christian mystical classics of all time and is the apotheosis of St. Teresa of Avila's life of interior and communal reform. As her *magnum opus*, it is one of the most reliable and beneficial spiritual companions for Christians at every possible stage of the spiritual life. For centuries readers have been charmed by Teresa's rambling writing style, at some moments conversational, at others contemplative and analytical, and again at others humorous and self-effacing, all the while interpolating her prose with prayerful ejaculations to her "Divine Majesty" on behalf of herself and her students. *Interior Castle* is perhaps best suited for those who, at the very least, have a regular habit of prayer. Those who wish to benefit from Teresa's direction but who have not yet established a habit of prayer may wish to begin with her prior work, *The Way of Perfection*. Many have found *The Way of Perfection* to be a more accessible preparation for *Interior Castle*.

As the title suggests, Teresa's principal analogy for the soul is that of a castle in the shape of a globe of purest crystal containing seven rooms—or *mansions*—each one successively closer to the central "throne room of the King." Like her analogy for the soul, *Interior Castle* itself has a sort multi-faceted prismatic quality that refracts its light differently at different stages of a reader's life. When her words are held up to the morning sun of early spiritual growth they refract one spectrum, but when held up at the noon-time of life they refract a different array of insights, and so on. There is a depth and richness to *Interior Castle* that merits many readings over the course of each successive season in a Christian life. Yet, Teresa cautions that progress is not purely linear, nor should one who is further advanced ever fear to return to the very first mansions where humility is learned.

As a result of the theological excellence of *Interior Castle*'s taxonomy of the soul, Pope Paul VI conferred on St. Teresa the ecclesial title of "Doctor." Popularly she has been called the "Doctor of Prayer." Many twenty-first-century Catholics, having endured decades of indiscriminate admixture of such popular disciplines as Jungian psychology and Gestalt therapy into their "spiritual direction," find themselves recoiling from their dismal results and have begun to return once more to the solid ground of Teresian spirituality. One of Teresa's own greatest concerns was the theological accuracy of her insights. To this end she regularly consulted men learned in those particular aspects of a soul's relationship to God, which she felt warranted such cautious attention. Yet in spite of *Interior Castle*'s thoroughness, theological orthodoxy, and technical reliability, it is important to understand that St. Teresa's primary aim was neither theoretical nor analytical, but practical. All of her insights were the direct fruit of the graces she herself received. She relied entirely on her own personal experience and the experience of others whom she observed and trusted. *Interior Castle* ultimately endeavors to guide the soul toward "the prayer of union" (also called "the prayer of quiet") in which the soul is united to God in the innermost mansion of the castle.

(Review by Christopher Candela)

Interior Castle by St. Teresa of Avila

St. Teresa of Avila, a Doctor of the Church, is renowned as a master teacher on prayer. *Interior Castle* is her final book (written in 1577), and what many consider her best synthesis of the life of prayer. In it she explains the stages that the persevering Christian is likely to pass through in order to attain the goal of the Christian life—union with God. The reformer of the Carmelite order discretely draws on her own spiritual journey to describe not only what the Christian must do to draw closer to God, but also the action of God in drawing the soul into this union and the wiles of the devil in his attempts to obstruct it.

Teresa compares the soul to an interior castle made up of many rooms, with Our Lord residing at the center. Outside the castle are reptiles, insects, and vermin—the foul things of this world that would prevent the soul from seeking her Lord. The door of entry to this castle is prayer and reflection.

Although she does provide extensive advice for those who achieve advanced forms of prayer, Teresa does not provide a manual for prayer as such. Rather, *Interior Castle* is largely a description of the necessary virtues (especially charity toward one's neighbor and humility), as well as the trials, temptations, graces, and consolations likely to be encountered as one progresses in prayer. While providing counsel and caution for each stage, Teresa also provides beautiful descriptions of the soul's transformation that encourage the reader to persevere and grow.

The book is easy to read, and reflects Teresa's humble and charming personality. Even though parts of the book clearly are directed to the cloistered religious, other parts are written expressly with those "in the world" in mind, and everyone can benefit from the spiritual insights and scriptural commentaries throughout the book.

In the first dwelling places are those who would like to see the beauty of the King's royal chamber, but who are enticed and distracted by many things in the world. Those who manage to enter the second dwellings take the first steps in the practice of prayer, and are more receptive to the promptings of Christ's grace. Those who enter the third dwelling places manage to become "good Christians." Of these, Teresa states that the Lord will not deny their entrance into the final dwelling place (there are seven in all) if they so desire—as long as they persevere through the demands and trials of the remaining dwellings.

Significant portions in the latter part of the book, especially the discussion of the sixth dwelling place, are devoted to extraordinary mystical experiences. These can be unsettling for those of us still in the initial dwellings, and some may be tempted to stop reading or to skim through them. However, Teresa considers that those who have not experienced these favors can still praise God for His goodness in granting them to other, more advanced souls. Knowing of these potential benefits also can motivate souls to make the sacrifices necessary to reach the inner chambers, though Teresa is careful to point out that these favors cannot be earned but are purely a gratuitous gift from God.

Some may criticize Teresa for being too demanding in her assessment of what is necessary to make spiritual progress. But Christ Himself warns us that "the gate is narrow and the way is hard that leads to life, and those who find it are few." For those who submit themselves to her guidance, St. Teresa makes that way a little easier, and perhaps more importantly, she gives one the courage to want to enter and undertake it.

(Review by A.M. Desprit)

Other works by St. Teresa of Avila are *Autobiography* and *The Way of Perfection* (both are reviewed in this volume).

Spiritual Letters by Dom John Chapman, OSB

The *Spiritual Letters* of Dom John Chapman are divided according to whom they were addressed: lay people, religious, and a Jesuit. In addition there are two appendices, one on contemplative prayer and another on mysticism.

Those who read the *Letters* slowly will find the letter format helpful, as the same theme is reinforced through various reiterations. Those who are reading the *Letters* to get an overview of the nature of contemplative prayer, however, are liable to wish that Chapman had systematically treated the various topics he takes up. (He does so to some extent in the appendix.) I read the *Letters* fairly quickly, wishing to compare Chapman's teaching on contemplative prayer with that found in Fr. Dubay's *Fire Within.* Dubay goes at lengths to accord St. Teresa of Avila and St. John of the Cross, while Chapman holds that the two are opposed on certain points. I am incapable of arbitrating this and other disagreements between the two, but observe that they largely agree, and what both say corresponds for the most part to teachings found in the great mystics. Both are worth reading in order to gain some understanding of the immensely important topic of contemplative prayer. Readers who are not at least somewhat practiced in lower forms of prayer, however, are liable to find Chapman's work puzzling.

Chapman maintains that meditation—he includes here spiritual reading and the devout study of theology, as well as meditation on the life of Christ, etc.—though "usually necessary in order to induce souls to love God, and to give themselves to Him," is not prayer. He softens this view somewhat, acknowledging that "people can get to very extraordinary sanctity . . . by the loftier kinds of meditation." In what he considers true prayer, one ceases all thinking; rather, "the time of prayer is passed by beginners in the act of *wanting God.*" As he explain, "thinking is directed by our will; and if we use our will to think of certain subjects rather than others, our will is occupied in keeping our mind on the subject; and therefore less occupied in loving God." Contemplative prayer depends on God's special grace, and not primarily on our will, though we can prepare ourselves for it both by practicing purity of heart and mortification and by spending long hours alone in prayer. Chapman lists the effects that contemplative prayer ought to produce, included among which is: "A desire for the *Will of God*, exactly corresponding to the irrational and unmeaning craving for God, which went on in prayer." (By "irrational" he means above reason.)

Chapman treats of the various problems that arise in prayer, such as distractions and the feeling we are doing nothing in prayer. He also gives advice concerning how to deal with suffering. For example, he notes that our Lord prayed that the chalice might be taken away, and not "I suffer, and I rejoice; I only want to suffer more," from which Chapman concludes that it is not against perfection to *feel* that suffering is intolerable, so long as with our will we trust in God and seek to do His will, confident that He will give us the grace necessary.

The third set of letters, written to a Jesuit, contains for the most part theological reflections on topics such as the relationship of philosophy to theology, of the natural to the supernatural, of faith to reason. A particularly long letter presents "a theology of the world on the Christian hypothesis."

The first appendix "On Contemplative Prayer" sums up Chapman's teachings. The second appendix on "Mysticism" explains how contemplative prayer is possible, given its non-reliance on images and rational discourse. Those with some familiarity with Aquinas's thought will find it fascinating; others may have difficulty following it.

(Review by Marie George)

Spiritual Letters by Dom John Chapman, OSB

Spiritual Letters is a compendium of letters of spiritual direction written by John Chapman, a priest and Benedictine monk, over a span of many years. It includes letters both to "lay folk" and religious, and concludes with a compilation of a number of letters to a Jesuit scholastic. The letters are contextualized with occasional footnotes, but largely stand on their own. Throughout the book, Abbot Chapman is writing primarily as a spiritual director to those he addresses—there is relatively little time spent on current events (though some, e.g. the First World War, occasionally merit mention) or other personal discussions. The purpose of these letters is to help their recipients deepen their life of faith and, most particularly, their life of prayer.

Prayer is without question the dominant concern of Chapman, and his writing on it is of one both deeply prayerful himself, and yet highly aware of the difficulties that deepening the practice of prayer presents to his correspondents. As such, though he is occasionally transcendent in his reflections, his advice is astonishingly practical, considering that contemplative prayer is his subject matter.

Chapman's main goal is to convince (again and again) his correspondents to pray more, to pray more deeply, and to pray with more perseverance. He instructs them on the practicalities of doing this in their various stations in life, with his overarching advice being quite simple: if you wish to pray better, you must practice! And moreover, you must not despair. Chapman constantly warns his correspondents (and us) that failed prayer is, too, prayer, and that the offering up of our failure to concentrate can be used by God as well as our transports or moments of emotion. We should not expect to enjoy prayer, he enjoins us, any more than a block of marble should expect to enjoy being sculpted—and like the marble, if we do persevere, we can hope to become beautiful in the sculptor's (God's) eyes. For Chapman, prayer is largely something that God does to us, if we let Him.

In addition to the direct, positive advice he offers, which is both nuanced and varied, Chapman cannot help but warn his interlocutors against certain methods of prayer that (he fears) prevent, rather than encourage, authentic prayer. These include too much activity in prayer, and too-formal systems for preparation. In his mind, there is often little reason to "warm up" for praying—one should simply get on with it. That said, he is careful to note that the mind must be given sufficient material to keep the imagination busy, lest it—left to its own devices—run wild and lead to greater distraction.

The form of this book, as a series of letters, lends itself primarily to steady, slow reading. A letter (or two) at each perusal gives one much to contemplate, whereas a quick reading at one or two sittings—though possible—would not be an ideal way of soaking up the experienced director's carefully wrought advice. It would also tend to emphasize the occasionally repetitiveness of the advice, which is less of a concern if the book is read slowly. In summation, I have personally never read another book that led me more often on my knees than this, or more fruitfully. A wonderful guide.

(Review by Mark Wyman)

The Third Spiritual Alphabet by Fr. Francisco de Osuna, OFM

I started *The Third Spiritual Alphabet*, only to soon set it aside. I was intimidated by its length (609 pages) and I found many of the interpretations of scripture it offered tedious or strained. If you are looking for a short book with a clear and direct message for your life on every page, this book is not for you. I also justified putting this book down on the grounds that it had been thoroughly combed over by Doctor of the Church, St. Teresa of Avila, who doubtlessly incorporated what is beneficial in it in her own spiritual writings. After picking up the book again, I no longer entirely agree with that view. There is a reason why this work (published in 1527) inspired St. Teresa of Avila. I do not recommend this book for the average beginner, both because it gets rather heavy at times (even for a person accustomed to reading ponderous philosophical works) and because it proposes a number of positions beyond the judgment of the average well-catechized reader (not to mention some odd views, such as that we ought to audibly sigh for God). In addition, some of the views it proposes are incorrect, e.g., "grace is one and the same with charity." Also, although much of what is said about contemplative prayer and recollection is directed to everyone, there is some material in the book that is of interest only to religious (e.g., the role of one's cell). However, for lay persons more advanced in the spiritual life who are endowed with a good store of patience and discernment, there are treasures to be found in this work, the chief of which is an understanding of the important practice of "recollection" and what fosters or hinders it.

Osuna wrote six alphabets in all, *The Third* being the most popular. Each chapter has a keynote sentence that begins with a different letter of the alphabet. Many chapters directly concern various aspects of recollection. Other themes include: giving thanks, detachment from created things, prudence, guarding one's thoughts, and controlling one's speech.

Osuna refers frequently to Scripture and to various saints: Augustine, Gregory, and especially Bernard, among others. His work is replete with images and similitudes, some of which are bound to strike the reader. For instance, I appreciated the analogy of prudent travel, which Osuna used to illustrate the importance of continually thinking of God and how to arrive at union with Him, as I had recently been meticulously planning a hike. These analogies may provide helpful starting points for meditation.

As for the main topic of his work, recollection, Osuna begins by offering various names more or less synonymous with it: hidden theology, wisdom, the art of love, prayer of union, concealment, and so forth. He then goes on to describe what recollection is: "It gathers together those who practice it and . . . makes them of one heart and love." "It gathers the exterior person within himself" by eliminating distractions and "recollects sensuality . . . and places it under the jurisdiction of reason." It invites "the one who enjoys it to go off to secret places." It "calms the senses," rendering vain gossip of no interest, as well as calming restlessness. It collects together the virtues in its practitioners. It prevents one from being overly concerned about what others do to one, keeping one intent on God alone. Lastly, it gathers God and the soul into one.

Osuna, contrary to *The Cloud of Unknowing*, maintains that reflection on Christ's sacred humanity is not an obstacle to recollection. His view that one should share one's experience of contemplation with others is questionable, however, since it seems that revealing spiritual favors that one has received from God can pose temptations against humility. And his view that we should ask for spiritual consolations seems ill-advised despite the many arguments he gives. Above all in prayer, we are to ask for love of God for Himself and to seek to do His will, which may mean to suffer dryness. Osuna's mistaken view contains some positive elements, however, e.g., we wouldn't know God as loving and desire to draw closer to Him if our experience of Him was devoid of consolation, and religion is not meant to be a sad, dreary thing. There are many other debatable points in this work, but this suffices to alert the reader to the difficulties involved in reading it.

(Review by Marie George)

The Third Spiritual Alphabet by Fr. Francisco de Osuna, OFM

Intellectuals make much of the fact that Thomas Jefferson had, next to his Bible, a well-worn copy of Thucydides' *History of the Peloponnesian War* on his nightstand. This devoted readership is the 18th century version of an excellent online review and continues to pique modern curiosity. How much more valuable to sample the book that inspired the mind and stirred the soul of St. Teresa of Avila: Francisco de Osuna's *The Third Spiritual Alphabet!*

De Osuna was a contemporary of Teresa's. She encountered his book just before his death. It was given to her by her pious uncle while she was staying with him and recovering from illness. De Osuna was a powerful and popular writer of the time, capturing and promoting the culture's interest in mysticism.

Modern day interest in mysticism is often muddied with heretical influences and the casual reader does well to note that de Osuna's era was not without conflict. The book's introduction gives us some understanding of the insidious influence of "quietism" on the age. De Osuna's work is an effort to guide the soul past the error and into real communion with God. He is writing for religious, but his examples can readily be applied to the lay community as well.

The Third Alphabet is an excellent companion to Jean-Pierre de Caussade's *Self-Abandonment to Divine Providence*. What de Caussade brings to the terrestrial, de Osuna brings to prayer. De Caussade instructs us how to live in the world with God as the center and de Osuna neatly dovetails with this worldview. De Caussade has the added advantage of building a bridge for the modern reader in understanding de Osuna. As one might expect in the case of an 18th century Jesuit, reading de Caussade is like eating a delicious cookie, all the best ingredients wrapped into a small, neat package. De Osuna is akin to eating spaghetti. Like Catherine of Siena, his writing is circular and repetitive. The reader's mouth becomes full while antici-pating an end point and it is best just to learn to stop when needed. This book is considered a classic on Franciscan mysticism and is well worth engaging, despite the author's occasional wandering.

You don't read de Osuna's work; you enter into a relationship with it. You don't start reading it any more than you finish reading it. Like any working alphabet, it's a tool with nuanced value for the many kinds of souls that dip into it or the same soul as it grows in understanding. You will read it again and again along with the notes you take in the margins, each time finding new ideas and under-standing.

Reading de Osuna guides the soul to infused prayer, a state where God becomes increasingly active and the soul more passive. Infused prayer guides the soul to understand what he sees in the world through the eyes of God's revealed nature. The contemplative does not rush out to serve soup to the poor because he believes the prob-lem is wealth imbalance, he begins to see that real poverty can be found in any man, just as the real God can be found in every situa-tion. De Osuna challenges the reader to go beyond an intellectual understanding that God can do all things and to experience God actively bringing good from the worst of human experience. He also addresses the fruits of this relationship and the outward manifesta-tions of deeper prayer.

Since de Osuna writes for religious, some topics may seem a bit harsh or extreme for the modern layperson; don't obsess over this as it is not the seminal message. De Osuna uses both the rod and the staff, always deferring to love as the great conqueror.

In the end, the book is just that, a book that can be used as flint to ignite the fire of contemplative prayer. It has no power to induce contemplation—that comes by the grace of God; it simply does a thorough job of orienting the reader's mind to fertile ground. The novelty of knowing that Teresa of Jesus held it in high esteem, along with the author's many references to the thought of leaders of an earlier Church, make this an excellent addition to your home library or, better yet, your bedside table.

(Review by Catherine Ryan)

The Way of Divine Love by Sr. Josefa Menéndez

Sr. Josefa Menéndez (1890–1923) was a Spanish-born sister of the Society of the Sacred Heart of Jesus. She had many visions of Our Lord, as well as of Mary. I believe them to be authentic as their basic message is very similar to that given to St. Margaret Mary Alacoque. This message is submerged, however, in a lengthy account that consists not only of what was said during the various apparitions, but also of a great deal of commentary on Josefa's life by her spiritual director.

Josefa had a vocation from an early age, but when her father died she stayed home to help support her family. She attempted to enter religion a couple of times, but deferred entrance due to her mother's appeals not to abandon her. Years later she once again asked for admission and was almost refused because of her previous vacillations. Sent to a house in France, she experienced severe temptations to abandon her vocation, as she missed her mother in Spain. What prevented her from doing so was Jesus, who had her enter into the wound of his Sacred Heart. He appeared to her on many other occasions, asking her to love him and to console him by making reparation for others who failed to love him as they ought. Josefa had to ask her superiors for permission to communicate with him, and she had to write down immediately afterward what was said. For a good while, Josefa repeatedly asks Christ to let her live the life of an ordinary religious—in other words, to stop appearing to her. She realizes the ingratitude of her requests: "I offered myself to comfort Him and to win souls . . . but, O Lord, do not forget that I am the most ungrateful and miserable of them all. 'I know it,' He said, 'but I am training you.'" Christ continually urges Josefa to be humble: "I permit your miseries and falls, so that in spite of the graces I bestow on you, you may never lose sight of your nothingness." He asks her to offer herself as a victim for souls in danger of being lost. His messages to her are for all of us: "Every soul can be instrumental in this sublime work. . . . Nothing great is required, the smallest acts suffice: a step taken, a straw picked up, a glance restrained, a service rendered, a cordial smile . . . all these offered to Love are in reality of great profit to souls. . . . No need to remind you of the fruits of prayer, of sacrifice, of any act offered to expiate the sins of mankind." Christ's repeated message is: "I am *Love*! My Heart can no longer contain its devouring flames. I love souls so dearly that I have sacrificed my life for them. . . . Now, I want something more, for if I long for love in response to My own, this is not the only return I desire from souls: I want them all to have confidence in my mercy. . . . Does not a father love a sick child with special affection? . . . So is the tenderness and compassion of My Heart more abundant for sinners than for the just. . . . I will teach sinners that the mercy of My Heart is inexhaustible." In addition, the visions contain a sobering message about hell, whose principle torment lies in the inability to love.

Once again, the spiritual content is woven into an extremely long account of Josefa's life. Perhaps one is more likely to derive profit from this book if one approaches it with the idea that one does not need to read every single page.

(Review by Marie George)

The Way of Perfection by St. Teresa of Avila

St. Teresa of Avila's stated intent is to propose a few remedies for small temptations coming from the devil, but she also talks extensively about prayer. A fair amount of what she says is directed to female religious, and doesn't have much applicability to the average lay person. While I find her an engaging writer of penetrating insight, at the same time I can see someone who is not liberally educated and/or who is under the age of forty having difficulty in drawing profit from this work (and this even though *The Way* is considered St. Teresa's most accessible work).

The work is not called the *Way of Perfection* for nothing. For example, Teresa does not mince her words over the desire for affection: "when we desire anyone's affection, we always seek it because of some interest, profit or pleasure of our own." She observes that while those of worldly affection are afflicted when they see their loved ones afflicted, those of spiritual affection realize that suffering can be beneficial to their loved ones and are not distressed so long as their loved ones are bearing their trials patiently. What distresses them is

185

when their friends commit faults. Those of spiritual affection bring to their friends' attention the error of their ways. St. Teresa notes that she benefited greatly by having people like this in her life, i.e., people whose concern for her spiritual welfare was detached from self-interest. She maintains that lack of self-interest makes individuals more compassionate and more truly loving.

Another example of how Teresa has perfection in her sights is seen in how she understands "our daily bread," to refer exclusively to the Eucharist, for she cannot believe that Our Lord had bread of bodily necessities in mind when he taught us the Our Father "as if he did not know that, once we begin to worry about the needs of the body, we shall forget the needs of the soul."

Teresa also talks a fair amount about the prayer of quiet, a gift of God that most faithful will not experience. However, she says many things about prayer useful to the average person.

The Way of Perfection is not an easy read. Some may be better off reading excerpted and annotated versions of Teresa's works such as are found in *When the Wells Runs Dry: Prayer Beyond the Beginnings* by Fr. Thomas Green and *The Fulfillment of All Desire* by Ralph Martin.

(Review by Marie George)

The Way of Perfection by St. Teresa of Avila

The Way of Perfection by St. Teresa of Avila, also known as St. Teresa of Jesus (1515–1582), is a spiritual classic of the 16th century Catholic Reformation. Teresa, a Discalced Carmelite nun, was canonized by Pope Gregory XV in 1622 and elevated to a Doctor of the Church by Pope Paul VI in 1970. In addition to earlier and later literary masterpieces such as her autobiography and *Interior Castle*, Saint Teresa is best known for founding convents that were administered according to a most rigorous interpretation of the Carmelite Rule.

As in the famous *Camino* of Santiago (St. James) St. Teresa's *Camino de Perfeccion* escorts the faithful reader on a pilgrimage toward the perfection of the soul through prayer. Prodded to write by her superiors for the perfection of the nuns under her own personal direction, the universality of her recommendations and remedies are of inestimable value to any spiritually mature person devoted to maximizing the spiritual benefits to be accrued from conversation with God. Teresa's counsels are guided by her own experience and routine observations, and in some cases by divine infusion. While this masterpiece of spiritual literature is mandatory for anyone compiling a regimen of serious spiritual reading, it is not a beginner's manual by any means; nevertheless, one should keep in mind that the degree of advancement in the spiritual life and not mere chronological age is the most important factor in deciding whether one is ready to pursue the Teresian path to perfection.

Humility prompts Teresa to deny full comprehension of her own writings. The book consists of a Prologue and forty-two brief chapters that are woven together into a spiritual tapestry from two distinct manuscripts. The saint guides her cohabitants and all future readers through a gauntlet of behaviors and dispositions to pursue and avoid so as to better implement the primary principle of the Natural Law to seek the good while avoiding evil. Strict observance of the Rule, humility, mutual love, renunciation of worldly matters, and a constant vigil for diabolical snares, prepare the individual for the spiritual medicine of contemplation and prayer.

The book ascends toward its Everest in its treatment of prayer, reaching its crescendo with the Lord's Prayer. Teresa takes pains to note the need for prayer in helping to combat the heresy and increasing secularization of her time, a lesson which should not be lost on us today. In Chapter 16 she employs a beautiful metaphor in likening the game of chess, which was then enjoying a renaissance in Spain under the sponsorship of the priest and bishop, Ruy Lopez, to a core set of contemplative concerns. Chess cannot be played without properly setting up the pieces, while the Queen is the most powerful piece in carrying out the goal of slaying the King. Analogously, to derive the full efficacy of undistracted prayerful contemplation a person must be properly cloaked with the virtues and fortified by a properly formed will. Humility, acting as the Queen of the virtues, offers us the cross with which we shall conquer and slay all obstacles in our ascent toward a loving communion with God.

In the final chapters (27–42) Teresa maps the steps of the soul's ascent toward God by means of an analysis of the Lord's Prayer.

Meditating upon each petition of the prayer given to the apostles by our Lord, the soul moves from a mindful withdrawal from all external stimuli, through a deep inner quiet, to being ecstatically seized by an all-consuming rapture in which it is pierced by God in a paradoxical union of pleasure and pain. St. Teresa's own rapture is best displayed in the Bernini sculpture known as "The Ecstasy of St. Teresa," which is permanently installed within Santa Maria della Vittoria in the heart of the Eternal City. The spear that pierces her soul captures the moment of sweet and salvific slaying.

(Review by Glenn Statile)

Other works by St. Teresa of Avila are *Autobiography* and *The Way of Perfection* (both are reviewed in this volume).

Words of Light: Inspiration from the letters of Padre Pio, compiled and with an introduction by Fr. Raniero Cantalamessa

My image of Padre Pio was based on his special gifts (such as reading souls), his upbeat sayings, e.g., "Pray, hope, and don't worry," and the novena he said to the Sacred Heart. I was in nowise prepared for *Words of Light*, compiled from his letters to his spiritual directors and arranged according to thirteen themes by Fr. Raniero Cantalamessa. I'm not really sure that the average Catholic can draw that much profit from the book, unless they are in a situation of intense suffering or are experiencing the "dark night of the soul." How many of us are consoled by the Christ Child after being physically attacked by demons? How many of us offer ourselves as victim souls? I think a lot of people are going to find themselves not ready for the lessons of the chapters entitled: "I suffer and I wish to suffer more," "I live in a perpetual night," and "Oh! What a beautiful thing it is to become a victim of love." I personally find discouraging the numerous statements in which Padre Pio expresses doubt about whether he loves God and whether he can hope to be saved (which amounts to the same thing)—and yes, I know we are to work out our salvation in fear and trembling. These statements are balanced by others in which St. Pio professes great confidence in God, as when he says even if he saw hell opening up at his feet, he would not despair, but place his trust in Jesus. Though most of the book seemed to me suitable only for those approaching some high degree of holiness, I did find here and there thoughts that the average Catholic can relate to. For example, if Padre Pio was horrified by how disfigured and vile he appeared when God revealed to him his hidden faults, how much more would we have reason to be concerned about ours? It is reassuring that Padre Pio, at a certain point of his spiritual journey, acknowledges that while he desires to suffer for Jesus, when put to the test he looks for relief despite himself. Also, he, like some of us, is on occasion tempted to call God cruel, and he weeps and sighs a lot. Some of his advice is quite accessible: e.g., he tells us to avoid anxiety and discouragement because they are rooted in selfishness and self-love, and belie a lack of trust in God. He astutely warns us of how the devil tries to mislead those who have drawn close to God and experienced divine consolation into thinking that they could never fall from this state with the result that they begin to lose a holy mistrust of themselves, something that ultimately can lead to their utter ruin. Overall, however, I think that for many readers, this book is liable to be difficult to digest.

(Review by Marie George)

Words of Light: Inspiration from the Letters of Padre Pio

Fr. Raniero Cantalamessa compiled this anthology of letters so that we could better know Padre Pio by allowing him to speak to us directly through his letters. What a gift he has given us. These letters provide great insight into Padre Pio's inner life, reveal the depth of his spirituality, and thereby contain so much for our own spiritual progress.

The Lord gave Padre Pio the gift of the Stigmata in 1918 when he was thirty-one years of age. He passed away in 1968, almost to the exact date of the 50th anniversary of receiving this gift. His life in between was one of constant prayer and intense suffering. Prayer was his center of gravity and from it he found the strength needed to fight both the constant struggles of the spirit and the constant assaults of the devil. These assaults—physical, mental, and spiritual—were intense. Seen in this light, Padre Pio's ability to carry out his daily duties, particularly his long hours in the confessional, becomes even more amazing.

The fear of offending God and the dangers to the soul by a fall gave him the desire to offer himself as a victim for souls and sinners. Padre Pio wrote that he desired never to tire of suffering and never to commit a venial sin. (WOW!) He believed that suffering was the only sure test of love and that the more one suffers, the more the sufferings of Jesus are lightened. Padre Pio bears a likeness to Simon of Cyrene in helping Jesus to carry his cross. He shows us that by carrying our own daily crosses without complaint, we too can become Simons of Cyrene. Padre Pio felt that love that is not fed and nourished by the cross is not true love and he did not want his own cross to be made lighter.

His asceticism and his mystical life were characterized by what is known as the "dark night of the soul." Padre Pio described it as a furious battle with no glimmer of light or comfort—a great desolation: the path of the Via Dolorosa. Yet occasional relief came from God's reassurance that "nothing can defeat those who groan beneath the cross for love of Me and whom I have striven to protect," and Padre Pio continued to entrust himself to the Lord. His devotion to Mary, mother of the "Man of Sorrows," was also one of the essential elements of his spirituality.

Padre Pio wonders what humanity would be without Christ in its midst. He relates the sorrow of Jesus who tells him: "I remain alone in the churches, by day and by night. They do not bother with the sacrament of the altar anymore. And even those who do speak of it, alas! with what indifference and coldness they speak." And Jesus then weeps that His heart has been forgotten. This should cause us great pain indeed and galvanize each and every one of us to visit Jesus often!

To quote Pope Benedict XVI, "the examples of the saints are our real life guides,"[1] and Padre Pio offers many lessons for us. As spiritual director, he focuses on simplicity of spirit and peace of soul so

---

1. Pope Benedict XVI, "Homily on the Solemnity of All Saints," November 1, 2006.

that we can approach all of life's ups and downs with calmness. We can learn so much from him in this book. That said, some of his writings can be challenging as they reveal a life experienced on a far deeper level than that to which most of us are accustomed.

(Review by Joan Lovett)

Prayer

Speaking with God from the Depths of the Heart: The Armenian Prayer Book of St. Gregory Narek

St. Gregory was a tenth century monk who belonged to the Armenian Church.[1] He was proclaimed a Doctor of the Church by Pope Francis on April 12, 2015. Mystic, theologian, and poet, St. Gregory is best known for *The Prayer Book*, which is sometimes simply called the "Narek" because it was so closely identified with its author, who himself says of it: "And since I leave readers this testament recording my misdeeds along the path of no return, that they might pray to God through my words day by day, may this book remain as a guide for repentance, continuously lifted in voice to you, almighty Lord, its letters like my body, its message like my soul (Prayer 54)." Replete with scriptural references, the Narek has been translated into thirty languages.

The Narek is composed of ninety-five psalm-like prayers, the vast majority of which are similar in theme to the penitential psalms (such as Ps. 51, the "Miserere"). They are accurately described in these words of St. Gregory: "look with favor upon this relentless expression of contrition for my wrongdoing and the reproach I heap upon myself from the depth of my heart" (Prayer 57). He is not exaggerating about the relentless self-reproach. A typical prayer starts out with St. Gregory sharply rebuking himself for a long list of failings, and ends with a word of hope or gratitude for the salvation offered to him by the all-merciful God; the following abbreviated excerpt serves to illustrate this pattern: "I did not fix the eye of my soul on the head of my life, Christ, who would have led me down the straight path. For in trying to run too quickly, I dug myself in deeper. In trying to reach the unreachable, I failed to reach my own level. In pretending to greatness, I slipped from where I was. . . . Only you are able to deliver me, a captive slave from these things. . . . For you alone, Lord Christ, revered doer of good, with the boundless glory of the Father and the Holy Spirit are blessed

---

1. The Armenian Church broke off from the Roman Catholic Church after the Council of Constantinople in 553; the Armenian Catholic Church was officially established in 1749.

forever and ever" (Prayer 55). This excerpt is also typical in that Gregory often offers thanks and praise to the Trinity and he frequently presents ideas in a series of juxtapositions ("your love calling even those despised like me, your word to steady those wavering like me," and so forth [Prayer 30]).

Whether or not one is liable to profit from the Narek depends on a number of factors. The first is whether one enjoys poetry, and then whether one enjoys St. Gregory's particular style. Gregory often incorporates in his poem-prayers long lists of similar ideas expressed in different words; some will find this repetitive, and others meditative. Secondly, the vast majority of the prayers are penitential in nature, and so if one were to read this book on a daily basis, one might grow weary of the lack of variety in theme. I find it a good book to use on those occasions when I am in a penitential mood. Lastly, despite their uplifting endings, some of the prayers are so intensely penitential it is questionable whether they make suitable reading for those who are inclined to excessive remorse. Some of us, though, could stand some beating ourselves up and entombing our hearts in sighs (to paraphrase Prayer 66). And we all do well to keep before our minds "the merciful lover of mankind" so frequently mentioned by St. Gregory.

(Review by Marie George)

Two other works by St. Gregory that have been translated include: *The Blessing of Blessings: Grigor of Narek's Commentary on the Song of Songs* and *The Festal Works of St. Gregory of Narek: Annotated Translation of the Odes, Litanies, and Encomia.*

The Art of Praying [Formerly entitled *Prayer in Practice*] by Fr. Romano Guardini

Fr. Romano Guardini was a prolific author, and a theologian who was greatly admired by Pope Benedict XVI. I chose to review a second of his works because of the importance of prayer in the spiritual life. I was initially a bit put off by Guardini's assertion that "generally speaking, man does not enjoy prayer." If our hearts are restless until they rest in God, if we are made in the image of God, prayer would seem to be something we desire to engage in. Guardini does not deny the latter, but, like the *Catechism of the Catholic Church*, which speaks of the "battle of prayer," he is realistic in noting that we do have a tendency to make lame excuses about lack of time or other important matters to attend to when really we just don't feel like praying. As he says later on: "At times, as we have said, prayer comes as easily as the heart's own language. But generally speaking and with the majority of people, this is not so. Mostly it must be willed and practiced, and the toil of this practice derives partly because we do not *experience* the real presence of God." Overall the book is a good introduction to prayer, which could be profitably read alongside the section on prayer in the *Catechism*. Even those who have received good instruction about prayer can draw some profit from this book. There are some places where Guardini makes statements that are vague, questionable, or even mistaken. "Mere existence is dark and brooding; value gives it light." "Man is . . . the very principle of life." "To it [popular devotion] belong Matins and Vespers." Still the overall merits of the book make it worth putting up with these minor flaws.

Guardini insists a lot on preparing for prayer, i.e., on becoming recollected, and rightly so. I wish, however, he had added the advice of not letting the effort to rid oneself of distractions become a distraction. He also places rightful emphasis on the holiness of God. I initially found it puzzling that he identifies our sense of sinfulness before the holiness of God as the first motive for prayer. This view is clarified when he speaks in terms of our need to be forgiven and renewed. People who do not feel a need for a savior do not often pray to Jesus. Guardini identifies as a second motive for prayer the desire for union with God. After that, he speaks of the various divine perfections, and how they elicit prayers of adoration, praise, petition, and thanksgiving. He then devotes a chapter to the Trinity and prayer. After treating oral prayer, he gives a nuanced treatment of contemplative prayer, acknowledging from the start that it takes different forms with different people. In the following chapter on divine providence, he explains well the importance of seeking primarily the realization of God's providential plan when it comes to making specific requests. In the same chapter he also makes helpful remarks regarding "praying always." The chapter on prayer in times of inca-pacity is full of judicious advice (with the exception of suggesting that a person unable to pray should show reverence toward all living things). The final chapter is devoted to showing the relationship among personal prayer, liturgical prayer, and popular devotion.

(Review by Marie George)

Other works by Guardini include *The Lord* and *Preparing Yourself for Mass* (reviewed in this volume).

Essence of Prayer by Sr. Ruth Burrows, OCD

The book consists of eighteen chapters, twelve of which are essays that appeared in various publications. Consequently, there is a cer-tain amount of repetition—which is sometimes helpful. Although Burrows mentions liturgical prayer and "praying always," her remarks are almost exclusively directed to solitary or personal prayer.

First, my reservations about *Essence of Prayer*: The book focuses on what prayer is and what its purpose is, while largely passing over the "how" of prayer. Burrows is not wrong in insisting that a method is not the prayer. However, a beginner also needs to be provided with some idea of how to pray. Burrows, at times, gives the impression that, so long as one is faithful to spending the time one has fixed each day for prayer, one's prayer is pleasing to God. But as other spiritual writers note, in the case of beginners in the spiritual life, that if nothing is perceptibly going on in their mind or heart, they shouldn't just sit there idle; Burrows herself acknowledges this. Bur-rows says "prayer is not a technique but a relationship. There is no handicap, no obstacle, no problem." But even the Apostles asked Jesus to teach them how to pray (Lk. 11:1).

Another reservation I have is that a fair number of chapters are devoted to explaining the life of a Carmelite, and so do not hold great interest for the average lay person (though I found "Carmel, a Stark Encounter with the Human Condition" and "Consecrated Life" helpful).

Lastly, the book contains a number of theological mistakes (e.g., that Jesus lived in faith) and some statements that at very least need to be nuanced, e.g., "Jesus . . . does not like his true disciples to think of themselves as servants of God" and "how vital we are—by His free choice—to His complete happiness."

While one can see from the above that this book is not suitable for most beginners, it can be read with benefit by those who are well catechized.

Burrows begins by presenting her main thesis: "Prayer . . . is not primarily something we are doing to God, something we are giving to God but what God is doing for us. And what God is doing for us is giving us the divine Self in love." She notes that a main obstacle to our receiving Him is that "we do not want him. We want our own version of him." What we need to do instead is have faith and trust that God is looking out for our best interest despite appearances to the contrary: "This is what it means to believe: to take that daily bread and eat it with love and gratitude no matter how bitter the taste." In a number of places Burrows elaborates on what faith entails. Her message is that we prefer to live according to our own limited perceptions of things because they afford us a certain comfort and security. We rely on our notion of who we are and who God is, and "we are unaware of how much of our life is lived from self, relying on self and not on faith in the Son of Man. We cannot rid ourselves of this deeply rooted pride and self-possession by our own strength." Burrows observes that only God can do this, but we must cooperate with Him through faith, by acknowledging His love at work at every moment of our lives, no matter how hum-drum, humiliating, or painful they may be. She also notes that we need to accept the destruction of our spiritual self-image, something God seeks to accomplish in us, so that we no longer live, but Christ lives in us; to this end, we need to love our spiritual poverty and trust in God's mercy.

(Review by Marie George)

Essence of Prayer by Ruth Burrows, OCD

This book looks like one of the glossy popular prayer guides churned out by the mainstream Christian Press. Its author, Ruth Burrows, chooses not to use her religious name, Sr. Rachel, in the book. Why does she do this? She also chose to have Sister Wendy, who was a popular TV art critic, write the foreword to this book. Wrong notes like these made me suspicious that this book would reflect the current popular trends in prayer life, like centering prayer, eastern spirituality, etc. However, the book in fact proved to be orthodox (as is Sr. Wendy).

This was a challenging book for me to read. Most of the ideas presented in this book are radical and were unfamiliar to me. To begin, Burrows quickly lances misconceptions you may have about what prayer is, as she starts to prepare you for some of the more complicated thoughts presented later.

The book's title leads one to believe that in this relatively short tome you will get a distilled set of instructions and tips on how to pray more deeply. The essence of vanilla, for example, is an extract of the vanilla bean, the essential oils of vanilla, distilled and concentrated. However, the essence of prayer that Burrows is talking about is not only the extract, not only the property of something that uniquely defines it, but something larger. After lunching with a friend, I will think about our interaction for hours after. The essence of our encounter has changed me, has taken me outside of my normal life and into his. The essence of prayer is what happens to you after praying; how God has transformed you through your prayer and His essence remains with you. It is still you, but you have been changed by the encounter. And what was your role in receiving the essence of your friend? Being there and open to him.

Let's cut to the chase and advance some of her radical ideas, so you can get an essence of Burrows thoughts and let them simmer: Prayer is primarily an act of God. (I still wrestle with this one). Our part is to receive. The Mother Superior of a convent wonders at times how God will provide them with grocery money for the next day. She also has to trust in God's providence to send novices to the community. Similarly, nuns have to abandon any delusion that they have anything to offer God; they have to accept that they have nothing to give, but to live with empty hands. "My giving could only be in allowing God to give." This is what "be it done unto me according thy Word" is all about (which explains why a picture of the Annunciation was chosen for the cover of this book).

At the end of the book, one has encountered a good friend in Sr. Rachel, whose essence will linger for a good long while and deeply influence you. It is an encounter that has changed you in a way that you can experience Him and allow Him to change you.

Whom is this book for? It is for readers who have the time to read a chapter a day or once a week and think deeply on the ideas presented. It is for those considering the religious life and all who are interested in Carmelite spirituality. It is perfect holy hour reading. It will frustrate those who are not willing to wrestle with the ideas presented and struggle to understand them. For me it was a difficult but rewarding book to read.

(Review by Hilary Cotter)

Other works by Burrows include *Before the Living God* and *To Believe in Jesus.*

How to Pray Always by Fr. Raoul Plus, SJ

Raoul Plus, SJ covers a lot of ground in this short and intense book (130 pp.), originally published in 1926. I would recommend this work to virtually anyone who is seeking to do spiritual reading. Yes, some parts may be too condensed for some readers, e.g., the section on Ignatian teachings on prayer. And, yes, there are a few claims that I find questionable, e.g., the only time Christ exercised choice was when he chose suffering. However, Plus dispels a number of misconceptions about prayer and breaks matters down in a common sense manner. I wish I had read this book when I was younger, as Plus elaborates on the teachings of a number of masters of prayer in a manner that is singularly insightful.

In "Part One: The Principles of Prayer," Plus distinguishes between the act of prayer and the state of prayer. While initially it is not entirely clear what he means by the latter, he certainly is clear about why people in general are not able to be continually engaging in the act of prayer. We have duties we need to attend to; a woman who spends her time in pious exercises while leaving the housework undone is not acting rightly. When it is not time for prayer, we must seek to act out of love of God and not for the sake of personal satisfaction: this is what it means to pray always. The continual direction of our will to God is what Plus means by a state of prayer. The direction of our will can be actual or habitual. Habitual pure intention, however, can only develop if we at times consciously make "an upward glance to God at the moment of action." We need to practice the presence of God which goes hand-in-hand with an "inner solitude" that arises from avoiding useless conversations and aimless occupations.

Plus begins "Part Two: The Practice of Prayer" by explaining the Ignatian methods for meditation and contemplation. He then goes through a number of prayer basics and eventually touches on the higher forms of prayer. One point he makes that is not so commonly seen in other books on prayer is that most of us often do not rely sufficiently on Christ our Mediator when we pray. We need to pray "through Him, with Him, and in Him." "There is not enough of Jesus Christ in our prayer as 'other Christs.'" Plus then speaks again about the importance of purity of intention and of the need to always do our best. He then goes on to address the role of aspirations, i.e., of frequent short spontaneous prayers, and he offers advice as to how to make this practice habitual. Among other things, he quotes Teresa of Avila who says that with God's help it may take six months to a year to acquire the habit of addressing and listening to Our Lord dwelling in our heart. Through purifying our intentions, through the practice of the presence of God, and through aspirations, we will continuously be either working for God or in conscious union with Him.

(Review by Marie George)

How to Pray Always by Fr. Raoul Plus, SJ

A daunting title, a daunting command, "Pray without ceasing" (1 Th. 5:17). I must confess, I took on such a title with a despairing skepticism, rather like when I read of the "Valiant Woman" in Proverbs. It all seems so far beyond me that I tend to assume the posture of the rich young man, walking quietly away from Our Lord when he was told, "Sell all that you own . . . then come, follow me" (Lk. 18:22).

But fear not! This little handbook is filled with useful ideas like, "the difficulty is less how to drive away useless impressions and ideas than [about] . . . [trying] to live habitually with a number of holy impressions and ideas stored in our minds." And another, "I cannot have my thoughts occupied with God without interruption. But my will should never be directed at any object except God. This direct orientation of the will is a form of union with [God] that is quite attainable and leads to perfection." When I told a priest friend that I had finished and liked this book, he smiled delightedly and said, "Yes, isn't it a relief?!" And yes, it is! It feels a little like being off the hook, to direct your will, but not always your thoughts to God—a tremendously more manageable goal.

How to Pray Always explains the way to accomplish Our Lord's command in an introduction and two parts. In the first, "The Principles of Prayer," Fr. Plus teaches the arts of recollection, submission to God's will, and maintaining an interior silence. In part two, "The Practice of Prayer," he teaches how to pray well by turning everything into prayer and living in a prayerful spirit. His advice is profound and yet seems quite doable.

Fr. Plus writes in an engaging and accessible way. For instance, "The imagination and feelings are a couple of giddypates. . . . At the very moment I am most anxious to be at peace . . . they worm their way in and sometimes take complete possession of my thoughts." He articulates difficulties and prescribes remedies with equally sympathetic and down-to-earth advice.

Feeling discouraged, but don't have time for a lot of reading? I think this book could be very helpful.

(Review by Ann Turner)

Other popular works by Plus include *How to Pray Well* and *Mary in Our Soul Life.*

Opening to God by Fr. Thomas Green, SJ

This book is directed to beginners at prayer. It contains a lot of solid and useful material, as Green draws on masters of prayer, such as Teresa of Avila. There are, though, things about the book that may displease certain readers. Green's comparisons are strained at times, and some of the questions he takes up hold little or no interest for most people nowadays (he wrote the book in the wake of confusions that arose after Vatican II). Overall, however, the book is an accessible and helpful guide for the beginner. In the first chapter he addresses what prayer is. He corrects certain common misconceptions about it, such as placing undue emphasis on our own effort and activity in prayer, rather than on God's action and our receptivity. In Chapter 2 he addresses whether Christians engaged in the world (as parents, pastors, etc.) really need prayer. He also puts his finger on the human tendency to pray for what we think is best, in effect using prayer as if it were a means of manipulating God to serve our ends. In Chapter 3 he talks about prayer serving the purpose of discerning what God wants us to be doing. He maintains that: (1) praying over Scripture is a privileged means of learning God's will for us; (2) recognizing the voice of God occurs when we are at peace in our prayers; (3) we usually need a spiritual director in order to learn to discern God's will. Chapters 4 and 5 speak of two ways in which we can dispose ourselves to being open to God. One consists in coming to attentive quiet. Here he suggests a variety of means from the traditional Ignatian method to Zen meditative techniques (the value of the latter is highly questionable; see *Jesus Christ the Bearer of the Water of Life: A Christian Reflection on the New Age*). The second way to dispose ourselves to hearing God is active purification of the soul. Green discusses traditional means from freeing ourselves from disordered attachments: penance, examination of conscience, and the sacrament of Reconciliation. Penance serves the purposes of making amends, of overcoming our selfish desires, and in a way of praying, insofar as the body, by its acts, reflect one's inner attitudes. The general examination of conscience allows us to acknowledge our sinfulness and open ourselves to God's forgiveness and healing. The particular examination of conscience is a useful means for rooting out our faults one at a time. As Green notes: "True knowledge of God always goes hand in hand with painful self-knowledge." Chapter 6 describes how to get to know God using the two Ignatian methods: meditation (in which we use reason) and contemplation (in which the imagination plays an important role). Green illustrates the two techniques with the Gospel passage about the woman at the well. This chapter is very helpful for those who are beginners at prayer. In the epilogue, he speaks briefly about prayer beyond the beginnings, a topic he develops at length in *When the Well Runs Dry*. He notes that, once prayer becomes joyous to us and our faults seem to be diminished, we can too readily attribute this to our efforts, at which point God often lets us experience difficulty in prayer and a resurgence of our failings. We must not yield to the temptation to think that prayer is vain, but persevere despite the seeming darkness; we need to trust that God will transform us through this process in His own good time.

(Review by Marie George)

Other works by Green include *Experiencing God* and *When the Well Runs Dry* (reviewed in this volume).

Prayer and the Will of God by Dom Hubert van Zeller

The first work by van Zeller that I ever read was *The Choice of God*. I liked it because it was hardcore, but at the same time found it severe, more for a religious than for a lay person. It turned out to be out of print. When I picked up this work I expected another dose of austerity, in addition to which I thought it would not hold a candle to my favorite on providence, *Trustful Surrender* by Fr. Jean Baptiste Saint-Jure. To the contrary, I found *Prayer and the Will of God* a delightful and generally clear work that makes one want to love God more. Van Zeller often employs engaging and simple comparisons, which makes the work readable for the average person.

In the first part, van Zeller treats basic topics concerning prayer, e.g., why we must pray, how we should pray, how we can tell if our prayer is fruitful, and what the error of "quietism" consists of. A point he makes repeatedly is: "Even the specific act of petition . . . is to be valued not for what it manages to get out of God, but for what it gets out of us. It cannot get out of God what God has not from all eternity wanted to give." Another point he makes repeatedly is how too often people speak of misfortunes as being "the will of God," whereas happy events are not identified in this way, as if God willed that we be unhappy. He devotes an entire chapter to a wonderful commentary on the Our Father.

In the second part, van Zeller speaks about the will of God. He explains why prayers for good things, such as that one's husband stop his excessive drinking, are not answered by pointing to unexpected benefits this might have in the big scheme of things, which is of course what God sees and wills. He goes through the various providential events in the life of Christ to help us realize that God has a plan for each of our lives, even if we cannot always see it the way we can in the life of Christ. Another reassuring point he makes in this section is that even when we have neglected to cooperate with God's grace we should not fear that God will treat us vindictively, for God will give us the grace we need for where we have landed as a result of our refusal. Van Zeller points out that putting God's will first means the death of self, but without this death man cannot truly live. One of his last observations is that we grow closer to understanding the mystery of the Father's will by entering into the Son's Passion through willingly accepting suffering.

(Review by Marie George)

Van Zeller is also author of *Holiness: A Guide for Beginners* and *Suffering: The Catholic Answer* (reviewed in this volume).

The Prayer of Love and Silence by a Carthusian, translated by a Monk of Parkminster

This book is simple, scriptural, passionate, and to the point, especially in the first part, "An Introduction to the Interior Life." It starts with our supernatural end and the basic principles of the spiritual life, and proceeds to offer a method of meditation so that we can pray always. Christ wants to be our life and wants of us our whole life. God Himself provides us the means of entering into intimacy with Him, primarily through the theological virtues. The simplest way for us to enter into this intimacy, then, is by making acts of faith, hope, and love. The author here is not referring to formal prayers with those names, but to personal prayers arising from our awareness of our relationship with God and Who He is to us individually. Our Carthusian counsels us to "keep ourselves as far as we can, during the rest of the day, in the presence of God, withdrawing from time to time within ourselves to adore him there by acts of faith, hope and love." He further tell us that we should get in the habit of lifting our hearts to God even without using words, but by an inward glance. Through these means we will gradually create an inner solitude where we can listen to God and make Him the focus of our thoughts and actions. Our Carthusian acknowledges that souls fear divine intimacy because it calls for sacrifice on their part, but urges us to recognize that of ourselves we can do nothing and to turn our lives over to God who can do all things. He advises that we make use of spiritual reading, study, and the sacraments (especially the Eucharist). In order to make our whole life a prayer, he counsels that before we begin any activity we should "stop for a moment and glance inwardly at the divine Guest within [our] soul," and when examining our conscience we should consider whether at any point we "have forgotten Our Lord for too long." In everything we do, be it spiritual reading, relaxing, going for a walk, etc., we should continually renew our "interior union with God, resting in his sacred intimacy," conscious that we are surrounded by His love. Certainly, it is necessary for us to obey the commandments, avoid temptations, do penance, and strive to detach ourselves from earthly things. Asceticism, however, is not an end in itself, but a means of emptying our hearts, so that God can fill them with his love. Our Carthusian quotes the passage in John's Gospel that speaks of the mutual indwelling of the Persons of the Trinity in each other, and Christ's desire that we share in the Trinitarian life; we are to enter into this life already: "the kingdom of God is within us" (Lk. 17:21).

The second part of the book consists of sermons delivered to monks. With very few exceptions, however, what is said is helpful to lay persons as well. Some of the themes treated are obsessions (and what to do about them), meekness, and simplicity. There are any number of insightful observations, e.g.: "Our suffering, for the most part, comes from revolt, from a want of adaptability and abandonment." The homily on Mary and the Presentation is especially inspiring.

The third part of the book, "The Blessed Trinity and the Supernatural Life," is somewhat more didactic. Its ultimate purpose is to help us root our prayer life in God's Trinitarian life.

(Review by Marie George)

The Prayer of Love and Silence by a Carthusian

The Prayer of Love and Silence contains the reflections on prayer and the spiritual life of an anonymous Carthusian monk of the same religious order as that depicted in the documentary movie "Into Great Silence." Some spiritual books focus on practical matters such as how to develop a plan of prayer, or how to correct various faults. It is important to practice good works and live a moral life, but the author pushes the reader to reach for something deeper and more profound: "There are, of course, many faithful souls who endeavor to lead good lives, and strive to attain a certain ideal of moral virtue. But how few know how to live a life of real faith, sustained by hope and aflame with the love of God."

The first section concerns "The Principles of the Spiritual Life." The most basic principle is that all asceticism should be focused on the love of God, and the author presents the gospel precept that we should love God with all of our heart, soul, and strength as fundamental. He contrasts this with a kind of asceticism that focuses on egocentric self-perfection. Rather, readers should understand that we cannot improve ourselves solely by our own efforts. The author elegantly states that "a purely natural principle can never produce supernatural results."

Other principles of the spiritual life are then presented, which concern recognizing that the presence of God is near us at all times, and most especially in our souls. Recognizing the divine life in our souls, the writer also asks us to reflect on the gravity of serious sin, which separates us from this life. Ultimately, the center of the author's approach to prayer is *faith*. If we have a sincere faith that God is always present, we will engage Him in deep and authentic prayer, and we will avoid sin lest we offend His presence within us.

The next sections help the reader reflect further on the aforementioned principles. In "Methods of Prayer" the author provides written acts of faith, hope, and love to provide starting points for prayer. He also discusses how we can pray throughout the day by taking the time to recognize God's presence. "Sermons in Chapter" includes sermons for various feast days. These sermons reinforce the spiritual principles already presented, and also may serve well as aids to prayer. The final section centers on the Trinity. This is a grand vision, which builds on the previous chapters to show that the goal of prayer is to enter into a relationship with the Trinitarian life of God through Jesus. Asceticism, prayer, the spiritual life these are means, not by which we attain God by force, but by which we clear away obstacles to allow Him to enter our hearts. It takes time, the author states, and continuous effort, and great difficulty, to overcome sin, selfishness, and most especially pride. But even our falls, we are told, can help in this journey as they lead us to rely only on God, and not on ourselves. It is worth persevering, as the end of our spiritual struggle is sublime and astoundingly beautiful: "The soul is thus ready to be penetrated with the uncreated light. Illumined and ablaze with these supernatural rays, we begin already on earth to taste the inheritance of the sons of God."

The *Prayer of Love and Silence* is an excellent book, refocusing the reader on the most essential aspects of Christianity and the spiritual life. Anyone who appreciates contemplative or monastic spirituality will love this book. This book is also strongly recommended for those with a more active spirituality by temperament. The Church is a great tapestry of vocations, all necessary and mysteriously interdependent. Anyone active in the world will benefit greatly from reading about a different perspective from this moving work, one that is clearly the fruit of a lifetime of silent contemplation.

(Review by Michael McCaffery)

Other works on Carthusian spirituality include *The Call of Silent Love* and *The Wound of Love*.

The Prayer of the Presence of God by Dom Augustin Guillerand, O. Cart.

The Carthusian Monk, Augustin Guillerand, did not compose this work as a book, though, perhaps he intended to, as it does reveal more structure than would be expected in notes written in a spiritual diary, and is far less repetitious than the editors lead us to believe. It is a short work, and shorter than its 169 pages, due to the blank pages between chapters. Although it contains a couple of exaggerated or poorly worded statements, they are unlikely to lead one astray, and the work exudes a focused and passionate love of God. By comparison with the Brother Lawrence's *Practice of the Presence of God*, Guillerand's work is more thorough when speaking about things that keep us from being present to God, and less so when speaking about recognizing God throughout one's daily routine. The two works complement each other. Virtually all except those advanced in the spiritual life stand to profit from Guillerand's book.

Guillerand opens by stating clearly that our goal is union with God. He says the first means to this is to pray that we may overcome the sins and vices that are an obstacle to this union. To this end, "we must ask for that frightening light which reveals them all—the sins we have committed knowingly and those, far more numerous, that we have committed almost unconsciously." Guillerand speaks repeatedly about praise: "This is the end of all prayer and of every movement of the soul: to praise God, to be united with Him, to be transformed into His likeness forever; to become forever His image and His child." Indeed, the entire last section is devoted to praising God, His goodness, wisdom, mercy, etc. Guillerand does a consummate job of articulating the importance of resuming our praise of God upon rising in the morning, in keeping with Scripture: "All ye works of the Lord, bless the Lord; praise and exalt Him above all forever" (Dn. 3:57). He exhorts us to consciously reconnect with God upon waking so that He may give supernatural value to our actions and the strength to overcome temptations.

Guillerand addresses a number of the things that can foster or hinder union with God: temptations, our response to natural evils, attachment to earthly things, humility, distractions in prayer, and desolation. Certainly, most of the things he says can be found in other spiritual authors; however, he often expresses them in a manner that is poignant and motivating. A recurring theme is that of "the filial and simple prayer of interior souls:" "To these God says in

210

the depths of their being, 'You are my beloved child. I am here. Let us talk.'" Guillerand cautions us, though, against addressing God as if he were a friend on our level; we need to pray to Him as a Father, i.e., as "someone from whom we receive everything; to whom we give only what He gives to us." We also need to recognize that God as Father knows that to love means "wanting what is good for one's offspring, not just what is pleasant." God is like the good human father who "in correcting he loved and he corrected by love."

(Review by Marie George)

The Prayer of the Presence of God by Dom Augustin Guillerand, O. Cart.

The central thesis in *The Prayer of the Presence of God* by Dom Augustin Guillerand is simple: Prayer is the path to holiness. Without prayer, any lasting advancement in the spiritual life and union with God—which is the goal of our life—is impossible. In his book, he describes in penetrating detail the prayer that occurs in the innermost parts of the soul, a practice found particularly among the Carthusians in their life of silence.

The book itself was organized and put together from Dom Guillerand's writings, which were discovered after his death. The writings themselves were not originally intended to be a book; each piece can stand on its own as a tiny treatise on prayer. But when they were organized and put together, they were arranged in a sound progression as short and thought-provoking chapters.

As Guillerand explains it, prayer is essentially approaching God, placing oneself in His presence, asking Him for Himself, and wanting only to be with Him. He writes that this desire for Him is the only thing ultimately worth asking for—as every single thing necessary to it will be given besides to the soul who loves and trusts our Lord entirely. Guillerand is not writing to a particular audience, nor is his method only for monastics: what he has to say is intended for anyone who cares to listen and learn. His idea of what prayer is and how it is practiced is very approachable, and could be incorporated by anyone into his daily life. This is the simple beauty of his work: prayer practiced in the silence of the soul is not for the monk alone but for the Church Militant as well, engaged with a flawed and sinful world.

The book is divided into four parts. The first explains what prayer is and what it does. Here Guillerand shows the reader just how important prayer is in order to advance in the spiritual life. The second part describes the ways in which one can or ought to pray. Here the reader is shown how prayer is done in the innermost chambers of the soul. The third outlines how to progress in prayer. In the fourth part Guillerand sings our Lord's praise, showing us the fruit of prayer, a taste of what the soul may discover in practicing true prayer. Throughout the whole, while he apologizes for being repetitive, Guillerand's message is so simple and clear. He dives right to the heart of all communication with Our Lord.

This book was amazing to read, and I could not recommend it enough! Dom Augustin Guillerand showed me an understanding of prayer that had not struck me before. Simply put, without prayer, there is no progression in holiness. Prayer is, at its heart, placing oneself in the presence of God—a silent conversation between the soul and its Maker. The love between God and the soul deepens until we are almost in heaven while still on earth. This collection of writings showed me not only how far I have to go to achieve this, but also described the way to do so.

(Review by Elizabeth Lademan)

The Practice of the Presence of God by Brother Lawrence of the Resurrection

The Practice of the Presence of God is a short spiritual classic suitable for most people. It is available in a wide variety of editions that are drawn from two works that in turn are drawn from letters and conversations with Brother Lawrence. *The Practice* is thus understandably somewhat repetitive, though often beneficially so. It is best to procure an edition that contains four conversations, fifteen or sixteen letters, plus the spiritual maxims (Br. Lawrence's biography by Joseph Beaufort is not essential). Avoid editions that are updated for the modern reader, as they often significantly alter the text, in some cases giving it a Protestant slant.

The book starts off slowly. It is only when one gets to the fourth conversation that one starts to get Lawrence's main point. The letters elaborate on it further. The maxims, at the end of the book, are the clearest and most helpful part, but perhaps they would not sink in as well if one did not read the previous parts of the book. (In passing, the maxim on the union of the soul with God looks like it was taken out of the *Summa Theologiae*, II-II 83.13.)

Br. Lawrence's central thesis is simple as it is profound: throughout the day, no matter what we are doing, we should endeavor to live in a continual communion of love with God by consciously recognizing His presence within us, by making acts of worship, praise, thanks, trust, resignation to His will, and by offering Him our suffering, and asking His help so that we know His will for us and are given the grace to accomplish it.

Other themes touched on include: distractions during prayer, lost time, the loss of friends, and suffering.

One has to exercise some discernment in reading this book. It would be a mistake to assume that certain things characteristics of Br. Lawrence's spiritual life are to be universally imitated or aspired to. For example, Br. Lawrence found no need for a spiritual director. Also, Br. Lawrence appears to have enjoyed perpetual consolation once the practice of the presence of God was firmly established in him, and in one place he says that God will not permit a soul determined to suffer all things for Him to experience long-lasting sufferings. He does remind us in the second letter that one should not undertake the practice in order to be consoled, but out of love of God; and in letters seven and eleven he makes comments about suffering that apply to the majority of us, who are called to suffer ways he never was. Lastly, while his choice not to reflect in advance on what he needed to do as far as mundane tasks were concerned was appropriate for him, as he had arrived at a stage where he was readily moved by divine inspiration, for most of us such a lack of reflection would constitute imprudence. These caveats aside, the popularity of this book is well-justified by the spiritual benefits one reaps from putting into practice its simple advice.

(Review by Marie George)

The Practice of the Presence of God by Brother Lawrence

One midwinter during the 1620s a young French soldier named Nicholas Herman was stopped in his tracks by a most extraordinary sight—a solitary tree, devoid of foliage. Of course he had seen such trees countless times before, but on this occasion he was led to contemplate its forthcoming budding and bearing of fruit, and that put him in mind of God's benevolence. The illuminating experience profoundly altered his life, and he entered a monastery as a lay brother. He spent most of his years in the kitchen where he was known as Brother Lawrence, and where he learned that the key to life is contained in a simple rule, namely, to train oneself to be conscious of God's presence all the time.

The simplicity does not connote ease however. He let a correspondent know that it took him ten years in the monastery to achieve that level of consciousness. And even though he lived until 1691, he was always learning more about humility and acceptance of God's ways of dealing with souls. The book in which his thoughts are recorded is artless in its spare construction. It is mainly composed of extracts from fifteen letters he wrote to various people, men and women, clerical and lay. But the artlessness frames all the more cogently the limpid message that the soul can truly rest in God at all times, regardless of the demands of worldly duty. Indeed Lawrence often felt closer to God in the bustle of the monastery kitchen than in the chapel. He was not an advocate of lengthy formal prayers, because he found they could easily lead to distractions. Rather the soul should speak and listen humbly to God.

In fact, for Br. Lawrence, life is meant to be a perpetual hymn to God, such as is attested to by St. John in his glimpse into heavenly adoration in *Revelations*. This is particularly so when we are visited with pain and disease. "Comfort yourself," he advises a friend who is ill, "with Him who holds you fastened to the cross . . . and seek from Him the strength to endure as much, and as long, as He shall judge to be necessary for you." He is confident that God will never forsake anyone who makes the effort to think of Him. The offering of afflictions, though difficult to do, is the highest gift we can make to our Creator, and is possible if we have made a habit of easy conversation with God. This advice he gave when he was himself near death, and could see that suffering actually bred consolation in the soul attentive to God.

Br. Lawrence's reflections are contained in a very small book of little more than sixty pages. He readily admits that he is always dispensing the same advice: do every action, however small and apparently insignificant, for God, and thank Him for everything you experience in life. For the past three hundred years, people of all walks of life, simple as well as learned, Protestant as well as Catholic, have continued to read that timeless message to good effect.

(Review by David Rooney)

Soul of My Soul: Reflections from a Life of Prayer by Catherine de Hueck Doherty (A later edition is subtitled: *Coming to the Heart of Prayer*)

Soul of my Soul does not rise to the level of the works of the great masters of prayer who are Doctors of the Church, such as St. Teresa of Avila and St. John of the Cross. One reason is that the book is more marked by the personality of Doherty, with whom one may or may not hit it off. The book suffers from stream of consciousness at times. And it contains some odd notions, such as that one can "become a prayer" and some theologically incorrect notions, such as "God is movement" and that: "Prayer and fasting can never be for oneself. They are always for the other." I find the book uneven; some chapters didn't nourish me at all, whereas others I found substantive. Each chapter ends with a short poem prayer. While I have reservations about the book, at the same time I can see a person who does not feel up to the heights of St. Teresa profiting from it. I do not think, however, that this is a good introductory book for a beginner in prayer.

Here are some of Doherty's insights: In Chapter 1, Doherty points out that: "Prayer will come when we fall in love with God. . . . Everything in us resists this falling in love. Who wants to fall in love with the Crucified one? . . . Who wants to be crucified on the other side of Christ's cross, even though this is his wedding bed?" In Chapter 4 she explains one of her favorite expressions (drawn from the Eastern tradition), namely, that when we pray we need to "put our head into our heart." What she means is that when our prayer life arrives at a mature stage of development the part of us that "endlessly dissects and analyzes and reasons about matters of faith has gone into your heart." This is her way of speaking about what some saints refer to as the prayer of quiet. Silence of heart is a recurring theme throughout the book. In Chapter 5 Doherty describes prayer as "my total faith in God as my Creator. I am his image, his icon, and without him I can do nothing. Prayer is my recognition of who I really am: a saved sinner, capable of breaking my friendship with God at any given moment, and likely even to revel in its breaking." Doherty also makes reflections on the Mass and on the name of Jesus (and the Jesus prayer) that are liable to touch some people's hearts.

(Review by Marie George)

Soul of my Soul: Reflections from a Life of Prayer by Catherine de Hueck Doherty

Soul of my Soul: Reflections from a Life of Prayer is exactly what it purports to be, a book of reflections. Catherine de Hueck Doherty shares her reflections on falling in love with God, surrendering to His love, meditating on His Word, plunging into silence, and contemplating Him while still being fully active in her love for her brothers and sisters.

She doesn't seem to hold herself bound to providing a rigorous, orderly development from one topic to the next, but rather, she flits from thought to thought, as a heart in contemplation might rest upon one attribute of God's gift of love this day, and then flow on to another the next. She says of herself that "I cannot write a dissertation, but I can share impressions with you." I am so glad she does.

Catherine engrosses her reader by expressing her "impressions" in a style reminiscent of G.K. Chesterton or even P.G. Wodehouse; who can predict where she will go next? She develops an idea with such a gift for words that one is caught up and delighted with her subject. Even the definition of prayer proffered in the introduction flows from the ordinary to a thing of poetic beauty: "How can you

216

define prayer, except by saying that it is love?" This sounds ordinary enough, and I may even feel inclined to start challenging her accuracy, but she goes on: "It is love expressed by speech, and love expressed in silence. To put it another way, prayer is the meeting of two loves: the love of God and our love. That's all there is to prayer." At this point, I have lost all inclination to confront her; I now want to sit at her feet and bask in her unconstrained exuberance.

There is beauty in her words, but also fun. Like G. K. Chesterton, Catherine continues to surprise her readers with paradoxes and unexpected descriptions. Here is a sample of one of her many gems: "If one stands in intercession with uplifted hands, as Moses did, then the miracle of God's action will take place. It seems strange, but the prostration of prayer, the dance of prayer, the rock-stillness of prayer, or whatever form prayer may take, floods the whole world with action. He who turns his face to God in prayer is in the eye of the hurricane, the eye of action."

Doherty is an artist with prose, but she doesn't confine herself to it. Each brief, beautifully penned chapter ends with a deeply felt and thought provoking prayer in which artistry and beauty are set free from the restraints of logical argumentation and order. They, too, are "Reflections," but reflections straight from the heart of a mystic who, for the moment, is busy meeting with the love of God. The chapter entitled "Answering Youth's Hunger" concludes with this:

What have you to offer me,
In whose blood flows wild anarchy?
Are you the sun with potent fire
To infiltrate my slow desire?
Are you the wind to sweep my blood
Gratuitously to such a flood?

If each delicately crafted closing hadn't had "Prayer" in its title, I might have thought I was reading poetry. And then again, perhaps I was.

(Review by Maureen Coughlin)

Other works by Doherty include *Bogoroditza: She Who Gave Birth To God* and *Poustinia* (reviewed in this volume).

When the Well Runs Dry: Prayer Beyond the Beginnings by Fr. Thomas H. Green, SJ

I read this book in one day. This fits with the author's view that books on prayer are not a substitute for the actual journey of praying, but provide a map that one can consult to make sure one is on the right route. As the subtitle indicates, this book is not meant for beginners in prayer. Much of what was said was lost on me. Still, it is worthwhile even for beginners to have some idea of how people's prayer lives typically develop, so that they will not be disconcerted if they experience certain changes in their prayer life. This book is superior to Green's earlier book on prayer *Opening to God* because he spends a lot of time on what the great saints have taught about prayer (especially St. Teresa of Avila and St. John of the Cross). Green fleshes out what they say in terms of his own experience as an individual and as a spiritual director in ways I found helpful. Green does occasionally make doubtful statements; e.g., I'm not sure "wasting time gracefully" is an appropriate way to talk about prayer at a certain stage. Overall, though, Green's words are reassuringly close to those of the great mystics.

Much of the beginning of the book is a development of the water metaphor that St. Teresa of Avila uses to explain spiritual growth in one's prayer life, as prayer moves from something we do to something that God does in us. In the first stage, beginners labor to draw water out of the well; eventually things get easier and they move to a stage where they have a windlass with which to draw the water out; in the third stage they are near a stream where the ground is moister and there is no need to water it as often; in the fourth stage comes heavy rain where God waters the garden and no effort is needed on our part. Green says that the third and fourth stages are probably indescribable to one who has not already experienced them. However, he describes the first, and talks at length about the second. At first, the person praying uses his imagination and intellect to contemplate and meditate on Scripture, the divine attributes, and so forth. After persevering over a certain period of time in engaging in such prayer, through the grace of God one starts to require less effort to encounter God in love. Those of too active a habit of mind often fail at this point to be receptive to what God gives them in prayer. Here Green quotes Teresa's humorous observation: "doves which are not pleased with the food given them by the owner of the dovecot, without their having worked for it, go in search of food elsewhere." A good portion of the rest of the book is devoted to treating causes of dryness in prayer. Among other things, he notes, following Teresa, that even though prayer may seem dry, if there is growth in supernatural virtues, then the water of prayer is in fact flowing and "watering the flowers" that are these virtues. Green predictably draws heavily on St. John of the Cross when examining the "dark night of the soul." What he says would be very helpful for a person undergoing this initially disturbing experience; e.g., he discusses, among other things, how one can know that this condition is not due to one's negligence, but rather to God working in one.

(Review by Marie George)

When the Well Runs Dry: Prayer Beyond the Beginnings by Fr. Thomas H. Green, SJ

When the Well Runs Dry is the companion and sequel to Fr. Green's first book, *Opening to God*. From the outset, the author acknowledges that this not a text for beginners. His explicit goal is to lead readers "beyond the beginnings" and toward "more intense living of the life of prayer." To accomplish his objective, Green employs the wisdom of three spiritual masters: Teresa of Avila, John of the Cross, and the author of *Cloud of Unknowing*. Drawing from their well-known texts and vivid metaphors, Green constructs a road map by which spiritual seekers can mark significant developments in their progress toward union with God. Despite occasional diversions into anecdotes and literary commentary that does not always seem germane to the overall point, Green accomplishes his objective well. *When the Well Runs Dry* slowly and steadily brings the reader to a deeper understanding of "the way God works in those he draws to love."

The first two chapters serve as a hinge between Fr. Green's two books, and they rely heavily on St. Teresa's teaching. Green rightly echoes Teresa's point that advancement in the life of prayer cannot happen without knowledge of self and knowledge of God in the Person of Jesus Christ. Therefore, the early stages of a rich and fruitful prayer life involve a person's intellect and memory. While these stages will bring many joys and consolations, the seeker must remember that the joys and consolations of mental prayer are not the goal of prayer. Here, Teresa's metaphor of a beautiful garden with flowers becomes iconic, and it provides a wealth of instruction. "The water is for the flowers," she writes in her autobiography, making the point that consolations are not the measure of a fruitful prayer life; growth in virtue is.

Still, this is not the primary point that Fr. Green wishes to illustrate. The third chapter, which bears the same title as the book, guides seekers across the "vast desert of purifying dryness" that comes after the early stages of growth. In these advanced stages, God allows aridity, suffering, and desolation to be the avenues by which seekers draw close to Him. Those who continue on the journey are the ones who desire the Lord enough to continue to seek him through these difficulties. These are the ones who learn "to seek the God of consolations and not the consolations of God," says Teresa.

At this point in the book, Green begins using the biblical image of clay in the hands of a potter as a metaphor for advancing in the spiritual life (cf. Jr. 18:1–6). Just as a potter moistens clay in order to shape it as he wishes, so God provides just enough consolation so that a faithful person continues to be pliable. These images of clay and pots open the way for the author's discussion of the two dark nights explained by St. John of the Cross. Ultimately, the dark night of the senses and dark night of the soul create a spiritual revolution in a seeker. "What a strange world we have entered," Green writes, "where loss is gain and darkness is light and all our human values seem turned upside down." This is the purification that God, the Divine Potter, intends for everyone who desires to grow close to Him.

One statement captures the overall trajectory of this book. "The art of praying, as we grow" states Green, "is really the art of *learning to waste time gracefully*—to be simply clay in the hands of the potter" (emphasis added). In the process of moving to the advanced stages of the spiritual life, one begins to realize that God does more and more of the work and we do less and less. This is precisely why, in the final chapter, the author employs the image that he believes captures the highest stage of prayer: floating in an ocean. In a seeker's life, the purpose of prayer is to let God take total control and become Lord, just as an ocean envelops one who floats. Therefore, the highest form of prayer, Fr. Green successfully reminds his audience, is to be carried away in God's will and to perform apostolic works wherever He leads. This is true of the mature seeker whether the rain of grace falls heavily or the well has run dry.

(Review by Derek Rotty)

Other books by Green include *Drinking From a Dry Well* and *Opening to God* (reviewed in this volume).

Retreats and Ignatian Spirituality

Consoling the Heart of Jesus: A Do-It-Yourself Retreat Inspired by the Spiritual Exercises of St. Ignatius by Fr. Michael E. Gaitley, MIC

This book is intended for people who for whatever reason could profit from a weekend retreat that requires no director and can be done at home. It takes its inspiration from the *Spiritual Exercises* of St. Ignatius, as well as from the writings of a number of other saints, e.g., St. Thérèse of Lisieux.

The first part of the retreat develops its central idea or foundation, drawn in part from Jesus's revelation to St. Margaret Mary: "Behold this Heart which loves so much yet is loved so little. Do me the kindness, you at least of making up for all their ingratitude, as far as you can." At the end of this section, Fr. Gaitley goes on to address how it is possible that we can console Jesus, given that He is perfectly happy in heaven. Fr. Gaitley draws on Pius XI, Origen, and St. Faustina, among others, in order to convince us that we can comfort Our Lord. Here is not the place to debate Fr. Gaitley's thoughtful arguments, but it is worth noting that those who have doubts on this point (as I do) are not likely to be attracted to a spirituality that is centered on consoling Jesus.

The second part of the retreat concerns five obstacles to living the foundation. In regard to two obstacles posed by suffering, one of the things Fr. Gaitley recommends for those of us who are little souls is that we accept the sufferings that God sends us instead of actively imposing them on ourselves. He says that we need to praise and thank God in our sufferings, trusting that they are sent for our benefit, as is the case when a father has his child undergo a painful operation in order to save the child's life. In regard to another category of obstacles, our sins and weaknesses, Fr. Gaitley suggests that we realize that they can keep us humble and provide us with a reason to turn to our Savior with trust. In doing the latter we console Jesus by allowing him to be our Savior. As for our attachments, he recommends that we go to Jesus, especially by adoring him in the Eucharist, and He will silently rid us of them. A fourth obstacle is the fear that if we get close to Jesus, we are more apt to hurt him by our failings. Here Fr. Gaitley suggests as remedies Marian consecration and making a spiritual communion of merciful love (which he explains at length). A fifth obstacle is the insensitivity of our hearts. Here Fr. Gaitley points out that consoling Jesus is incompatible with treating other people who are members of his Body (or at least potentially members of it) without compassion. He offers an examination of conscience regarding our hard-heartedness toward our neighbor, not surprisingly recommending that we go to Confession.

The concluding portion of the retreat goes over what was covered with a view to future practice. It recommends (1) consoling Jesus "by giving him my trust and acts of mercy"; (2) keeping a simple schedule for daily prayer (what he recommends is really not that simple); (3) frequenting the sacraments, meditating on divine mercy, and doing some spiritual reading. Two appendices follow, one on St. Ignatius's rules for the discernment of spirit and another comprised of excerpts from St. Faustina's diary.

The book draws many important teachings directly from the saints, and its insistence that mistrust of Jesus's merciful love is more offensive to him than any other sin is well-placed. Still, I did not particularly like the book. I found the tone annoying—patronizing one moment, sophomoric the next. It is irreverent to say, as Fr. Gaitley does, that "Jesus snapped." A number of his analogies did not make things clearer, and thus were distracting. My other problem was that despite being familiar with the ideas Fr. Gaitley drew from the saints, I felt there was too much material to ponder in too little time. Also, Fr. Gaitley never makes it clear that all the various practices he advocates are not a package deal; while one person may draw closer to God through the chaplet, another may do so by reciting the Divine Office (something he does not mention) or the Rosary (which gets only a passing mention). While this won't be a book I'll come back to, it did do me considerable good, and many others attest to the same.

(Review by Marie George)

Consoling the Heart of Jesus: A Do-It-Yourself Retreat Inspired by the Spiritual Exercises of St. Ignatius by Fr. Michael E. Gaitley, MIC

How many of us are able to drop everything and attend a thirty-day retreat? Save the rare priest who belongs to a monastic order, I do not know of anyone. This book, *Consoling the Heart of Jesus: A Do-It-Yourself Retreat* opens by stating exactly that—and giving us, normal, ordinary people, a feasible option for a retreat we are able to "attend" on our own individual schedules.

The book is actually much shorter than it seems at a first glance, as there are hefty appendices added at the end. This may be consoling to the busy housewife and mother of many little kids who may be discouraged at first.

The main part of *Consoling the Heart of Jesus* is the modified retreat itself, ending on page 196. It is divided into four main parts. The introduction tells the reader about the retreat they will be finding within, and Part One begins to dive into the Ignatian spirituality retreat itself. Part Two goes through the five obstacles a soul may find in the attempt to console the Heart of Jesus, and the Conclusion goes over the material, giving practical insights and tips for the reader to apply to daily life.

The rest of the book consists of appendices for support, and references. The first appendix is a retelling by the author of St. Ignatius's rules for the discernment of spirits, and the second is composed of selections from St. Faustina's diary.

Before I read it, I had heard for a long time about this book. In a very active Catholic Homeschool Moms' online group, where lots of book references are procured and given, *Consoling the Heart of Jesus* is mentioned and recommended so often as the best book for spiritual reading. I am very pleased I was asked to write this review, as after I read it I came to understand why this book is so admired and beloved by so many.

The simple, clear, and helpful language of the author, I believe, is what is behind its popularity. Fr. Gaitley uses simple analogies and his masterful gift in storytelling to convey to the reader the ideas in the book. He is at once constantly challenging us toward a higher, more profound spiritual relationship with Our Lord Jesus, while at the same time showing us in many different ways how achievable that is. For example, he counsels that: "We trust God to gently send his crosses that most benefit us and then we strive to accept them with a smile." I loved this statement, and it exemplifies the clear and truthful—and joyful—teaching of Fr. Gaitley in this book. There are so many spiritual truths that we already know, yet reading his words makes them come alive again.

Fr. Gaitley somehow brings to the reader a simpler, clear version of the famous Ignatian spirituality. The author takes us through many meditations, placing us in a specific time and place, be it in the contemporary world or in biblical times: "We are at the bottom of the hill of Calvary, also known as Golgotha, look up the hill and see Jesus at the top, hanging on the cross. . . . He doesn't see us because He is surrounded by a huge crowd of people." In this manner the author opens one of his many meditations. Readers can easily follow and enter the scene and benefit from the experience. Some are longer and some shorter, but all bring us another lesson to take in.

This book was born out of the author having given a one-day retreat at his parish, a retreat that was so well received that people begged him to write it down into a book.

I am so glad he did!

(Review by Ana Braga-Henebry)

Other works by Fr. Gaitley include *You Did It to Me: A Practical Guide to Mercy in Action* and 33 *Days to Morning Glory* (reviewed in this volume).

A Do-It-At-Home Retreat: The Spiritual Exercises of St. Ignatius of Loyola by Fr. André Ravier, SJ

Fr. Ravier counsels that this do-it-at-home retreat should be done under "the direction of a competent spiritual guide." Though this is certainly highly desirable, his book, for the most part, does a sufficiently good job of explaining the various elements in an Ignatian retreat that a well-catechized person can gain profit from doing the *Exercises* even without a guide. One of the book's particular strengths is the reflections that provide fruit for thought for doing the various scriptural contemplations. Indeed I used that part of the book as a source of meditations without making a retreat. The main weakness of the book is that it never makes clear to the reader that some of what Fr. Ravier presents is taken directly out of the *Exercises*, while some of it is not, but is either a summary of what Ignatius said, expands on it, or are thoughts of Fr. Ravier that find no counterpart in Ignatius's text. (An example of the latter is: "The first Beatitude summarized the rest because those that follow are simply repeating the first under different names.") It is true that Fr. Ravier sometimes indicates Ignatius's own words by using italics, but this is not always the case, nor was it immediately evident to me that he was using italics to serve that purpose. Fr. Ravier, like Ignatius, numbers his points. This gives the impression he is quoting Ignatius, which is not the case (the numbering in the two works do not even correspond to each other). Also, Fr. Ravier breaks up the very important "first principle and foundation" with his own commentary when he should have quoted it in its entirely, and then commented upon it. Despite these shortcomings, overall, Fr. Ravier's book offers a helpful alternative for those who cannot make an Ignatian retreat in the typical retreat setting.

(Review by Marie George)

A Do-It-At-Home Retreat: The Spiritual Exercises of St. Ignatius of Loyola by Fr. André Ravier, SJ

The title of this book might be misleading. It *is* a do-it-at-home retreat manual, but it is not a do-it-yourself project. Fr. Ravier makes it clear that a person attempting this retreat needs the guidance of a spiritual director. And I can see how that would be true—to ensure a commitment to the daily practice of the retreat and to aid with spiritual discernment. But on its own, this book is great spiritual reading whether or not the reader actually completes the retreat in earnest.

The book presents an at-home version of what you might experience if you were to attend an Ignatian retreat. The full retreat for discernment is thirty days, which many religious are expected to complete, and requires seclusion and hours of prayer each day. This book puts the benefits of that retreat within reach of the layperson with minimal expenditure of time, so that the retreatant could still go on with the normal events of daily life. Most Ignatian-style retreats I have attended have been for a long weekend. In those weekends, the presentation of the meditations is abbreviated. This book allows the retreatant to experience the full breadth of the *Exercises*.

The book is divided into three parts. The first includes an explanation of the method of completing the retreat, which includes a thorough description of the framework of the daily prayer, as well as prayer in general. Fr. Ravier points out that what we consider the "Ignatian method" was not really made up by Ignatius at all, but a reflection of what was common practice in his day, and in fact quite similar to St. Teresa of Avila's method of mental prayer. The Ignatian plan includes a four-part preparation and then a three-point meditation on prearranged topics. To complete the day's exercises, the retreatant is called to a colloquy with God. The goal is to move the will to more fervent love of God and, perhaps, to make a discernment.

In the second part of the book, meditations and contemplations following this framework are provided for each one of thirty-two days. In the first week the meditations lead the retreatant to a realistic understanding of sin and hell and the necessity of mercy. Immediately at the end of week one—when these realities are freshly impressed upon the retreatant—Fr. Ravier recommends that he make a general confession (instructions are included in the book). In the second week, the retreatant contemplates the early as well as the public life of Christ and considers the implications of Christ as king. The third week focuses on the passion and death of Jesus and the fourth week, the Resurrection, Ascension, and Pentecost. All throughout the book, the author pauses at critical points between meditations and explains to the retreatant where he is in the process and what he should be experiencing along the way.

The last section of the book includes some prayers, notes for the spiritual director, and a lovely essay on discerning God's will, which includes "rules" for discerning spirits and understanding movements of the soul. Lastly, there is an article on dealing with scruples.

This whole last section, I think, would be worth the price of the book.

This book makes the *Spiritual Exercises* of St. Ignatius doable and inviting. If a reader were unable to find a spiritual director, it would still be fruitful to contemplate the life of Christ and one's own place in the Kingdom as described in the book. Perhaps more importantly, Fr. Ravier provides an irresistible view of the intimate union with God possible through meditative prayer: "Love of its very nature seeks union."

(Review by Margot Davidson)

Fr. Ravier is also author of *As a Little Child: The Mysticism of "Little Children"* and of *"Those Who Are Like Them."*

The Examen Prayer: Ignatian Wisdom for Our Lives Today by Fr. Timothy M. Gallagher, OMV

Plainly not every spiritual practice is for everyone. The examen prayer, however, is definitely one that most everyone should give a try. Fr. Gallagher's book provides a clear, accessible, and inspiring introduction to it. Those who already practice the examen also stand to gain considerable profit from this book. Gallagher ingeniously weaves an excerpt from St. Ignatius's spiritual diary into general explanations about the examen. He provides many concrete illustrations of the various aspects of the examen drawn from people he has met when giving retreats and from his own practice of this prayer.

The book opens by explaining the benefit offered by this prayer. Growth in relationship with God depends on mutual self-revelation. That means that we must listen to what God is saying to us and that we must reveal ourselves fully and openly to God. The examen is a means of doing both these things. In the opening section Fr. Gallagher walks us through reflections for a given day that St. Ignatius recorded in his spiritual diary. We see how Ignatius is aware of the stirrings of his heart, that he discerns which are from God and which are not, and that he strives to act according to God's will, all of which things are fundamental to the examen prayer. The next section goes into detail about each step of the examen: gratitude, petition, review, forgiveness, and renewal. The first step is to review the gifts God has given me that day with a grateful eye. When I realize God's love for me, my love for God and desire to do His will naturally increases. The second step is to ask God for the light and strength to see my day as He sees it. Without God's aid I can have no spiritual insight. The third step is to review my day: How was God present to me in the different events of the day and the different motions of my heart? How did I respond to them? Did I have thoughts or feelings that didn't come from God? How did I respond to them? The fourth step is to ask God's forgiveness for my failings. I seek forgiveness in the context of a God who I know loves me and wants my salvation. Step four does not simply consists in asking pardon, but in being aware of God's loving embrace in forgiving us. It is not simply a self-evaluation, but a "dialogue between two hearts." The fifth step is to prepare for the following day in the light of the steps that preceded it. Again, the explanations of all the steps are illustrated by concrete real life examples.

A third section is devoted to treating things that optimize our ability to fully enter into the examen, such as the time and place we choose to do it, and the utility of spiritual accompaniment. Important advice about beginning and concluding the examen is also offered. The fourth section treats difficulties in praying the examen; among other things it briefly develops the notions of spiritual desolation and consolation. The final section speaks of the spiritual fruits of the examen, such as increased awareness of God's loving presence in the midst of one's daily activities and the direction one receives for one's apostolate as a result of being in tune with God's will.

(Review by Marie George)

The Examen Prayer: Ignatian Wisdom for Our Lives Today, by Fr. Timothy M. Gallagher, OMV

I found myself to be at war with *The Examen Prayer: Ignatian Wisdom for Our Lives Today*. I think it is because its guidance is not about a pocket of your spiritual life, such as having to overcome a specific vice. Rather it is about revising your whole life, one day at a time. I find that a fearsome journey to begin, though in his book Fr.

Gallagher shows it shouldn't be so. The Examen prayer carries the individual's formal prayers into his daily activities, by considering the day's events in terms of one's relationship with God: Did I move closer to or further from God as I progressed through this day?

The book is a slim 192 pages, containing an explanation of the "Examen Prayer," first written about in the 1500s by St. Ignatius of Loyola, the founder of the Jesuits. The book is in five parts, the first two describing the method of the prayer, and the last three looking at the prayer in practice through the writings of those who have prayed it for years. As he considers the words of the various people he has met and talked with (from every walk of life), Fr. Gallagher takes the reader through the possible difficulties that might arise as one begins and perseveres with the Examen.

The language is simple and straightforward, accessible to most. Father uses many examples, but none so much as that of one particular day in the life of St. Ignatius. Honestly, I found the writing to be a bit tedious; it seemed repetitive, and lacked variety in sentence structure. I was often anxious for a section to end, as I was distracted by the style. And yes, I am that person who would rather re-write the novena than pray it, so take my words with that grain of salt, un-recollected English teacher that I am.

I have read the book twice, and I appreciate the grace that Fr. Gallagher affords the reader who is not swept away. While I look with longing at the voices of those who have prayed the Examen for thirty years, Fr. Gallagher encourages newcomers by speaking freely of the struggles he himself had in persevering. At times he would not really be looking for it, and the Examen would "find him." Another religious he quotes had quit praying the prayer years before, when she suddenly realized that she had settled into a routine of prayerfully reviewing her day. "The examen found me!" Such stories make a beginning easier.

And so we begin again.

(Review by Ann Turner)

Fr. Gallagher is also author of *The Discernment of Spirits: A Reader's Guide: An Ignatian Guide for Everyday Living* and *An Ignatian Introduction to Prayer* (reviewed in this volume).

Poustinia: Christian Spirituality of the East for Western Man by Catherine de Hueck Doherty

Servant of God, Catherine de Hueck Doherty (1896–1985) was born in Russia to a deeply religious family. After WWI she immigrated first to England and then to Canada. She founded the Madonna House Apostolate in 1947. Her book *Poustinia* is divided into four parts, the first explains what poustinia is. Poustinia means "desert." The Russian "poustinik" was a person from any walk of life who felt a call to give up everything and live a solitary life in a rudimentary dwelling, generally on the outskirts of town, the purpose being to be with God, but at the same time to pray for others and help them as well. The individual would pray, fast, and read the Bible; he (or she) would also welcome anyone who came to visit him and, if need be, would help the townspeople with things like harvesting their crops. Sometimes after years of living this way, a poustinik might feel called to become a pilgrim and bring the wisdom acquired through prayer to others.

Doherty adapted for Westerners this way of meeting God in solitude. She invited individuals to pray in silence in a room devoid of decoration, apart from an icon of Our Lady and a cross on the wall (one without a corpus, to symbolize one's own crucifixion). In the room there would be a cot for a bed and a Bible. Those coming to the poustinia for one or several days were given, each day, water and a loaf of bread to be divided in three for meals. One feature of the poustinia that I find odd is that one does not attend Mass, but simply remains in silent prayer the whole time (I suppose this was true of some of the fathers of the desert). Doherty suggests that those who have an attic or spare room turn it into a poustinia. I find that any room that is devoid of enticing distractions serves the purpose.

The idea of poustinia, however, is more than that of a somewhat novel silent retreat. Doherty points out that one doesn't need "a hut" or solitude to live a life of prayer; "prayer is a contact of love between God and man." Doherty observes: "There is a poustinia of the heart. Why should my heart be removed from God while I am talking to you? When you are in love with someone, it seems that the face of the beloved is before you when you drive, when you type . . . and so on. Somehow or other we can encompass these two realities, the face of the beloved and whatever we happen to be doing." To achieve the poustinia of the heart requires shutting up one's chattering intellect and listening to the silence of God; it requires *kenosis*, emptying oneself, especially of oneself. Only then when filled by God can one effectively reach out to people searching for God.

In the second part of the book, Doherty elaborates on the latter themes for those who have a life-long vocation as poustinikki. In the third part, she shares some of the "words" that she received while in poustinia. Some of these words were more helpful than others to my own prayer, as typically happens when one person is trying to draw spiritual insight from someone else's spiritual diary. In the last chapter, Doherty speaks of her own vocation and returns to the theme of poustinia of the heart.

Occasionally I find it hard to follow what Doherty is trying to say. And occasionally the language she uses tells us she writing in the 70s. However, for the most part she has a simple, straightforward style. The book will appeal to those who seek a deep relationship with God in the silence of their hearts.

(Review by Marie George)

Other works by Doherty include *God in the Nitty-Gritty Life* and *Soul of My Soul* (reviewed in this volume).

A Retreat for Lay People by Fr. Ronald Knox

I used *A Retreat for Lay People* as part of a weekend stay-at-home retreat, and it worked splendidly; the book could equally well be read over a longer period. The book's twenty-four short chapters were written at different times for different audiences and they cover a wide variety of topics. Knox subsequently arranged them in three groups, one on foundations of the spiritual life, a second on the life of Christ, and a third on everyday life. As Knox observes, the wide variety of moods in which the meditations were written increases the chances that some of them fit the mood of the reader. I found this to be the case. While certain meditations did not do much for me, others struck a deep chord. This was also true of the two "holy hours" that divide the sections; the holy hour on how God hides himself in creation, in his dealings with men, in his Incarnation, and in the Eucharist contained messages I needed to hear, whereas the second one on the Mass and the Life of Christ not so much. Knox is very down to earth (in a way which I suspect makes him especially appealing to a male audience) and understands what things pose a problem to the average Christian, e.g., people wondering whether they love God because they do not feel love for God. He offers some simple, but striking comparisons to make his points. For example, he tells us that we need to be like dogs in that they are continually focused on their masters, whereas we tend to take ourselves, and not our Master, as primary point of reference. And he uses as one of his starting point for a reflection on hell the experience of starting a day with some event that puts us in a foul mood, which escalates with every subsequent little annoyance. Such a lack of peace within oneself and with the entire world, extended for all eternity, gives some idea of what hell is like. Knox's suggestions are eminently practical, e.g., he observes that it would be good to rehearse beforehand the act of acceptance of God's will that one should be making on one's deathbed. He advises us to avoid falling into the rut of formal pieties when we pray, but to approach God in the spontaneous manner of a child. And he provides a number of rules so that we may hit a balance between using created things with grateful appreciation and mortifying ourselves. Some of the other topics he covers include: fear of death, our love of keeping up appearances, the Passion seen from our Lord's point of view, the problem of suffering, minor trials, the Rosary, and Mary's serenity.

I accidentally started reading another book by Knox entitled *A Retreat for Beginners*, which unfortunately is currently out of print. Its target audience is high school boys (which can be mildly distracting to those of us who do not belong to this group). Appropriately, the book contains a certain amount of didactic material concerning spiritual basics. Still much of the content is also helpful to the well-catechized adult. And the presentation is even more sparkling than is the case of the *A Retreat for Lay Persons*. One can imagine the twinkle in Knox's eye when he was giving parts of it to a live audience. Though there is the occasional arcane joke liable to go over the heads of the majority of young people, for the most part the work is accessible and apt to appeal to any young man with even a slight interest in knowing and loving God.

(Review by Marie George)

A Retreat for Lay People: Spiritual Guidance for Christian Living by Fr. Ronald Knox

Going on retreat is a traditional exercise of the Christian, and yet the opportunity for lay people to do so may be rare, given the constraints on time because of raising children, fulfilling workplace duties, or facing the physical limitations of advanced age.

But a solution is at hand, courtesy of the English writer Ronald Knox (1888–1957). Knox was not only renowned as a translator of the Bible, as an eloquent expositor of Catholic truth, and as a consummate homilist, he was also very much in demand as a retreat director, and many of his talks were collected in a series of books for varied audiences. The present title, composed of talks given to lay retreatants, was first published in 1955, and its profound insights into human nature and its gentle kindling of a deeper love for Our Lord have resulted in its being reprinted a number of times.

This is a book that could be read profitably once every year, perhaps in Lent. Knox's prose is conversational, not stilted or tied to a given era. The reader can well imagine him speaking directly to him or her, as he unerringly yet unobtrusively zeroes in on those shortcomings in the spiritual life that are retarding holiness. There is no preaching; just a clear evocation of defects of nature, character faults, and creeping acceptance of sinful attitudes that weigh us down. But he will not leave the reader despondent or scrupulous. Instead he gives practical advice about how to turn toward God in daily actions. Two small examples will suffice. When minor setbacks occur, suppress the self-pride that wells up, and recollect how insignificant we are. And conversely, when things go right, just remember to thank God, even for trivial things.

At the same time he emphasizes that Divine Grace often operates unseen and unfelt. Part of becoming a better person is accepting that God is in charge, that we cannot expect to order our lives neatly along a pre-determined path to goodness. Knox is suspicious of perfectionists in spirituality. Such an attitude often leads to pride and exclusivity—even to schism and heresy in the annals of the past two thousand years. Nor, of course, does he advocate the polar opposite, what is called Quietism, that passivity that opens the way to acquiescence in sin.

In a meditation on St. Mary Magdalen, Knox asks the reader to consider her response to Our Lord under the three categories of contrition, resignation, and hope. Her, and our, expressions of sorrow for past sins may seem incomplete. Her, and our, acceptance of His will may seem half-hearted. Her, and our, hope may seem a forced effort in a world bent on thwarting His will. But he reminds us that Our Lord himself said of her that she did what she could, and that was enough to shower His mercy on her, and therefore on us if we do likewise.

In a brief appreciation of this book, it is impossible to do justice to his approach. After all, Knox was not an aphorist, and quoting from him would necessitate lengthy selections that space limitations prohibit. Suffice it to say that *A Retreat for Lay People* is a gem, and a splendid doorway to the rest of Knox's writings.

(Review by David Rooney)

Other works by Knox include *Pastoral and Occasional Sermons* and *The Creed in Slow Motion*.

Retreat with the Lord: A Popular Guide to the Spiritual Exercises of Ignatius of Loyola by Fr. John A. Hardon, SJ

Fr. Hardon tells us that his guide is for people who are doing the exercises individually (generally at home) rather than in a group, *with help from a spiritual director*. He provides general information about the purpose of the spiritual exercises and how one is to proceed. His guide supposes that one has a copy of the *Spiritual Exercises*. Hardon provides ninety brief reflections (three per day for a thirty day retreat), each a condensed version of what would be offered by the person leading an Ignatian retreat. Each reflection is closed with a maxim or maxims from St. Ignatius or other saints. I find them very helpful. For the most part I find that Fr. Hardon's explanations are also helpful. Occasionally I find what he says questionable or that he could have sounded the topic more deeply. For example, Ignatius tells us that we exist to praise, reverence, and serve God. Hardon simply put in parentheses after praise, "know," and after reverence, "love" without any further comment. Yet these pairs are not synonyms, and it would be interesting to reflect on why St. Ignatius chooses "to praise and reverence" in preference to "to know and love." Also, when Hardon talks about purity of heart, he speaks of it in terms of being sinless, but he never mentions the more subtle forms of attachment that we often suffer from even when we are not clearly breaking any commandment. In order for the book to be short—it is only 225 pages—there are many themes Hardon cannot expand much on. The book's brevity can, however, be a plus for those who cannot take time off to spend thirty days in a retreat house, yet desire to profit from the richness of the Exercises.

(Review by Marie George)

The Spiritual Exercises of Ignatius of Loyola by Ignatius of Loyola, translated by Fr. Louis J. Puhl, SJ

The Spiritual Exercises of Ignatius of Loyola is not a book to read on one's own. Indeed, the *Spiritual Exercises* is liable to appear to be a series of notes and odd rules to those who have not made an Ignatian retreat. Immense profit, however, can be derived by actually doing the exercises with the help of a knowledgeable spiritual director. I know this from personal experience. St. Francis de Sales, who made quite a number of such retreats, would heartily agree as to their benefits.

There are books that can be used for self-guided Ignatian retreats, three of which are reviewed in this volume. There is Fr. John Hardon's *Retreat with the Lord*. Then there is Fr. Michael Gaitley's *Consoling the Heart of Jesus*—it is of Ignatian inspiration, while drawing on other spiritualities as well. Lastly, there is *Do It At Home Ignatian Retreat* by Fr. André Ravier. Note that both Hardon and Ravier recommend that one makes the retreat with the help of a spiritual director. However, even if one is unable to find a director, one may nevertheless derive much profit from such a retreat.

Books from which one can gain an understanding of the Ignatian methods of prayer include Fr. Timothy Gallagher's *Meditation and Contemplation: An Ignatian Guide to Praying with Scripture* and *The Examen Prayer: Ignatian Wisdom for Our Lives Today.* Another book by Fr. Gallagher, *An Ignatian Introduction to Prayer: Scriptural Reflections According to the* Spiritual Exercises, offers specific subjects of contemplation.

(Review by Marie George)

The Spiritual Life

The Art of Loving God by St. Francis de Sales

The Art of Loving God contains seventeen short chapters drawn from conferences that St. Francis gave to Visitation nuns. All the chapters can be read with profit by lay people, except, perhaps the third. This work is more accessible to the young reader than the *Introduction to the Devout Life*, as de Sales (aided by the editor) limits himself to what is most essential, and expresses himself in a succinct manner, without the flowery language and sometimes strained comparisons that he employs in the *Introduction*. De Sales addresses the themes of having confidence in God's mercy, embracing the will of God with equanimity (holy indifference), being patient with ourselves, exhibiting modesty in bearing and speech, practicing simplicity, being untroubled by what others think of us, abandoning ourselves to God, having the right attitudes toward crosses, and avoiding anxious introspection. He mentions at several points the difference between movements of the lower and higher parts of the soul (between the emotions and the will)—useful knowledge for beginners in the spiritual life. Several chapters are devoted to the theme from which the book takes its name: love of God. Among other things, de Sales warns against searching for methods of loving God and thinking about loving God when the thing to be doing is loving God. We love God simply when we do what pleases God in accord with our vocation in life with the sole motive of loving God. I particularly appreciated the chapters on how we are to accept reproof, deal with distractions, and behave when we are sick.

(Review by Marie George)

Beginnings in Spiritual Life by Fr. Dominic H. Hoffman, OP

Beginnings in Spiritual Life treats virtually all of the various aspects of the spiritual life centering them on the theme of love. It is addressed to relative beginners, and I could see it as being especially helpful to the young person who decides to take the spiritual life seriously and who seeks systematic guidance in doing so, or even to an older person who has recently made this decision, as well as for a new convert. Those of us who have been working on our spiritual life for a good while will find some of the book's contents elementary; many topics are treated at greater length and depth by other authors. However, even people in this category can profit from Hoffman's practical and balanced advice. The book is divided into forty-nine chapters of about five pages each, and so could be read in a year, if one read a chapter per week, or in a couple of months, if one read a chapter a day. Each chapter ends with a "practical reflection."

Hoffman begins by talking about God's love for us. Here he makes a statement that will puzzle those who are accustomed to think that God's love is unconditional, namely, that "some of us are loved actually [by God], and some are not." What Hoffman means is that God does not wish for persons who are in the state of mortal sin the greatest good, which is Himself; God no longer dwells in them through grace, and He will not let them share in the beatific vision if they die unrepentant. At the same time, God calls all those who are not actually his friends to make their peace with Him. In the sections that follow, Hoffman elaborates on different aspects of love: "Preparations for Love" (treating among other things, temptation and suffering), "Prayer: The Language of Love," "The Mass and Sacraments: The Lifeblood of Love," and "The Heart of the True Lover: The Nature of Christian Perfection." Then there are two sections on the virtues (including one on modest dress), one on the apostolate, and a final section on "Perseverance in Love," which includes a chapter on Mary and on the importance of spiritual reading.

Here are a couple of examples of Hoffman's down-to-earth advice: "We sometimes feel that in order to merit from our sufferings . . . we must endure gloriously, riding into the battle on white stallions with banners flying. But 'what an illusion,' one of the saints has told us, Thérèse of Lisieux. Her life has shown us that sufferings are not always borne, even by a great saint, with a joyful song on the lips, but often with the grimness of mere endurance. Our Lord himself, lonely in the Garden, is not singing praises of suffering either. . . . If we are sometimes discouraged by the praises of suffering coming from some of the saints, let us take comfort from the example of Christ." In regard to how far we ought to extend ourselves to others, Hoffman notes: "There are no set rules to determine what Christ wants, but the law of love requires a balanced judgment as well as a heart sincerely willing to please him. . . . And in this we have his [Christ's] example. Although he gave himself to the healing of the sick, he did not do this to the exclusion of the instruction and companionship of his own spiritual family, the apostles, and to his own need of solitude and prayer."

Too often we are intimidated by our false conceptions of the spiritual life. Hoffman, by dispelling these misconceptions, calms our needless fears. *Beginnings in Spiritual Life*, while not minimizing the difficulties of this life, is a book that is eminently encouraging.

(Review by Marie George)

Beginnings in Spiritual Life by Fr. Dominic Hoffman

I liked *Beginnings in Spiritual Life* so well when I read it in my late twenties that I bought extra copies to give out and I even had a friend take my copy with her on a trip to get it autographed by the author—and I'm not the groupie sort! Its short chapters and clear, practical advice were very helpful and inspiring to me.

But perusing this book now in my sixties, I find that I have moved beyond its advice. I don't know that I am any holier now, but I found myself reading impatiently, saying, "Yes, yes, I know all of this." Some of this knowledge, though, doubtlessly came from reading *Beginnings*.

In *Beginnings*, Fr. Hoffman addresses himself to the layman. He says that it is written "for those making a start in the spiritual life" and "it presupposes only a minimum of good will. Not everyone who makes a beginning is on fire with spiritual enthusiasm. Some will begin out of a grim sense of duty. Others may not want to make a beginning at all, but do so only as a vague hope in an empty life."

The book is really a concrete manual about how to start to love God; whence the titles of its various sections: "Preparation for Love," "Prayer: the Language of Love," "The Mass and Sacraments: the Lifeblood of Love," and so forth. In these sections, Fr. Hoffman helps us surmount hurdles in the spiritual life that we laymen often have, such as: lack of time; loving people we see as unlovable; sexuality for the layman, either in the single life or married state; practical suggestions for confession, etc.

I would recommend reading it to see if it helps you come to know the love of God in your life.

(Review by Barbara Doran)

The Fulfillment of All Desire: A Guidebook for the Journey to God Based on the Wisdom of the Saints, by Ralph Martin

Ralph Martin divides this guidebook for the journey to God according to the commonly used division of the spiritual life into the purgative, illuminative, and unitive ways. He defines these stages in the first chapter and shows how they correspond to the ideas set forth by five saints. He then goes on to quote copiously seven saints as to the different aspects of each of these ways: Francis de Sales, John of the Cross, Teresa of Avila, Thérèse of Lisieux, Bernard of Clairvaux, Catherine of Siena, and Augustine. The book is long and the average length of its seventeen chapters is around twenty-five pages. Some are going to find even the part on the purgative way tough reading; and much of what was said about the illuminative and unitive ways are going to be lost on those who, like me, plod along the purgative way. I do not think the typical young person will find it engaging. Some people, however, will be delighted with its comprehensive treatment of the spiritual life drawn directly from the wisdom of great saints; Martin does a wonderful job of showing the complementarity of their thought on central points. It is a very meaty work.

Part I, "Transformation Begins (The Purgative Way)," opens with a chapter entitled "Awakening and Conversion." Here Martin recounts Augustine's struggle to break with sin and the importance of avoiding deliberate venial sin. He also speaks of the primacy of grace and the obstacle that self-reliance poses to spiritual progress. The next chapter, "The Biblical Worldview of the Saints," insists on the reality of heaven and hell, and on our inability to get to heaven without relying on Christ. Subsequent chapters deal with the transformation of our desires, prayer, and temptations and trials.

Part II, "Reaching Stability But Moving On (The Illuminative

Way)," opens with a chapter on knowledge of self and knowledge of God, after which is a chapter on detachment. Chapter 11 outlines the different kinds of love we can have for God; it also contains helpful sections on godly friendships and on married love. Chapter 12 is on growing in prayer. The section devoted to the practice of the presence of God (which Martin refers to as "recollection") did not seem to do justice to its importance. Later parts of this chapter were too lofty for me, as was also the case of most of Chapter 13, one exception being the idea of forming a spiritual support group of friends to keep us grounded. Chapter 14, "A Deeper Purification," goes into John of the Cross's passive night of the spirit.

Part III, "Transforming Union (The Unitive Way)" was mostly beyond me. I have to say that even in sections that were mostly beyond me, I could relate to some of what was being said; for example, what John of the Cross said about inordinate affections. As Martin points out, the same person can experience aspects of two or even all three stages at a given time of life. Also, the parts I little understood were not without interest as they indicate what we should aspire to and describe places we can expect to eventually arrive at if we continue progressing.

(Review by Marie George)

The Fulfillment of All Desire: A Guidebook for the Journey to God Based on the Wisdom of the Saints, by Ralph Martin

The fulfillment of all our desires will be enjoyed when we complete our journey toward a state of union with God, the achieving of which is the purpose of this life. Ralph Martin's book gives us a spiritual road map for the journey using the writings of seven saints who have been recognized as Doctors of the Church: Augustine, Teresa of Avila, John of the Cross, Bernard of Clairvaux, Thérèse of Lisieux, Catherine of Siena, and Francis de Sales. Traditionally, the spiritual journey has been divided into three stages: purgative, illuminative, and unitive. Teresa of Avila elaborates further by introducing the concept of the seven mansions of the soul. Following these stages, Martin offers us instruction on spiritual growth. What makes this book such a treasure is that the author allows the saints to speak for themselves, while his commentary serves only to provide background information, to connect, and to clarify.

The saints understand reality with great lucidity and so their instruction is of the utmost value. If, for instance, you are tempted to think you're doing okay because you view your sins as venial, and so not too serious, listen to what Teresa of Avila thinks of venial sin: "It seems to me a sin is very deliberate when . . . one says: 'Lord, you see it, and I know you do not want it, . . . but I want to follow my whim' . . . it doesn't seem to me possible that something like this can be called little, however light the fault; but it's serious, very serious." She is not speaking here of inadvertent sin.

The first part of this book outlines the purification process of the purgative way, which is the stage where we experience a true conversion and try to turn away from sin. Awakening to God, carelessness about sin, avoiding near occasions of sin, self-reliance, the primacy of grace, prayer; these are basic topics the saints considered of supreme importance as we begin our spiritual journey. We need to undergo a transformation of what we desire and fear. Although our saintly guides lived in times and cultures so different from our own, their practical advice for avoiding habitual sin and increasing devotion is as useful now as it was then. Their writings consistently nudge the reader to abandon any attachments not pleasing to God, and to follow Jesus with an undivided heart.

Purified in the purgative way, Teresa's third mansion, we attain stability as we enter the illuminative way. At this point a twofold knowledge is essential: knowledge of self and knowledge of God. The greatest obstacle to further progress is lack of desire. Catherine of Siena stresses that: "If you would make progress, then, you must be thirsty, because only those who are thirsty are called: 'Let anyone who is thirsty come to me and drink.' Those who are not thirsty will never persevere in their journey. Either weariness or pleasure will make them stop."

Finally, after having experienced the grace of conversion, having grown in virtue, the soul longs for more, it longs for union. The saints' words concerning the unitive way are especially helpful to increase our own desire for union.

The true beauty of this excellent book is that it assures the reader that, although the journey toward holiness requires great effort, union with God is possible to any one of us. Teresa of Avila says: "Have great confidence . . . if we try we shall little by little . . . reach the state the saints did with His help."

This is a book that I am not putting back on the shelf, but am keeping it at hand, in order to frequently return to its plethora of good quotes. I would recommend it to any mature Christian desiring to learn more about the mystical tradition within the Church.

(Review by Mathilde Misko)

Martin is also author of *Hungry for God: Practical Help in Personal Prayer* and *The Urgency of the New Evangelization: Answering the Call.*

I Believe in Love by Fr. Jean du Coeur de Jésus D'Elbée, translated by Marilyn Teichert, with Madeleine Stebbins

I Believe in Love consists of ten retreat conferences given by Fr. D'Elbée to women religious. Virtually all of what he says is applicable to everyone. The book has a warm tone, is easy to follow, and is a favorite of many, including myself. If you have been laboring under the impression that God is just waiting for you to do something to condemn you to hell, this book will help you realize, to the contrary, that: "Not a single soul falls into hell that has not torn itself out of my [Jesus's] arms." D'Elbée supports what he says with copious quotations from Scripture and he draws on the teachings of many saints, especially that of St. Thérèse of Lisieux.

Fr. D'Elbée opens the retreat with the theme "Love for Love." "God loved us first that we might love him." God's love is the cause of creation and of our redemption and of other blessings specific to ourselves as individuals. What we need to do is love him in return. We need to examine ourselves not only as to keeping the commandments, but also as to our love of God, e.g., have we failed "to believe in God's merciful love and to live in it." The following chapter, "Humble Confidence," expands on the necessity of trust in Jesus. We must humbly recognize our weakness while at the same time realizing that with Jesus's help we can love God and neighbor as we ought. It is our lack of trust in his mercy and love that offends him more than our other sins. D'Elbée elaborates further on this theme in the following chapter, "Unshakeable Confidence." Jesus wants to save us; he wants to be our friend. What we need to do is trust him, and especially because we are weak and sinful. We should love our spiritual poverty and powerlessness as things that motivate us to rely on God's mercy and power. The next chapter, entitled, abandonment, speaks of our need to allow Christ to work in us and to embrace his will in all things. We need to thank God for everything, even those things that are most contrary to our will, because it is His will; moreover, He knows what is best for us and wants us to have life abundantly. Chapter 5 returns to the theme of humility. Chapter 6, on fraternal charity, develops the advice of St. Thérèse to focus on people's good points and to realize that what may appear to you as faults may in fact not be. Here D'Elbée also proposes the consoling truth that Jesus can remedy the harm that we have done to others by our bad actions, and even draw a greater good out of them. Chapter 7 is on the apostolate. The basic message is that Jesus saves souls when we pray and make sacrifices for them; any successful apostolate is rooted in God's love received in our hearts. Chapter 8 is a succinct, but clear treatment of the place of suffering in our lives. Among its insights is that the cross is not found without the Crucified; to reject the former is to reject the latter. Chapter 9 contains a clear exposition of Church teaching on the Eucharist and the Mass, source and center of the Christian life. The final chapter reiterates the desire of Jesus to be our friend, and also speaks of Mary and the saints. My summary here in no-wise does justice to the rich teaching of this book.

(Review by Marie George)

I Believe in Love by Père Jean du Coeur de Jésus D'Elbée

This short book, subtitled "A Retreat Conference on the Interior Life," is, in the words of H. Lyman Stebbins in the Preface to the American Edition, "a guide to happiness based on the teaching of one who found it entire: St. Thérèse of Lisieux." The author, a priest of the Congregation of the Sacred Hearts, presents it as a retreat about confident love, based on the teaching of the Little Flower.

The book is divided into ten chapters. The first three share similar themes. In "Love for Love," we are reminded of the total love of God for each one of us, and of His desire to be loved in return, emphasizing that we must have an audacious confidence in this love, which reaches us in a particular way when we recognize our weakness. In Chapter 2, "Humble Confidence," the author shows through several stories from the Gospels how this combination of humility and confidence works all miracles. Chapter 3, "Unshakeable Confidence," insists on the immensity of God's mercy, which allows us to remain firmly confident, even as we recognize the depth of our own weakness.

In the next chapters, the author broadens his scope to some attitudes that flow from this foundation of confident love. Chapter 4, "Abandonment," notes that complete confidence leads to total abandonment: in seeing the will of God in everything, we learn to stop worrying, a habit hurtful to God's Heart, and to leave the result of all our actions to Him. In Chapter 5, "Great Desires, Humility, Peace," the author points out that great results only come about through great desires, yet we need to start with humility, which draws Jesus irresistibly into a soul, and leads that soul to obedience, and hence to peace.

In Chapters 6, "Fraternal Charity," and 7, "The Apostolate," the focus extends to our relations with others. We need to change ourselves if we want to change the world. We start by loving Jesus, learning from him meekness and humility. This leads to forgetting ourselves, seeing the good in others and forgiving them. Our Apostolate likewise begins interiorly, with holiness: prayer and suffering come before words and actions, and can save many sinners. And of all prayers, the Mass is the most powerful for the Apostolate. Finally, we must believe, even if we don't see its fruits.

The next two chapters take a closer look at suffering and at the Mass. Chapter 8, "The Cross," reminds us of the benefits of suffering: it buys souls and salvation, detaches us from earth and purifies for Heaven, and teaches compassion. The author points out, however, that crosses must be borne out of love, and that we shouldn't seek them, but rather accept them. In Chapter 9, "The Eucharist," he notes that Jesus offers his infinite love first on the Cross, and then in the Eucharist. This sacrament offers us the opportunity to offer to Jesus his own Heart, and to become what we consume.

Finally, Chapter 10, "Jesus, Mary, the Saints," focuses in particular on Mary, whom the author calls the most imitable of the saints, because of the ordinariness of her life. Her jewels—her simplicity, abandonment, love of the cross, and thirst for souls—hearken back to the themes with which this book began. And because Jesus looks at the giver more than the gift, so it should be Mary who presents him ours. As for the saints, they became so because they too believed in love.

In conclusion, this book, full of quotes from scripture, St. Thérèse, and the saints, is both accessible to the most ordinary Christians and profound enough for intellectuals and members of religious communities (as witnessed by the comments of several of these at the beginning). It helps us find the very heart of our faith, while laying the ground for holiness, a successful apostolate, and inner peace.

(Review by Mark Murray)

Introduction to the Devout Life by St. Francis de Sales, translated and edited by John K. Ryan

The *Introduction to the Devout Life* is a practical how-to manual for living a life entirely oriented toward growing in holiness and attaining the ultimate goal of heaven. It is suitable for anyone who either is looking for advice as to how to begin or is sensing that years of effort are not achieving the goal. The central genius of this book is that it was written for those who are living in the world and have to deal with all the challenges and temptations that this entails. Arguably, the most important part of this book is de Sales's explanation as to why "devotion is possible in every vocation and profession."

The *Introduction* is divided into five parts: instructions and exercises designed to help the soul embrace the devout life; instructions on prayer and receiving the sacraments; instructions on the practice of virtue; counsels against temptation; and, exercises and instructions for confirming the soul in devotion. Through this format, de

Sales provides clear and profound advice on every aspect of life, ranging from how to order one's prayer life and remain attentive at Mass, to how to choose one's friends and forms of entertainment.

De Sales's counsel is extremely practical, and includes, for example, the best times and means for prayer, and how to avoid common temptations. His advice is also timeless—one quickly appreciates why the Saint is a Doctor of the Church—though today's reader obviously will need to practice some discernment to apply de Sales's principles to modern challenges. For example, exposure to certain television programs, video games, and popular lyrics clearly violate de Sales's exhortation regarding conduct necessary to practice the virtue of chastity.

The reader will be reminded frequently that de Sales wrote this book 400 years ago. Some of his explanations make reference to science and other sources of knowledge that are out of date. Although some readers will find this merely quaint, others, especially younger people, might be turned off by it. It also is interesting to note the differences in religious practices between his time and ours, which provide occasions for reflection. For example, de Sales does not recommend that everyone receive Communion on a daily basis, and does not even assume that everyone should receive when attending Sunday Mass.

Several objections might be made to de Sales's advice. One is that there simply is not enough time in the day to do everything that he asserts is essential to the devout life. His response would likely be that which he gave to one of his directees in a letter: "[i]f you are faithful to God, he will never fail you; even though he has to stop the sun and the moon, he will give you enough time to perform your exercises and all else that you must do" (translator's introduction, quoting a letter to Mme. de Charmoisy). One might also surmise that if one is faithful, God will provide the wisdom to understand how to reorder one's priorities, together with the courage to do so, in order to practice the devout life.

The second objection may arise from de Sales's "most important of all words of advice," the need for a spiritual guide. At various points in the book, de Sales comments on the need to consult with and follow the advice of a spiritual counselor. While most everyone will agree on the importance of having a trustworthy guide, many experience frustration at their inability to find one in this day and age. Even so, if one cannot find a spiritual director immediately or even after some time of trying, this should not discourage anyone from persevering with respect to de Sales's other advice (and continuing to pray for a competent counselor).

A final objection may be that de Sales gives too much advice in this one treatise to enable one to absorb it all after one reading. This only underlines the recommendation that this book be read not just once, but repeatedly in the course of the spiritual journey, and kept close at hand as a trustworthy aid to overcome the innumerable obstacles that arise along the way.

(Review by A. M. Desprit)

Introduction to the Devout Life by St. Francis de Sales

St. Francis de Sales's *Introduction to the Devout Life* has known widespread appeal since its first publication in 1609. At a time when the idea of holiness and books devoted to it were associated with those in the religious life, St. Francis wrote for a general audience. This is evident not only by the advice he gives, but also by his lively and accessible style. In fact, the draft on which this work is based was originally written for a lay French widow, Madame de Charmoisy, who saw its value and convinced the saint to publish it for the general public.

Francis himself had a long experience of bringing others to God: as bishop of Geneva (but exiled to the small French town of Annecy, as the Protestants controlled his Episcopal seat), he was responsible for the return of many thousands of Protestants to the Church.

Part I guides the reader, through reflections and exercises, from an aspiration to the devout life to the firm resolution to follow it. Here Francis explains what he means by devotion, noting that this term means different things to different people, but that true devotion is in fact a prompt and easy practice of charity, and that its form will vary, depending on the vocation and situation of each person, so that devotion for a religious will be different from that of a lay person, and so forth. This broad and flexible view of what it means to be devout is what makes this book suitable to readers of all stations and backgrounds.

Part II is on prayer and the sacraments, as the means *par excellence* to move from a resolution to live a devout life to its attainment. This is also a reminder that God is the ultimate architect of our personal holiness.

Part III, the longest by far, is on the practice of virtues. By using many specific examples, and by a balanced, measured, and common sense approach to concrete situations, the saint demonstrates that his advice is meant for ordinary people who live in the world. His recommendations on fasting, for example, are surprisingly practical.

Part IV consists of advice on how to fight common temptations, and discusses the difference between temptation and consent, how to become stronger in resisting temptations, and how to handle anxiety, depression, consolation, and dryness.

Finally, Part V is a short compendium of advice and exercises to help us renew and confirm our soul in devotion.

The above synopsis brings out many of the reasons why this book has been so popular for the past 400 years, and why it is still recommended to the faithful today. Although the occasional passage seems dated, the great bulk of this work is either directly relevant to the modern reader, or can become so with a simple adaptation to our 21st century lifestyle. Human nature has not changed, nor has what it means to be holy. Francis's direct style, his use of exercises, concrete stories and examples, and his sense of what is reasonable, all make this book accessible to a broad audience. In addition, each part is divided into many very short chapters, which allows it to be read by small increments, should time be a factor. In essence, this work can be seen as a "handbook of holiness" that has proven its worth through the past four centuries, and should be on every Catholic's list of "must read" books.

(Review by Mark T. Murray)

Other works by St. Francis de Sales include *Treatise on the Love of God, Consoling Thoughts on Trials of An Interior Life*, and *The Art of Loving God* (reviewed in this volume).

Mother Angelica's Answers Not Promises by Mother M. Angelica with Christine Allison

Mother Angelica's works most closely resemble those of venerable Archbishop Fulton Sheen. This is not surprising given the similarities between the two. Both of these Americans used the media to evangelize. Both addressed the average person using everyday language, sprinkled with folksy humor. While Sheen was certainly the more educated of the two, Mother Angelica rivals and perhaps surpasses Sheen when it comes to first-hand knowledge of what troubles people about the truths of the Catholic faith and what they find challenging when it comes to living it. For those who feel intimidated by the thought of doing spiritual reading, this book is a good one to start with. If one is looking for a dense, meditative text or a magisterial treatment of prayer or some other aspect of the spiritual life, one would do better to look elsewhere.

Answers Not Promises covers a fair number of the essentials of the spiritual life. The book is divided into three sections of four chapters. The chapters average twenty-three pages in length and are easy to read; the text contains many anecdotes and examples. In the first section, "First Things," Mother Angelica treats things that we often struggle with: believing in God, finding our way to God, coming to grips with unanswered prayers, and dealing with suffering. The chapter on suffering presents eight different types of suffering ranging from "corrective suffering," which detaches us from our worldliness and willfulness, to "personal suffering," which we bring upon ourselves by following the natural bent of our personality type (e.g., the person who complains so much about his problems that he alienates those around him). The descriptions of the different sorts of suffering help us better understand the utility of suffering. The remedies offered include: praying, imitating Christ, and uniting our sufferings with those of Christ.

In the second section, "Life and Love," Mother Angelica treats two capital sins: lust and pride. She also devotes a chapter each to forgiveness and guilt. In the chapter on lust, Mother Angelica pulls no punches as to what is and isn't a sin, nor does she sugarcoat the difficulties of overcoming this vice. She emphasizes prayer and striving to reform oneself moment by moment. The chapter on guilt could be very helpful for people who labor under the illusion they are doing God's work by beating themselves up. Mother Angelica distinguishes between good guilt and bad guilt; good guilt motivates us to repent, whereas bad guilt leads to despair and self-hatred. The chapter on pride is chockfull of examples apt to disabuse us of any illusion we might have as to not being proud, such as, the driver enraged by someone who took his parking spot, perhaps unwittingly (how anyone could dare to inconvenience me!), the parent who badgers his child to pursue a prestigious profession, and the husband who "interrupts his wife . . . as if his opinions were the only ones worth listening to." The chapter on forgiveness makes the important point that forgiveness is a choice, an act of the will, and it does not instantly rid one of all bad feelings.

In the third section, "Last Things," Mother Angelica treats the subjects of death, why purgatory, what heaven is like, and why people go to hell.

Mother Angelica is not a theologian (she had two people check the book for theological accuracy), and there is the occasional theological slip. For example, in response to the question: "'Are you really telling me that every time I sin, God is hurt, truly hurt?'" she responds: "'That is exactly what I am saying.'" Christ was able to be hurt in his human nature, but not in his divine nature, and the other Divine Persons cannot be hurt at all (though they can be offended). Such mistakes are few, however, and for the most part Mother Angelica's uncomplicated faith serves to shed ample light on problems that so many of us wrestle with, and her down-to-earth manner makes her "answers" easy to follow.

(Review by Marie George)

Mother Angelica's Answers Not Promises by Mother M. Angelica with Christine Allison

Just to be clear, I have not been a Mother Angelica "groupie." Before reading this book I had only listened to parts of a handful of her radio shows as I drove my children around. Still, I found amazing the few stories I had heard about the overt interventions of Providence in her life, and I could not help admiring her accomplishments. That coupled with her own faithful determination, which had such an impact on the world, made me want to learn more about her.

Mother Angelica's Answers Not Promises is a good introduction, evoking her feisty personality, her warmth, her straightforward dead-on catechesis, and some very sympathetic advice about the spiritual life. The book is 273 pages long, divided into three parts, roughly equal in length. I found the first two parts to be more interesting, though the third part contains a powerful story about angels.

Part I, "First Things," addresses our relationship with God: faith, purpose, suffering, and silence. Mother deals with these issues by recounting stories from her own life and from the lives of the many, many people she has met through her ministry. These stories come from the context of our culture, dealing with issues that arise due to the time in which we live.

Part II, "Life and Love," deals with overcoming obstacles to a closer relationship with God: lust, guilt, inability to forgive, and our propensity for sin in general. Her message is simple and not at all new: seek God's help and He will be with you. Yet the message is made incarnate through true stories, such as that of Catherine of Sienna who once spent a grueling night fighting temptations against purity. The next day, she called on our Lord to complain of his absence from her in the night. He contradicted her, stating that he was the strength with which she had been able to fend off the temptations. She had not been alone at all. Saints and sinners, you and me and Mother Angelica included, have his aid whenever we ask. Simple. Startling. A profound meditation on the fact, that if you are seeking God, He is already there with you.

Part III, "Last Things," deals with Catholic teachings thereon and whether we must believe in them: angels, saints, purgatory, heaven, hell. Mother Angelica makes the point that the existence of these things points to the great mercy of God. We each have the free will to choose God or not, and these beautiful creations (and the scary ones) all help us to choose correctly.

It is a pleasure to read about a woman whose faith is clearly the center of her life, the source of her strength and determination. She tells of God's graciousness to her personally and to others who have crossed her path over the years. I could imagine this book as an aid to catechists who are trying to get their students to see God's workings in the present world. Story after story convinces us that it happens. We all need to know when to say, with John in the Gospel, "It is the Lord" (Jn. 21:7), and how to have Peter's faith as he takes up his outer garment and jumps into the water to get to Christ on the shore. I think this book helps.

(Review by Ann Turner)

Other books by Mother Angelica are *Praying with Mother Angelica* and *Mother Angelica's Private and Pithy Lessons from the Scriptures*.

The Road of Hope: A Gospel from Prison by Cardinal Francis Xavier Nguyen Van Thuan

Archbishop Van Thuan was incarcerated by the North Vietnamese from 1975–1988. This book consists of messages he wrote while in prison in order to encourage his flock. After his release he edited these messages into a collection of short thoughts organized around thirty-seven themes ranging from duty to joy, from ordinary work to studies, from new life to perseverance. The book lends itself to being read a few thoughts at a time or a section at a time (either sequentially or on the specific topic one feels drawn to at the moment). The content of the thoughts is reminiscent of the works of the American archbishop, Fulton Sheen, who deals with the trials and opportunities for spiritual growth that belong to the average person in the pews. Thus, the book is liable to be helpful to the average Catholic with a family who works in or outside the home, and especially for one who is beginning to do spiritual reading— Van Thuan's suggestions are short, simple, and to the point. The book is also apt to be useful for those interested in evangelization, as many of the themes treated are related to it: leadership, the apostle, dedication, and renewal. Van Thuan is insistent on the role the family plays here: "The Christian family must be apostolic in its witness. It must show that it has been called to holiness and that it can live a married life pleasing to God. It must share with other families the grace and happiness with which God has blessed it."

259

In one thousand thoughts there are bound to be some that one will find trite. However, sometimes one does need to be reminded of the obvious or near-obvious, e.g., "Other people do not need your help or your possessions as much as they need your love." There are a couple pensées that I find questionable, e.g., the assertion that "it is never necessary to criticize [or] distrust others." However, the vast majority hit home and I ended up copying over two dozen of them, e.g.: "Complaining is a contagious disease whose symptoms are pessimism, loss of peace, doubts, and a decrease in the zeal which comes from close union with God." There is such a wide variety of themes covered, everyone is bound to find thoughts they need to hear. I especially appreciated the section, "Happy Child," in which Van Thuan develops the theme of being like little children.

(Review by Marie George)

The Road of Hope: A Gospel from Prison by Francis Xavier Cardinal Nguyen Van Thuan

I am not sure that this book is what one would call a "read." After beginning it, I changed course and began to read it by way of using it for meditation at the end of day as an examination of conscience tool, concentrating on a section or a page at a time, mulling over the words. It would be a great book to read for Advent or Lenten season meditations.

How the book *The Road of Hope: A Gospel from Prison* was created is inspiring in and of itself. What is contained therein, even more so. Originally written and smuggled out of prison, these exhortations, little teachings, or proverbs, if you will, were intended to encourage the orphaned faithful of a diocese in Vietnam. However, these collected writings of Francis Xavier Cardinal Nguyen Van Thuan, speak to all of us. He writes "as a father who does not have anything new to say" to his children, but with words that need to be heard again and again. Knowing that his people will be without his presence, he wanted to write these thoughts in order to help them persevere as apostles—persevere on the Road we must all walk in order to win the Prize. The Road is long, but it one of Hope; coaxing us along it is the prize of eternal life and God. However, there are also obstacles on this road of Hope. Cardinal Van Thuan addresses all of these things. His fatherly love is obvious; his leadership and intelligence—both spiritual and practical—are evident. He is often humorous and sometimes very direct and blunt. He seems to have had Scripture memorized and the saints' lives as well. This priestly shepherd's wisdom is a wonderful companion as we march on the pilgrim's path. A good "read" for all on their walk of life, on the Road of Hope.

(Review by Austen Fitz)

Van Thuan is also author of *Five Loaves and Two Fish: Meditations on the Eucharist.*

Spiritual Combat by Lorenzo Scupoli (Sophia Institute Press, 2002; this edition has been abridged and edited)

Spiritual Combat, a favorite of St. Francis de Sales, may not work well for certain (relative) beginners in the spiritual life, as at times Scupoli proposes very elevated goals; for example, he tells us we "must love to be despised by others, detesting their compliments, delighting in their blame, and stooping, whenever an opportunity offers, to do that which others regard with contempt." Also, in a few instances Scupoli's advice is ambiguous and his theological positions questionable, which may confuse some. Overall, however, what he says is insightful and eminently practical.

Scupoli offers advice that I have rarely or never seen in other authors. For example, a number of authors speak of the importance of trust in God, but Scupoli in addition explicitly names as central to the spiritual life distrust of self. Indeed he insists that we can easily delude ourselves into thinking we trust God when really we are relying on ourselves, if we do not "consider first your own weakness; then, full of self-distrust, turn to the divine power, wisdom, and goodness, and in reliance on these, commence the action or conflict with fearlessness." He provides us with concrete means we can adopt to acquire self-distrust and trust in God, as well as an astute way of monitoring whether we have done so; namely, by looking to whether after a fall we are vexed and despondent or whether we are humbly and calmly sorry, resuming immediately our efforts to please God.

Another great piece of advice concerns purity of intention. Scupoli first notes that we like to do good and spiritual things, and so there is the risk that we do them not because we want to please God, but because we derive satisfaction from them. He goes on to advise us how to avoid this trap: "When anything presents itself as in accordance with the will of God, do not bring yourself to will it until you have first lifted up your thoughts to God, to ascertain whether it is His will that you should will it, and whether you will it because He does and with the view of pleasing Him alone. Then let your will—thus moved and drawn by His—be bent upon willing it, because He wills it, and with the sole object of pleasing and glorifying Him." Scupoli then offers a way of assessing our purity of intention, i.e., if we are vexed when our work is impeded, it shows that our aim is not purely to please God, but to satisfy ourselves: "For every soul that moves as God moves it, and aims at pleasing Him only, does not wish for this more than for that, nor to have anything unless God wills to give it. . . . Such a soul is equally contented, whether having or not having it. For in either case, it obtains its purpose, and its wish is fulfilled, which was nothing else but the good pleasure of God."

Space does not allow me to continue recounting Scupoli's astute counsel. Two more things that I found especially helpful are, first, his identification of the various ruses of self-love, "our first and greatest foe" and how to evade them; and second, his suggestions on preparing ourselves for death by determining what is most likely to separate us from God and mentally preparing ourselves to combat it. Other topics he address are suffering, the Eucharist, prayer, how to recover from a fall, the danger of relying on the "idol of one's judgment," combating temptations (including those of the flesh), peace of soul, meditation on the Cross, seeing God in all things, the utility of the particular Examen for acquiring virtue, and dryness (desolation). Many readers will find *Spiritual Combat* a blockbuster.

(Review by Marie George)

The Spiritual Combat by Dom Lorenzo Scupoli

This little book from the sixteenth century is a manual for self-assessment, resisting temptations, and coming closer to the Lord. The combat in the title is not so much with the devils as with our very selves, or our personal "devils:" our self-will, moral blindness, and wayward desires. (The cover of my copy shows an etching of Jacob wrestling with the angel, so perhaps in another sense the combat is with God, a combat we should hope to lose.)

Nor does this work simply recommend ways to remove dangerous habits, since habits are rarely overcome without replacing them with new ones. Thus, practices of self-sacrifice and diffuse charity are presented as the appropriate replacements. Nevertheless, Scupoli emphasizes that exterior works do not themselves constitute true devotion to God. Interior renunciation of our will—self-surrender—is the key, and thus here is where most of the spiritual combat takes place. Thus, a recurring theme is the distrust of self and trust of God.

The manual is realistic in acknowledging that spiritual growth does not usually progress in a straight line. The battle plan often does not survive first contact with the enemy. We stumble, sometimes grievously and repeatedly, leaving spiritual wreckage whose repair itself takes a lifetime. Thus, Scupoli does not focus directly on a linear ascent in the spiritual life, the way St. Teresa of Avila or other advanced contemplatives might. Rather, he devotes several chapters to our falls, and even what a fall's purpose may have been in the divine plan. A point the manual repeats is that a fall is a sign of residual pride, that we trust ourselves too much, expecting too much from our own strength, and that it is a grace that we did not fall further. That is, the fall humbles us, and redirects us to trust in God's enduring presence at our side, showing us mercy even when we are not asking for it. A sign that we have placed our confidence in God is that we can accept even our fall as somehow integral to our reaching spiritual perfection.

The manual is organized in a very usable way. The whole of it is not long: less than 150 pages. The chapters are brief, some less than a page. The language is straightforward and the advice is concrete, filled with examples. The book's encouragement of self-criticism, while not excessive, is constant, and so perhaps it is not ideal for someone prone to self-absorption or to scrupulosity. In general, however, this little book deserves a wide audience, being suitable both for the beginner and for the advanced; indeed, it is said that St. Francis de Sales carried a copy of this book at all times, calling it the "golden book." It merits reading and rereading for years.

(Review by Christopher Decaen)

The Spiritual Direction of Saint Claude de la Colombière, translated and arranged by Mother M. Philip, IBVM

Despite being recently out of print, this short book nonetheless merits a brief note. It is divided into two parts, the first, and longer of which, is addressed to a general audience, and the second to religious. I found some of the latter quite applicable to lay persons as well, though not all of it—which I regard as a drawback, but only a minor one. Each chapter consists of short excerpts from St. Claude's letters, retreat notes, spiritual reflections, etc., a helpful format for readers whose attention tends to wander. St. Claude generally speaks in a direct and down-to-earth manner that is readily understandable. The volume covers more than thirty themes pertinent to the Christian life, e.g., vanity, temptation, zeal, pusillanimity, and friendship with Christ.

St. Claude was the spiritual director of St. Margaret Mary Alacoque, and so not surprisingly one chapter is on devotion to the Sacred Heart. Probably the theme St. Claude is best known for addressing, however, is trust in Divine Providence. Though part of me would be more inclined to direct someone interested in this theme to *Trustful Surrender*, still this volume contains many striking words of wisdom thereon, as well as a beautiful prayer of radical trust in Providence composed by the saint. I suppose that those who have done a lot of spiritual reading will find some of St. Claude's advice on other topics to repeat what they have already read elsewhere. However, some of what he says is especially penetrating or worded in a manner that strikes one to the quick, and so even veteran readers of spiritual works can profit from this book. His advice on the practice of the presence of God, detachment, humility, and simplicity is particularly astute. I admire his radicalness, e.g., "I have promised with God's grace not to begin any action without remembering that he is witness of it—that he performs it together with me and gives me the means to do it; never to conclude any without the same thought, offering it to him as belonging to him, and in the course of the action whenever the same thought shall occur, to stop for a moment and renew the desire of pleasing him."

(Review by Marie George)

Treatise on the Spiritual Life by St. Vincent Ferrer

I confess that I did not get much out of the *Treatise on the Spiritual Life*. This cannot be simply due to the brevity of the work, as I drew much more profit from the equally brief *Thoughts of the Curé d'Ars*. No doubt St. Vincent makes some good points, e.g., about judging others and on how to preach, but these points are found in other authors who, to my mind, present them in a more engaging way. Even what is perhaps the most useful part of the work, namely, the section on motives to excite us to perfection, didn't move me that much. Also, I have a hard time understanding the contempt of self that St. Vincent enjoins upon on us in graphic terms: "He who would escape the snares and temptations of the devil, particularly at the close of his life, should . . . consider himself a corpse, full of worms, and a prey to corruption. . . . It is thus, my dear brother, that you and I should always esteem ourselves . . . and consequently [we should be] ready to accepts contempt." Far be it from me to speak disparagingly of the work of a Dominican saint. Perhaps I will be better able to assimilate St. Vincent's messages later in my spiritual journey.

(Review by Marie George)

Treatise on the Spiritual Life by St. Vincent Ferrer

St. Vincent Ferrer's spirituality is partly in his sermons and partly in a little book called the *Treatise on the Spiritual Life*, the latter being the only one of his works that seems to have any circulation today. Vincent, "the messenger of the Apocalypse," announced that the end of the world is very near if people will not reform their lives and give up schism, heresy, ecclesiastical corruption, and personal sin. Vincent also shows us what we must do to reform; he basically preaches a preliminary purification under the impulse of God's grace. The content of this purification is discussed in the *Treatise of the Spiritual Life*, a book clearly designed for Dominican religious in their convents. We thus have to draw implications about how some of his strictures for religious would apply in lay Christians' lives.

Vincent calls for a spirit of poverty and mortification in many areas. For example, he advises: "Should that which is served to you appear insipid and without relish—through want of salt, for example, leave it as it is, without wishing to season it yourself . . . secretly deprive yourself of all condiments, whose properties are only to excite pleasure in eating." At such times, we are to recall the vinegar and gall given to Christ.

Vincent also preached about the value of silence, but not in today's sense of meditation or centering prayer. He argued, as did the Letter of James, that the tongue is the source of many sins; thus, silence prevents many evils and preserves sanctity. At the same time, however, a friar should speak up when charity requires it.

While it is not clear whether Vincent expected lay people to avoid condiments and sleep on straw mats, it is clear that he raises issues of mortification, self-renunciation, and detachment from worldly goods that are too often forgotten today. He also introduces prudence into his asceticism. He warns us that the devil often tempts religious to overdo fasting, leading them to give up religious life when too much fasting makes them ill. A friar must examine his "bodily temperament" and take what is necessary for his health.

Vincent also warns against trying to use fasting and other good works to obtain "revelations" and ecstasies. Such visions are pure gifts from God, not the results of our own efforts.

St. Vincent Ferrer is less appreciated nowadays than he should be. We live in a world that fears apocalypses such as nuclear war, environmental disaster, and real or imagined economic collapses, but doesn't believe in an apocalypse that includes the return of

Jesus Christ and His General Judgment. Today's world does not normally take its bearings from the standards of a next, transcendent world, and we often operate on the assumption that there is no such world. Thus, it is not surprising that we fail to practice the self-denial that, according to Vincent, prepares us to enter that transcendent world.

(Review by Robert F. Cuervo)

The Twelve Steps: A Spiritual Journey by Friends in Recovery

Contrary to popular belief, the Twelve Steps are not only for people who suffer from "classic" addictions; they are for everyone who struggles with the same sins over and over. If you are a person who is "carrying baggage" or who would identify yourself as "damaged goods" this book may well be for you. The book does not condone the victim mentality of blaming our choices and behavior on things that happened to us in the past. Rather it helps us identify past traumas and recognize the powerful influence that they have had on our image of and relationship with God. The insights we gain by working the steps can thus help us improve our relationship with God. Working the steps also helps us identify our weaknesses and strengths, and it helps us accepts ourselves as the sinful creatures we are in light of the hope that God will remedy the defects that we cannot change on our own. It motivates us to trust more and more fully on God, and is conducive to humility. Many of the steps have to do with our relationship with others, e.g., step nine urges us to make direct amends to people we have injured unless it would harm them or others.

No doubt some people will be more motivated to work the steps in a group setting, and a group generally does offer more input and more support. However, some of us do not like group settings. I worked the first steps with just one other person, and later continued on my own with profit. Doing so with another person afforded more opportunities to identify and comes to grips with denial—a huge advantage given how prone to self-deception most of us are. However, those inclined to brutal honesty will probably do fairly well even on their own. I would rank this as one of the more helpful spiritual readings that I have done (and I do not suffer from a classical addiction).

(Review by Marie George)

The Twelve Steps: A Spiritual Journey by Friends in Recovery

Who in the English-speaking world has not heard of the Twelve Step programs that help those suffering from addictions and/or those who love them? There are Twelve Steps for all kinds of addictions based on the original Twelve Steps which dealt with alcoholism. This help is offered in books, the original being the "Big Book" called *Alcoholics Anonymous* (for the addicted person), and *One Day at a Time* (for the families/friends of the alcoholic). There is also now website help and meetings (even online) with others who face the same problems. Fr. Emmerich Vogt, OP and his Twelve Step retreats (available on CD) also comes to mind.

I find it incredible that there are those in the Christian world who denigrate this help. I have heard several reasons for the distrust, many of them somewhat valid, but many are based on ignorance, bad experiences at "unhealthy" meetings (yes, there are those too), and the belief that "if I just say my prayers," the problem will go away.

In no way do I want to belittle the power of prayer and the miraculous acts that our merciful God can do. However, it seems clear to me that the normal way God works is to remind us that when we are sick, we should get help. For physical illness, we see a doctor. For a spiritual illness we go to the priest and the sacraments. Chemical addictions, however, are a spiritual, emotional, and physical illness combined. No one knows this better than the person who has an addiction and lives with it day to day, trusting each day that God will help him or her through the day to stay clean, for that one day.

Two valid reasons I have heard from those who do not go to meetings are that there is no meeting available in the area or that going to a meeting could jeopardize one's reputation in a very small town. These reasons lead me to recommend *The Twelve Steps, A Spiritual Journey*. It can be used by those who need to see the Scriptural truths that are manifested by those who live the Twelve Steps in their lives. Moreover, it is a good book to use in a general group setting with no particular addiction in mind.

The book has a text book/workbook format. Each step is explained and advice is provided as to how it can be lived in one's life. There are then thoughtful questions and reflection aids so that one can honestly analyze the ways in which one's life can be lived more fully and joyously. Peace and joy can come as a result of "working the steps" despite our sins and weak natures and paradoxically even because of them, as we try to overcome our faults and make amends for past acts through the help of a "Power greater than ourselves." All of this is done with a biblical basis and the understanding that Jesus is our Lord and Savior and it is to Him we turn as He asked us to do.

I once was talking to a pastor in a very small town who regretted the fact that anonymity would be impossible if particular meetings for addictions were established. Consequently, he found this book helpful to use in a monthly retreat format. Many parishioners attended the retreats, and then at a later time went to the priest to speak privately about their particular needs.

As with all spiritual tools, the book can be used incorrectly or poorly. Meetings can turn into "gripe" sessions or "woe is me" time. Participants need to be seeking practical ways to know, love, and serve God, not themselves, through the particular cross they bear.

Two further reservations: the suggested group activities often do in fact "break the ice" and also illustrate some point, but some will have a hard time with them. However, a "trusted servant" who is leading the studies can take what he wants to use in these areas and leave the rest. The second reservation is that this book is "Christian" in nature, not specifically Catholic. That being said, if one is a Catholic, one can still see the universal truths within the Twelve Steps and use them as an enhancement to the sacramental life.

(Review by Austen Fitz)

Way to Happiness by Archbishop Fulton J. Sheen

I figured that since the cause for canonization of Archbishop Sheen is underway, I should review another one of his works. I can well believe he is a saint, but I can't say I'm a fan of his books. I found *Way to Happiness* similar, but somewhat more substantial than *Way to Inner Peace*. Sheen again is simple, straightforward, and folksy. His social commentary, though dated at times, often remains pertinent to the contemporary scene, e.g., what he says about tolerance. He organizes his thoughts in bite-size chapters, which makes for unintimidating reading, but at times leaves one wishing that he would have treated the topic in more depth. Sometimes his portrayal of human failings is so exaggerated that one may well not see that it applies to oneself in the cases that it does. The book does contain a lot of common sense advice and some gems, e.g.: "Once a week, man, reposing from work, does well to come before his God to admit how much of what he did during the week was the work of his Creator; he can remind himself, then, that the material on which he labored came from Other hands, that the ideas he employed entered his mind from a Higher source, that the very energy which he employed was a gift of God."

(Review by Marie George)

Included among Fulton J. Sheen's many works are *Victory Over Vice*, *The World's First Love* (reviewed in this volume), and *The Way to Inner Peace* (reviewed in this volume).

Virtues

The Hidden Power of Kindness by Fr. Lawrence G. Lovasik

Fr. Lovasik expands on a theme previously developed by Fr. Frederick Faber, sometimes drawing explicitly on Faber. He covers in more detail the things kindness encompasses, e.g., punctuality, cheerfulness (or affability), courtesy (including being a good listener and calling people by their names), smiling, and a host of other things that we might overlook in our dealings with others. At times, though, he is more diffuse than Faber; this is especially true in the section that treats the benefits of kindness. I suppose it is not fair to complain that Fr. Lovasik's attempt to bring out everything that has a bearing on kindness results in summary coverage of numerous spiritual matters that are worthy of treatment in their own right. However, it does seem to me that the work (which has already been abridged from the full version, *Kindness*) would be more effective if it was shorter and more tightly organized. For the most part, Fr. Lovasik gives solid advice, as for example when he points out that undue mistrust of people is a particular form of unkindness. The general solidity of his advice stems from the extensive use he makes of scriptures and the writings of the saints in discussing various issues. (I do think, however, that Fr. Lovasik is mistaken when he suggests that in order to correct people in a kindly manner, one should make what they need to do seem easy; if what they need to do is in fact difficult, making light of it is often more likely to make them feel discouraged than anything else, and it may also be somewhat untruthful.)

A summary of the work can be drawn from the table of contents. Part one, on developing a kind attitude, includes chapters on practicing the elements of kindness, avoiding passing judgment, resisting greed, envy, and vainglory, controlling inordinate anger, bearing other's offenses, founding one's thoughts on virtue, and discovering the transforming power of kind thoughts. Part two, on learning to speak kindly, includes chapters on dedicating oneself to truth, being charitable in speech, learning to avoid speaking unkindly, using kindness in correcting others, and seeking the blessing of kind words. Part three, on showing love in kind deeds, includes chapters on avoiding giving bad example, cultivating a love that overflows in kinds deeds, performing works of mercy, and reaping the rewards of kind deeds. Appended is a useful self-quiz on how kind one is.

The book is easy to follow as the topic it covers is not an abstract one. It is certainly a topic we should all have interest in, since kindness is a fruit of the Holy Spirit.

(Review by Marie George)

The Hidden Power of Kindness by Fr. Lawrence G. Lovasik

I picked up the book, *The Hidden Power of Kindness*, years ago, at the suggestion of my spiritual director. It was during a difficult time in my marriage when, of course, I thought the problem was on the side of my spouse. In the midst of many conflicts, I realized that much of the problem lay in my husband's personal psychological issues. There was nothing I could do about them and I felt that I'd hit a brick wall, and saw nothing but despair in the future with this person.

My spiritual director suggested that I read this book and apply the principles. He told me that he'd seen families who had everything money could offer, but the parents could not, or would not, get along or be kind to each other. His experience was that these children never matured completely because their parents, the foundation of their lives, were constantly at each other's throats. Their foundation was insecure and unpleasant. However, he had seen families with many problems, but the parents were determined to establish the practice of being very kind to each other, avoiding external conflict, especially in front of the children. These children, he noticed, were able to mature in what the world would refer to as impossible conditions, looked at from a financial, psychological, physical, or emotional standpoint.

I read the book and put into place, or attempted to do so, a practice of being as kind as possible, ignoring many times little personal insults from my spouse when he was in a bad mood, or simply trying to help him through his personal difficulties, which were many. It was not easy at first, because we are trained to be defensive and proactive for our own benefit. I think the modern phrase is, "Don't let anyone take advantage of you."

Over the years, it became a habit to be gentle and kind toward my husband. In return, I saw his effort to be gentle, kind, and thoughtful toward me, even though the external issues and differences didn't go away. It seemed they just became less important.

When my husband died suddenly earlier this year, I realized that we had twenty-seven years of marriage, most of which were peaceful and beautiful. His children did not remember conflict, but mentioned in their eulogy at the graveside that they felt loved; they remembered their father, who was not an easy man, as a loving man. I know this had a lot to do with the fact that we cultivated the habit of being kind to each other. I think this book is an excellent meditation for anyone who finds himself in an "impossible" situation. We can always make it better with kindness, and this book is a great guide to that habit.

(Review by Mary Ann Shapiro)

Another work by Fr. Lovasik is *Mary My Hope: A Manual of Devotion to God's Mother and Ours.*

Humility of Heart by Fr. Cajetan Mary da Bergamo

We cannot doubt the importance of the topic when Christ himself says, "learn of me for I am meek and humble of heart" (Mt. 11:29). And there is much that is helpful in this book which to a large extent is a resume of teachings of Thomas Aquinas and which makes frequent references to relevant passages in Scripture. However, da Bergamo sometimes skips over important points found in Aquinas, while overemphasizing certain others, and for this reason I cannot whole-heartedly recommend this book. Perhaps one might be better off simply reading Aquinas. For example, da Bergamo says: "So the soul . . . aware . . . that from one moment to another it may be condemned to hell by divine justice, fears the wrath of God, and this fear causes the soul to remain humble before Him." He fails to mention, as Aquinas does, that of the three kinds of fear of God, the most perfect form, filial fear, excludes a fear of punishment (see *Summa Theologiae* II-II 19.7). To give another example, he says: "When I do evil it is entirely my own work, when I do good it belongs to God alone." Then what would it mean to cooperate with the grace of God? Or again, he affirms that: "The truly humble believes that he is ... a greater sinner than others"; St. Thomas, however, says that this is not necessarily so (see *Summa*, II-II, 161.3). Or yet again he quotes Aquinas saying that Christ "recommended humility to us above everything else," but does not include Aquinas's affirmation in the same question that humility ranks after the theological virtues and legal justice. Numerous problems such as these make me uneasy about claims that da Bergamo makes that are unfamiliar to me. Nonetheless, the book does contain many pieces of useful advice. Here are some paraphrased examples: It is certainly conducive to not despising others to reflect on the fact that although they might be wicked at the moment, they might repent and end up in heaven, while though one might be in the state of grace at the moment, it only takes one un-repented mortal sin to end up in hell. In general, reflecting on our past sins, especially those that might have landed us in hell, if by God's grace and mercy we had not repented, is conducive of humility; similarly, with reflecting on the fact that our sins were responsible for the passion and death of Jesus. The lack of humility manifests itself in a wide variety of ways. When we are agitated at falling into sin and at the slowness of our spiritual progress, this is due to a lack of humility. The same is true when act in a humble manner so that people will think that we are humble or when we pretend to have no interest in a coveted office or honor so that people do not look down on us for our ambition. Self-righteousness, i.e., setting oneself up as a model of virtue to be followed is another manifestation of the lack of humility.

Da Bergamo stresses the importance of both praying for humility and confessing our sins of pride if we are to become humble. His advice to learn humility from the life of our Lord is eminently sound. The book closes with a useful treatment of the four species of pride described by Aquinas, as well of eight vices related to pride, e.g., presumption, ambition, and envy.

(Review by Marie George)

Humility of Heart by Fr. Cajetan Mary da Bergamo

Among the virtues, humility has little appeal. We imagine the humble man to be like Dickens's Uriah Heep, a poor groveling, obsequious clerk, slithering below the more powerful, resenting his low station. Or we imagine a man like Scrooge's poor, ignominious clerk Bob Cratchit, beaten, abject, affecting cheer despite misfortunes. Humility seems to be not a virtue worth cultivating, but rather a coping skill for small spirits, dealt a harsh lot by fortune.

Bergamo dispels these popular but erroneous notions: "humility is not a sickly virtue, timid and feeble, as some imagine; on the contrary, it is strong, magnanimous, generous and constant." He explains that self-acclaimed humble men, like Uriah Heep, are hypocrites because "he who thinks himself humble is no longer so . . . so to flatter ourselves that we are humble is the beginning of pride, and the more humble we think ourselves, the greater is our pride."

Humility is "true knowledge of God and oneself." To know ourselves as we truly are, we should compare ourselves to Jesus Christ, the Word made flesh—the exemplar of humility.

The author manifests the true nature of humility and establishes its absolute necessity for salvation. Bergamo explains that one may become a saint having various deficiencies, but lacking humility, no one is saved. He says, quoting St. Thomas: "'Acquired humility is in a certain sense the greatest good.' Therefore whoever possesses this virtue may be said, as to his proximate disposition, to possess all virtues, and he who lacks it, lacks all."

Humility of Heart, like *The Imitation of Christ* by Thomas à Kempis, is not a book read through in one or two sittings. Such are best read—savored—a meditation a day. Each paragraph is richly laden, with explanations of common interior struggles, for example: "To fix our thoughts solely on our own wretchedness might cause us to fall into self-distrust and despair, and in the same way to fix our thoughts solely on the contemplation of the Divine Goodness might cause us to be presumptuous and rash. True humility lies between the two: 'Humility,' says St. Thomas, 'checks presumption and strengthens the soul against despair.'"

Also, anomalies of human conduct are explained. For example:

We read of many who, after being renowned for their holiness, fervent in the exercise of prayer, great penances, signal virtues, and who after being favored by God with gifts of ecstasy, revelations and miracles, have nevertheless fallen into the hideous vice of impurity at the slightest approach of temptation. And when I consider it, I find that there is no sin that degrades the soul so much as this impure sin of the senses, because the soul, from being reasoning and spiritual like the angels, becomes thereby carnal, sensual and like brute beasts "who have no understanding. . . ." (Ps. 31:9) The soul is humbled according to the measure of its self-exaltation, and great must have been the pride which was followed by such a tremendous and abominable humiliation.

This meditation book is divided into six chapters: "Thoughts and Sentiments on Humility," "Practical Examen on the Virtue of Humility," "Examen on Humility Toward God," "Examen on Humility Toward our Neighbor," "Examen on Humility Toward Oneself," and "Moral Doctrine." Meditations are numbered and fairly short—the right length for a fifteen-minute reflection in a busy day.

This book strips away illusions about our standing as regards humility and manifests hidden cavities of pride in our souls. But it offers useful remedies and aids for the journey to eternity.

(Review by Jeanette M. Roberts)

The Screwtape Letters & Screwtape Proposes a Toast by C. S. Lewis

I was a little skeptical when a friend suggested the *Screwtape Letters* as spiritual reading. I wondered if people would be able to see themselves as having fallen into or liable to fall into the various spiritual traps Lewis describes. For example, Lewis opens with Screwtape advising his nephew not to rely on arguments to convince his victims of the truth of materialism, partly because the weekly press and the like have rendered them incapable of following an argument, but mainly because using arguments gives the Enemy (God) the advantage. My reaction to this astute observation was not to reflect on my own behavior, but rather to observe that things have gotten far worse since Lewis's day due to the internet. I feared the rest of the book would have me cheering Lewis on without feeling at all convicted myself. This proved not to be the case, as for example, when Screwtape remarks that "The Enemy will also try to render real in the patient's mind a doctrine which they all profess but find it difficult to bring home to their feelings—the doctrine that they did not create themselves, that their talents were given them, and that they might as well be proud of the colour of their hair," and also when Screwtape tells his nephew to "zealously guard in his [the patient's] mind the curious assumption that 'My time is my own.'" For the most part, Lewis's treatment of vices, as well as of pitfalls in one's prayer life corresponds to advice given by the best spiritual authors. And some people may find his manner of conveying this advice through fictive letters of an older devil to his nephew more engaging and accessible than the expository writing typically used by spiritual authors. Those who are not adequately catechized, however, may end up erroneously taking some of Lewis's ironic comments at face value.

In addition to showing how to deal with various challenges in the spiritual life, Lewis is also successful in conveying God's great love for us, something he does via Screwtape's musings about the foibles of humans and his frustration in being unable to understand why God bothered to make such feeble creatures. One of my favorite lines is: "Remember always that He really likes the little vermin, and sets an absurd value on the distinctness of every one of them. When He talks of their losing their selves, He means only abandoning the clamour of self-will; once they have done that, He really gives them back all their personality, and boasts (I am afraid, sincerely) that when they are wholly His they will be more themselves than ever."

Certainly Lewis is not everyone's cup of tea, and fiction is not going to satisfy every reader's tastes in spiritual reading. When it comes to content, however, *The Screwtape Letters* contains a significant amount of accessible and solid spiritual nourishment.

(Review by Marie George)

The Screwtape Letters by C.S. Lewis

Outside of his Narnia chronicles, this short little book is certainly Lewis's most famous work of fiction. Yet, it's not fiction in the ordinary sense, which is why it is fittingly included in this book. *The Screwtape Letters* purports to be the record of a collection of letters from one demon to another, specifically advice to a low-level demon, named Wormwood, charged with the custody and destruction of a certain man's soul, written by his "affectionate uncle" Screwtape.

At the level of wit and irony, this book can be read simply out of an appreciation of Lewis's writing style, or for insight into his theological views, or as an excellent allegorical way of describing how demons think about God and us. Limiting yourself to these ways of reading the book, however, misses its most important use. *The Screwtape Letters* is best read as an opportunity to examine one's own conscience, for the human being that the lesser demon has been assigned is recognizable as *me*. The demon can see the man's thoughts and desires, and tries to manipulate or direct them, or even simply to distract him from them; whence the reader can watch objectively how our minds often work, to rationalize ourselves into sin or to draw ourselves away from the good. Although Lewis is explicit in his introduction to say that he does believe devils are real, the mode of this book would work just as well as a metaphor of "sin speaking to the sinner in the silence of his heart." The book is less demonology than spiritual psychology, though it is implicitly also a work on spiritual combat. For Lewis's real focus is on us, not on the devils, as tempting as it is to read the book for its cleverness.

Thus, if this book is read as spiritual reading, then, like all spiritual reading, it needs to be read slowly and reflectively, and not at the speed to which the prose and the drama it conveys lend themselves. Indeed, it takes some effort to read this book properly, meditatively, in part because one has to keep translating uncle Screwtape's counsel into that of "the Enemy," Christ. Likewise, the chapters are not headed by a topic, so the reader has to be especially attentive to discern Lewis's lesson in each chapter. There are chapters that are about the human "patient's" temptation to hypocrisy, to laziness, to impatience in adversity, and to superficiality (especially in one's choice of friends). More than one chapter implicitly offers advice about the role of interruptions in one's life, and the absurdity of us thinking that our time is "ours." There are helpful sections on the difference between healthy and unhealthy fear (for example, Lewis implies that the fear and anxieties the devil wants us to have are about the future or the past, whereas Christian fear is principally about the present), and on how we should and should not pray for people who irritate us (pray for their daily needs, not so much for their immortal souls). Many of these counsels are counter-intuitive, but upon reflection there are deep truths here.

The accessibility of this book is perhaps its greatest virtue. It could be read by a teenager or an adult, a beginner in the spiritual life or someone advanced—though it seems more suitable for the former. Any Christian could profit from it, and Catholics need not worry about Lewis's Anglicanism exerting a problematic influence, as there is nothing distinctively protestant about the theology or the counsel the book offers. As has been said before, in many ways Lewis is more Catholic than protestant; indeed, many contemporary Protestants might be shocked at sections that talk about the importance of kneeling while praying or of using formula-prayers over improvised spontaneous prayer!

(Review by Christopher Decaen)

Lewis is also author of *Mere Christianity* and *The Weight of Glory*.

Self-Knowledge and Self-Discipline by Fr. B. W. Maturin

Fr. Basil W. Maturin, a former Anglican clergyman, wrote this book in 1909. Accustomed as I am to reading Aquinas, I found Maturin wordy, diffuse, and poorly organized. Maturin too often rests in vague generalities, making it hard to apply what he is saying to oneself. To my mind, he does not bring our Lord sufficiently into the picture. Still Maturin does offer some sound advice on mortification, advice that especially beginners in the spiritual life can profit from. Two constant themes are: the little things matter and true mortification should not be regarded as something negative. Although one could hope for a more penetrating treatment of this topic, there is no doubt as to its importance: "You cannot belong to Jesus Christ unless you crucify all self-indulgent passions" (Ga. 5:24).

The book is divided into nine chapters of around 30–35 pages each. The first chapter goes on at length about how common and multi-form self-deception is and eventually offers some advice as to how to acquire true self-knowledge.

Chapter 2 develops the thesis that self-discipline does not consist in destroying something in us that is evil, but in ceasing to misuse our God-given powers, through mortification; the purpose of self-discipline is "to restore to the soul the exercise of its full power." In this task we need to exercise patience and prudence as bad habits cannot be expected to disappear at our first efforts, but we must wear them down by small, continual efforts, seeking constantly the assistance of divine grace.

Chapter 3 takes off from St. Paul's reference to four laws. The first, the law of the members, consists of little acts of self-indulgence which leave the soul weakened to resist temptations to sin. The second is the law according to which sin operates, namely, growing like a cancer throughout the soul. The law of the mind is one's conscience. Conscience is an essential aid to avoiding sin, but to follow it we need the law of the Spirit of Life in Christ, the grace of Christ. Maturin maintains that the direct conflict is between the law of the members and the law of the mind, whence the need to be attentive to "the trifling acts of self-indulgence or self-will against which conscience so vehemently protests" and to accordingly mortify ourselves.

Chapter 4, on the discipline of the will, goes on quite a while until Maturin finally tells us again that we have to strengthen our will in every little decision we make throughout the day, and mortification is key here, as is reliance on the Divine Healer of souls.

Chapter 5, on discipline of the mind, speaks about the importance of controlling our thoughts. An event can trigger thoughts of discontent and/or rebellion alongside thoughts of acceptance and penitence. The thoughts we hold on to color our perceptions of other things and contribute to our character; thus, we need to discipline ourselves to fill our mind with healthy thoughts, leaving little room for unhealthy ones.

Chapter 6 on the discipline of the affections is mainly about love and hate; it contains some useful reflections on anger. Chapter 7 is on the discipline of the body; it was never clear to me exactly what Maturin understood the war between spirit and flesh to consist in.

Chapter 8 clarifies that mortification is not about giving up things that are bad or about inflicting suffering on ourselves as if suffering were intrinsically good. We part with earthly goods in order to gain heavenly ones. Chapter 9 shows how mortification is a preparation for understanding divine love. Maturin points out how the Israelites went from a group of whiners in the desert to a people devoutly saying the Psalms, attributing this change to the discipline of following the law.

(Review by Marie George)

Self-Knowledge and Self-Discipline by Fr. Basil W. Maturin

Many people fail to see that there can be no such thing as self-help that does not include divine help. Likewise, many seek divine assistance without recognizing the need for self-knowledge. In the terrific little book *Self-Knowledge and Self-Discipline*, Fr. B.W. Maturin offers us a straightforward guide, which rings as true today as it did when it was first published in 1909. Maturin's style is clear and understandable; his meaning is unmistakable and his perception is inspirational.

I venture to say that if you read this book, Fr. Maturin will reveal some features of "self" in a way no other book has done. Maturin demonstrates familiarity with the uncertainty surrounding the pitfalls and joys along the way of our spiritual development, and he gives us a clear message of how to understand ourselves in order to become strong, disciplined, and loving. Maturin asserts, "There are two spheres of knowledge in which everyone who is endeavoring after any growth in the spiritual life must be making some advance: the knowledge of God and the knowledge of self." *Self-Knowledge and Self-Discipline* is a book that helps one grow in the latter in order to gain leverage to achieve the former.

The lessons from *Self-Knowledge and Self-Discipline* teach us to become attentive to the elusive thoughts we are only vaguely aware of, yet allow to rule over our minds. As Maturin notes, these subliminal thoughts have a profound effect on our behavior. Maturin offers very practical ways to recognize such ideas and to discipline ourselves to deal with them. He argues, in fact, that the very purpose of the temptations in our lives is for us to be questioned: "What kind of being are you? Do you love God, or the following of your own inclinations?"

Self-discipline is well known to be a powerful force; however, it is poorly understood. Self-discipline that is not based on accurate self-knowledge is fruitless. Self-knowledge and self-discipline do not just mystically happen. If you have ever made an effort to discern your path, but felt something was missing, something important was eluding you, this book may be for you. Maturin's methodical lessons are steeped in a realistic awareness of the tangible grit of the human condition, not some otherworldly power of self-denial. They are based on scripture and the doctrines of the Church. The crucial hinge of the book is in the third section where Maturin comments on the part of Romans where Paul reveals his own internal conflicts. Maturin reflects on how Paul's self-knowledge and the inner response to it are key to spiritual growth.

Anyone concerned with growing in the spiritual life and advancing in knowledge of God and of self will derive benefit from reading *Self-Knowledge*.

(Review by Bruce Roeder)

Maturin is also author of *Laws of the Spiritual Life* and *Sermons and Sermon Notes*.

The Steps of Humility by St. Bernard of Clairvaux

Sometimes St. Bernard's interpretations of Scripture seemed strained to me, and he retracts his interpretation of "the Son of Man knows not the hour." Some of the things he says are interesting in themselves, but seem tangential to his topic; indeed, on two occasions he admits to digressing. It also took me a while to figure out how his steps of humility correspond to the steps of pride, not to mention where his three steps of truth fit in. Once I got the step system figured out, I had to resist debating whether his steps were really in the correct order, instead of reflecting on my own shortcoming vis-à-vis the steps. In short, there are many things that can distract the reader from the spiritual profit to be drawn from this book.

I will explain here the ordering of the steps to remove a couple distractions. The book opens by indicating the goal humility leads to, namely, truth. Bernard then goes on to distinguish three steps or grades of truth in order to show more clearly to which the twelfth and final step of humility leads. The first grade of truth coincides with the highest level of humility (getting rid of the beam in one's eye and finding oneself in truth through self-examination); the next grade is compassion for others (rooted in the knowledge of universal human weakness, including one's own); the final grade is contemplation. Bernard nicely accords these grades with the beatitudes: the beatitude concerning meekness precedes the one concerning mercy which precedes the one concerning purity of heart. Bernard then speaks about the steps of pride. They are as follows, starting from the least degree (1) to the highest degree (12): (1) curiosity; (2) frivolity; (3) foolish mirth; (4) boastfulness; (5) singularity; (6) conceit; (7) audacity; (8) excusing sin; (9) hypocritical confession; (10) defiance; (11) freedom to sin; (12) habitual sin. The path of humility runs in the exact opposite direction. Step 1 is to overcome habitual sin; step 2 to overcome freedom to sin and so forth, with step 11 (overcoming frivolity) and step 12 (overcoming curiosity) being the steps hardest to achieve, according to Bernard. Of the four species of pride Aquinas speaks of, Bernard only makes explicit reference to boasting.

What are some of Bernard insights? He identifies the curious person as one who has grown weary of attending to his spiritual condition and who seeks distraction from this essential task by inspecting what others are doing. It is wearying to constantly be monitoring one's thoughts, desires, and actions. Although we who fail to do so may be far from the pride that habitually casts God's law aside, we have taken a step in that direction. The next step is frivolity. There is a kind of superficiality that installs itself once we are no longer sobered by self-examination, preferring rather to look at what others are doing: at one moment we are elated because we find ourselves wonderful, and at the next moment we are sad because we realize that our neighbor has some excellence we lack. Foolish mirth goes one step further: we become so self-complacent that we only see what is good in ourselves while focusing exclusively on what is bad in our neighbors so that we no longer see them as rivaling us in any way—gone is the sorrow of envy characteristic of the previous step. Similarly useful descriptions are given of the other steps. Overall, Bernard helped me to size up many of my shortcomings in regard to humility. While I think the benefits to be derived from his work well offset its editorial weaknesses, a less dedicated reader might beg to differ.

(Review by Marie George)

The Steps of Humility and Pride by St. Bernard of Clairvaux

This short treatise was young Bernard's first published work, written for his fellow Cistercian abbot Godfrey of Langres. *The Steps of Humility and Pride* takes its organizing principle from the seventh chapter of Benedict's *Rule*, with its delineation of twelve steps of humility that the monk must progressively embody in his quest for holiness. Recovering the primitive Benedictine vocation was the guiding principle of the early Cistercians; Bernard's writing here breaths forth that devotion to the Father of Western Monasticism. Humility and pride stand in a precisely inverted spiritual relationship for Bernard; by humility one ascends to Christ but with pride one is separated from Christ. "You see now there is a way down and a way up, a way to evil and a way to good." Each of these two dispositions drives its opposite out of the human spirit. Early manuscripts of *The Steps of Humility* summarize these contrasting pairs of twelve steps at the beginning of the treatise. Humility is not a pietistic disposition for Bernard, but is rather a function of self-knowledge that leads to truth: "Humility is a virtue by which a man has a low opinion of himself because he knows himself well."

There are three degrees of truth in Bernard's recounting: truth in oneself, truth in one's neighbor, and truth in itself. Judging oneself and having sympathy for one's neighbor purify a Christian so that one may contemplate the Savior who is Truth. As Truth, Christ embodied humility; Jesus's obedience is what the Cistercian monk tries to imitate. By contrast, pride obscures spiritual vision; pride is the beam in one's eye that Jesus warns against in the Sermon on the Mount. In promoting humility Bernard is not denigrating human dignity. Instead he insists that only by removing pride can one clear interior space to make compassion for one's neighbor possible. At the apex of the spiritual ascent lies the union with the Holy Spirit, and here Bernard draws upon the medieval tradition of allegorical exegesis of the Song of Songs to describe this union as a romantic rapturous ascent of the soul to God.

True to his Augustinian leanings, Bernard privileges interior knowledge; pride is defined as the desire to appear exteriorly virtuous in the sight of others. In accord with the *Rule of Benedict*'s twelfth degree of humility, a humble monk must shun curiosity and not even raise his eyes toward others, lest he imitate Eve's glance at the forbidden fruit, or Satan's longing to displace God in heaven. Satan is addressed and denounced directly in a section that will confirm interpreters' judgment of Bernard's fiery temperament. Pride shuns productive sober introspection in favor of outward concerns. Such vanity invites successive degrees of instability that Bernard characterizes as levity and giddiness, which themselves mark the early stages of sin that eventually culminate in rebellion against one's religious superior and ingrained sinful habits.

Bernard wrote his treatise for monks in a reform movement that tried to restore the practice of the Benedictine charism in its austere simplicity. Most twenty-first century readers of Bernard will not follow his footsteps and join a monastic community. How might Bernard's treatise speak to contemporary readers today? Those who turn to this saint in search of what is called "self-help" in the popular style of therapeutic consumerism will certainly be disappointed, but unreasonably so. Bernard's insistence that humility is the path to inner peace is a timely message in an era where individualism is running up against social and ecological limits. Though committed to a well-defined tradition of contemplative spirituality, Bernard's writing is accessible to lay readers willing to join him in a considered examination of their interior lives. His prose is neither esoteric nor complicated, and should be appreciated by both beginning students and seasoned veterans who have embarked on the religious quest for meaning and truth.

(Review by Christopher Denny)

Other works by St. Bernard include *On Loving God* and *Sermons for Advent and the Christmas Season.*

Timeline of Authors

St. Augustine 354–430

St. Bernard of Clairvaux, OCist. 1090–1153

St. Gregory Narek 950–1003

Bl. Henry Suso 1290–1365

Julian of Norwich 1342–1416

St. Catherine of Siena 1347–1380

St. Vincent Ferrer 1350–1419

Fr. Thomas à Kempis 1380–1471

St. Ignatius of Loyola 1491–1556

Fr. Francisco de Osuna (1492 or 1497–c. 1540)

St. Peter Alcántara 1499–1562

St. Teresa of Avila 1515–1582

Fr. Lorenzo Scupoli 1530–1610

St. John of the Cross 1542–1591

St. Francis de Sales 1567–1622

Fr. Jean Baptiste Saint Jure, SJ 1588–1657

Br. Lawrence of the Resurrection 1614–1691

Bishop Jacques-Bénigne Bossuet 1627–1704

St. Claude de la Colombière, SJ 1641–1682

Fr. François Fénelon 1651–1715

Fr. Cajetan Mary da Bergamo 1660–1753

St. Louis-Marie Grignion de Montfort 1673–1716

Fr. Jean-Pierre de Caussade 1675–1751

St. Alphonsus Liguori 1696–1787

St. John Vianney 1786–1859

Bl. John Henry Newman 1801–1890

St. Peter Julian Eymard 1811–1868

Fr. Frederick Faber 1814–1863

Fr. Charles Arminjon 1824–1885

Fr. B.W. Maturin 1847–1915

Bl. Columba Marmion 1858–1923

Dom John Chapman, OSB 1865–1933

Elizabeth Leseur 1866–1914

Fr. Robert Hugh Benson 1871–1914

St. Thérèse of Lisieux 1873–1897

Gabrielle Bossis 1874–1950

Dom Augustin Guillerand, O Cart. 1877–1945

St. Elizabeth of the Trinity, OCD 1880–1906

Fr. Jarrett Bede, OP 1881–1934

Fr. Raoul Plus 1882–1958

Fr. Romano Guardini 1885–1968

St. Pio 1887–1968

Fr. Ronald Knox 1888–1957

Sr. Josefa Menéndez 1890–1923

J.R.R. Tolkien 1892–1973

Fr. Jean du Coeur de Jésus D'Elbée 1892–1982

Fr. Gabriel of St. Mary Magdalen, OCD 1893–1953

Archbishop Fulton J. Sheen 1895–1979

Catherine de Hueck Doherty 1896–1985

C.S. Lewis 1898–1963

Caryll Houselander 1901–1954

Dom M. Eugene Boylan, OCR 1904–1964

Fr. Walter J. Ciszek, SJ 1904–1984

St. Faustina Kowalska 1905–1938

Dom Hubert van Zeller 1905–1984

Fr. André Ravier, SJ 1905–1999

St. Teresa of Calcutta 1910–1997

Fr. Lawrence G. Lovasik 1913–1986

Fr. John Hardon 1914–2000

Fr. Thomas Dubay, SM 1921–2010

Mother Mary Angelica, PCPA 1923–2016

Fr. Peter Thomas Rohrbach 1926–

Cardinal Francis Xavier Nguyen Van Thuan 1928–2002

Fr. André Louf, OSCO 1929–2010

Fr. Thomas Green, SJ 1932–2009

Fr. Stefano M. Manelli, FI 1933–

Fr. Anthony J. Paone date of birth and death unknown (*My Daily Bread* was published in 1954)

Ralph Martin 1942–

Fr. Simeon Leiva-Merikakis 1946–

Fr. Jacques Philippe 1947–

Sr. Ruth Burrows, OCD date of birth unknown (*To Believe Jesus* was first published in 1978)

Fr. Timothy M. Gallagher, OMV 1954–

Fr. Michael E. Gaitley, MIC 1977–

Reviewer Biographies

Bernhoft, Alison

Alison is stunned to find that she's in her early sixties. How did that happen? She graduated in piano from the Royal Northern College of Music, England, and from Oxford University, where she read music. She has a Master's in the History of Mediaeval Music from UCLA.

Alison has been unleashing the choleric aspect of her melancholic/choleric nature, and has found that when not vying for emotional space with Eeyore, she has quite a knack for getting things done. This came in very handy homeschooling her six children, including a second-born son with Down's. Alison has just published the key to making your house do half the teaching automatically: *Entropy Academy, or How to Succeed at Homeschooling Even If You Don't Homeschool.* As Catholic converts of some thirty years, she and her husband are in their first year of formation as Third Order Dominicans. Her activities beyond (and within) the home have been severely curtailed by early onset Parkinson's. She now types incredibly slowly with one hand and copious mistakes.

Braga-Henebry, Ana

Ana grew up in Rio de Janeiro and received a Master's degree in Aesthetic Studies from the University of Texas at Dallas where she met her husband. The family of seven children moved around the country following dad's academic career, and make their home now in South Dakota, where Ana is almost done being an educator at home. Ana has reviewed books for over twenty years and enjoys writing.

Biondi, Sabino

Sabino is in his mid-forties. He's been practicing law since 1998 and heads the Trusts & Estates Group at Wilk Auslander, LLP, in NYC. He is a parishioner and volunteer at Our Lady of Lourdes, Malverne, where he and his wife, Wendy, are also pre-Cana instructors. He volunteers his time as a CYO soccer coach and little league baseball. Although raised a Catholic, he credits his wife as his inspiration to be a better Catholic. His favorite pastime is spending time with Wendy and their four children.

Biondi, Wendy

Wendy is in her mid-forties and received the Sacrament of Confirmation as an adult. Once a stay-at-home mom to her four children, whose ages range from seven to twelve, she has recently returned to the work force. Previously a Private Investigator of fifteen years, she is currently an Executive Assistant to the CCO and Managing Director of Media Influence at Ogilvy Public Relations. Through her local parish she is also a volunteer pre-Cana instructor along with her husband Sabino. She enjoys spending time with her children, cooking lavish meals with her husband, and playing with her dachshund/chihuahua rescue, Rhett Butler.

Candela, Christopher M.

Chris (b. 1976) is a single Lay Dominican from New Hampshire living in Manhattan who has dedicated his life to the Church's liturgy. Raised in a non-religious home, Christopher eventually sought out the Catholic faith in his teens. He received a scholarship to study organ, voice, and chant at the Catholic University of America in Washington, DC. Twenty years later, he is in school again pursuing a degree in philosophy. Christopher also enjoys his regular volunteer work with the Franciscan Friars of the Renewal at their shelter for men in the Bronx. He has recently become the Director of Music at St. Peter Church in Omaha, NE.

Cotter, Hilary

Hilary is in his late fifties, married with five children. His wife and he homeschool their children and participate in a co-op where he teaches and assists in a French, Kitchen Science, and a biology class. He is an avid reader and enjoys playing the piano. He works in IT.

Coughlin, Maureen C.

Maureen is a home schooling wife and mother of nine with a BA from Thomas Aquinas College and some postgraduate work in

English Literature at Loyola Marymount University. She is a Third Order Dominican and a member of the Board of Directors for her Public Library. She also volunteers, arranging altar flowers for the parish, teaching Confirmation students, and coordinating the home school First Penance and First Holy Communion program. Her hobbies include gardening, swimming, traveling, quilting, lace making, and videotaping the frolics of her rambunctious tortoise.

Cuervo, Robert F.

Robert is single, in his late sixties, and of a visionary but prudent temperament. He is a member and former chapter president of the Lay Fraternities of St. Dominic, and a Knight of Columbus. He has a BA and an MA from St. John's University, and a PhD in political science from Fordham University. He is a retired associate professor of political science at St. John's University, and was an adjunct associate professor of political science and history at Pace University. His interests include numismatics, urban mass transit, and Bible/prayer book collecting.

Davidson, Daniel P.

Dan is a Catholic in his late forties who received a BA from Thomas Aquinas College. He currently resides in Lake Ariel, PA with his wife and five children. Certified in Latin, History, and English, Dan taught at St. Gregory's Academy in Elmhurst, PA for many years until its closure in 2012. He currently teaches Latin and History at Tunkhannock Area public high school where he also coaches basketball and lacrosse. He enjoys gardening, woodworking, hunting, and fishing.

Davidson, Margot

Margot is the owner of Hillside Education, a small publishing company that serves the Catholic home educating community. She has a Masters of Education in Children's Literature and is the former editor of both *mater et magistra* and *Laudamus Te* magazines. After having homeschooled her children, she is currently the director of a small Catholic Montessori school in northeast Pennsylvania and is a Level 1 and 2 Catechist for the Catechesis of the Good Shepherd.

Decaen, Christopher

Christopher is a cradle Catholic in his mid-forties, living with his wife and four children in Southern California. Temperamentally, he seems to be melancholic with a significant touch of choleric. He teaches a wide range of subjects at Thomas Aquinas College, where he is presently also the Assistant Dean for Student Affairs. He is also a life professed Lay Dominican, and his hobbies include painting, reading, gardening, and moderate hiking (since his kids are still pretty little).

Denny, Christopher

Chris is a middle-aged Generation X Catholic working in the Department of Theology and Religious Studies at St. John's University in New York City. A one-time monotheist tout court, he owes his return to the Catholic Church to divine grace and an undergraduate education in philosophy and comparative literature. Recipient of a PhD in theology from the Catholic University of America, he is a happy husband and father of three daughters who travel and hike where the roads and paths lead them.

Desprit, A. M. (*pseudonym*)

A.M. is in her fifties. An attorney by profession, she is now living a life of prayer and penance with a community of monastic sisters.

Doran, Barbara

Barbara is in her early sixties and of melancholic temperament. She is married and has one child, a daughter. She holds a BA from Thomas Aquinas College and an MA in Religious Studies from St. Joseph's Seminary Institute of Religious Studies, Yonkers, NY. She is author of the fourth grade text, activity book, and teachers' manual for Ignatius Press's Faith and Life series. She worked for Catholic United for the Faith and was a director of a religious education program. She is now a homemaker and has a part-time job caring for an elderly lady. She loves reading and listening to audible books while doing housework, and also enjoys walking.

Fitz, Austen (pseudonym)

Austen Fitz is a wife, mother of six adult children, and ten (at present) grandchildren, all practicing Catholics. Depending on her depth of trust in God (too often minimal), the child (all "just normal" intelligence, but each unique), the year (varied), her virtue of patience (mostly nil), and prudence (touch and go), and prayer (her knees are not quite worn out), the family used all options for education: homeschool, parochial school, or boarding school over the years. She is a graduate from Thomas Aquinas College and has a Master's degree from St. John's University in New York in Catechetics, and is not a writer. Interests include her grandkids, all things Catholic, working for the needs in the local Church, El Camino de Santiago, reading (Augustine to Wodehouse), music (chant to jazz), hiking, and the Benedictines and Carmelites.

Furhman, Angela

Angela is a married woman in her late twenties with two children; she is melancholic/choleric in temperament. A cradle-Catholic, Angela has a BA from Thomas Aquinas College, and is currently a stay-at-home mom out on a farm in windy, rural Kansas. She loves to read, live and think intensely, analyze stories, write stories, bake, and spend time outdoors.

George, Marie I.

Marie is single, in her late fifties, and of choleric/melancholic temperament. She is a member of the Lay Fraternities of St. Dominic and has a BA from Thomas Aquinas College, a PhD in philosophy from Laval University, plus master's degrees in biology and pastoral theology. She is a professor of philosophy at St. John's University, NY. A past volunteer instructor for RCIA, she currently teaches CCD. She loves the outdoors and is an avid walker and an amateur botanist.

Iacoviello, Lucy

Lucy is in her late forties. She has a PhD in Cellular and Molecular Biology from McGill University where she met her husband. She recently finished homeschooling the youngest of their five children and now teaches 10th-grade biology at Trivium School in Lancaster, MA. She lives in Lunenburg, MA where she and her family enjoy the four seasons in all their New England glory: tending the vegetable garden in the summer, harvesting in the fall, skiing in the winter, and making maple syrup in the spring.

Lademan, Elizabeth

Elizabeth lives and works in Arlington, VA as the administrative assistant to the Director of Campus Ministry at Marymount University. She was awarded her bachelor's degree in liberal arts from Thomas Aquinas College in 2008, and is profoundly grateful for the classical education she received there. She is active in music, performing on both the classical violin and Celtic fiddle in several bands in the DC area. In her spare time, she enjoys composing music and reading great literature.

Langley, Mark

Mark is a melancholic Catholic in his late forties. Having earned his BA from Thomas Aquinas College he considers himself fortunate in his marriage to his childhood sweetheart with whom he has raised twelve children. Mark is the founder of a classical high school, The Lyceum, where he teaches in Cleveland, Ohio. Aside from singing polyphony and chant, and playing the organ as a church music director, he enjoys brewing beer, blogging, and gardening.

Lovett, Joan

Joan is a cradle Catholic, educated at Catholic schools, who took a "leave of absence" from the church after college. Thanks be to God, He called her back through the people He placed in her life. She is single, has just crossed the "70-mark" in age, and is now retired from a career in banking. She has a BA in political science and an MA in economics. She is a lay member of the Dominican Order and a Eucharistic Minister at her church. She loves to read and is in her third year of yoga, where she will always be a beginner.

McCaffery, Michael

Michael is a business professional. He is married and in his mid-thirties. He is a lifelong Catholic who has a special interest in Ignatian spirituality. In his free time he enjoys running, tennis, and reading about history and philosophy.

Misko, Mathilde

Mathilde is in her late fifties and of very mixed temperament. She earned a BA at Thomas Aquinas College. For the past ten years she has been a lay associate of the Franciscan Friars of the Renewal. She is nearly finished homeschooling the youngest of her six children, and she and her husband are the happy grandparents of three grandchildren. She has always been actively engaged in her parish, has taught CCD classes for many years, and is now helping to develop an adult catechesis program. Mathilde loves gardening and hiking (especially on the nearby Appalachian Trail). Having recently finished treatment for cancer, she has a renewed appreciation for the joy of life, the gift of friends, and the necessity of living the spiritual life with earnestness.

Murray, Mark T.

Mark is single and in his mid-fifties. He has an MA in Roman History from Laval University, and currently works in the Telecommunications industry in Calgary, Alberta. He is a lector and RCIA instructor at his parish, and in his spare time enjoys reading and travel.

O'Reilly, Lise A.

Lise is married to Kevin; they have five children ranging from thirteen to twenty-one years of age. Her days are filled raising her children Catholic, homeschooling, enjoying living in the mountains, weekly hiking, filling their home with music from their various instruments, and working around her boys' many hunting trips. In another life, she is a graduate of Thomas Aquinas College, and has an MA in Philosophy from Laval University. In recent months, she is managing to squeeze in a hobby: piano lessons.

Roberts, Jeanette M.

Jeanette holds a BA from Thomas Aquinas College and an MA in world literature from the University of Dallas. Married for thirty-one years to Mark Roberts, she resides in Bloomingdale, Ohio on a small horse farm, where they homeschooled seven children. She and her youngest daughters currently train and show five quarter horses, and she is an avid hand spinner and member of the Fort Steuben Fiber Arts Guild.

Roeder, Bruce

Bruce is a cradle Catholic from Baltimore, Maryland and a 1983 graduate of West Point. He is now a retired Military Police officer and Assistant Professor at the US Army Command and General Staff College at Fort Leavenworth, Kansas. He and his wife Suzy have ten children and one grandchild, and are members of St. Benedict's Catholic Church in Atchison, Kansas where Bruce also teaches RCIA.

Rooney, David

David lives in New York City and teaches engineering at Hofstra University. He and his wife have five grown children. He is a long-time member of the American Catholic Historical Association, and is interested primarily in modern English Catholic history. He is author of *The Wine of Certitude: A Literary Biography of Ronald Knox* (2008).

Rotty, Derek

Derek is in his mid-thirties. He is husband to a wonderful wife who helped guide him into the Catholic Church twelve years ago, in 2004. He is a father to four energetic and hungry children. He earned BA and MA degrees in History from the University of Memphis, and an MA in Theology from the Augustine Institute. He currently serves as Director of Faith Formation at St. Pius the Tenth Catholic Church in Greensboro, NC. In his spare time, Derek enjoys baseball, cooking, classic movies, and naps.

Ryan, Catherine

Cathie is in her early fifties, of melancholic/choleric temperament, and a single mother to one delightful, teenage son. She was a stay-at-home mom for many years before starting a small financial planning business. She holds an MBA from Boston College, and is grateful for the fine orthodox catechesis given to her by the tireless Presentation Sisters of the Blessed Virgin Mary in NY. She likes to travel and read.

Savage, Deborah

Deborah is in her early sixties, married, with one child, a daughter whom she adores. She has been a faithful Catholic for most of her life, though she didn't really fall in love with the Church until she went to graduate school. She has a PhD in Religious Studies from Marquette University which she completed at the age of fifty-three, having spent most of her previous life working in the business sector. She is currently a member of the faculty at the St. Paul Seminary School of Divinity where she teaches philosophy and theology and also serves as the Program Director of the Master's Degree in Pastoral Ministry. Outside of caring for her family and her writing and research, Deborah is an avid fitness enthusiast. She has been a competitive athlete since childhood, is a Master's swimmer, and has run a number of marathons. She continues to work out vigorously in various ways whenever she can.

Shapiro, Mary Ann Halpin

Mary Ann is in her late fifties and is recently widowed. She was married for twenty-seven years to Andy Shapiro. They have six children together; two in heaven, Michael Joseph and Daniel Brendan, Patrick (26), Caecilia (24), Dominic (22), and Antoinette (18). She is a lifelong practicing Catholic. She has a BA from Thomas Aquinas College and holds a Lifetime California Multiple Subject credential. She has been involved in education for thirty-six years, the majority working with homeschool families. For the last twelve years, she has been involved in the Independent Study Charter movement with Ocean Grove Charter School, where she now serves as an Advisor to twenty-one teachers.

Short, William G.

Bill, a graduate of Thomas Aquinas College and the University of Notre Dame Law School, practices law in Ventura County, California. He and his wife Katie, also a lawyer, have nine children, and live in Ojai with sheep, chickens, turkeys, and white doves.

Statile, Glenn

Glenn is married to a wonderful wife, Agnes, a retired award-winning librarian. He is an optimist by temperament, which is a euphemistic way of camouflaging the fact that he is not as much of a realist as he ought to be. He has a BA from Fordham University and a PhD from the CUNY Graduate Center. He is a member of the philosophy department at St. John's University. He is an avid chess player and dog lover. His love of music might have something to do with the fact that he was named, not for a saint, but for a bandleader: Glenn Miller.

Stehn, John L.

John is in his early fifties, and of melancholic temperament. He is a member of the Lay Fraternities of St. Dominic. He is a US Army veteran, and holds a BS from the Virginia Military Institute and an M.S. from the University of Kentucky, both in mechanical engineering. He is a licensed professional engineer and serves as an engineering manager at a major US engineering firm. He is recently divorced, and loves spending time with his two children, hiking, running, and cycling. He has an amateur interest in the history of the liturgy of the Dominican Order, particularly the Dominican Divine Office.

Turner, Ann

Ann is in her early sixties. She has an MA in English from the University of Dallas (UD), did a brief stint at the Dallas Theatre Center, and has a BA in psychology from the University of Missouri in Kansas City. She met her husband at UD; they have been married thirty-five years, and have eight children and seven grandchildren. She has home schooled all the children, helped start a school in Texas, and is currently a part time English teacher at the Trivium

School in Massachusetts. Ann is a cradle Catholic and attends the Extraordinary Form Mass, singing in the choir whenever possible. An avid reader, she loves fiction, biographies, and spiritual works.

Wyman, Mark C.

Mark, in his late thirties, is a sanguine/phlegmatic married father of three (two boys and a girl, so far). An adult convert to Catholicism from Episcopalianism, he holds a PhD in theoretical physics from Cornell University and presently works in quantitative finance in New York City. When not writing computer code or changing diapers, he enjoys learning about biology from his wife, cooking at their house in Westchester county, and rereading the poetry he enjoyed in his undergraduate days as a double major in English literature at McNeese State University in his native Louisiana.

Index of Authors

Index of Reviewers

Printed in Great Britain
by Amazon